Diagnosing 'Disorderly' Children

The practice of diagnosing children and young people as 'disorderly' is becoming increasingly commonplace. Once labelled as disorderly, troublesome or emotionally disturbed, such children are seen as problems for schools and the education system. They can even find themselves connected to practices that claim to predict further mental disorders or the likelihood of becoming potential perpetrators of violence and crime. *Diagnosing 'Disorderly' Children* explores the effects of this trend, and questions whether what is being done is right for the child and for society.

Based on the author's in-depth research with young people diagnosed as disorderly, this book provides a thorough critique of today's practices, and examines:

- the traditional analysis of behavioural disorders and the making of 'disorderly' children
- the influence of 'expert knowledge' on behavioural disorders and its influence on schools, communities and a new generation of teachers
- the effect of discourses of mental disorder on children and young people
- the increasing medicalisation of young children with drugs such as Ritalin.

Diagnosing 'Disorderly' Children offers an innovative, accessible and timely analysis of a critical issue facing schools and society today, using Foucauldian notions to pose critical questions of the practices that make children disorderly. Rich in case studies and interviews with young people, it will make fascinating reading for students, academics and researchers working in the fields of education, inclusion, educational psychology and youth studies.

Dr Valerie Harwood is Lecturer in Education at the University of Wollongong, Australia.

Diagnosing 'Disorderly' Children

A critique of behaviour disorder discourses

Valerie Harwood

 Routledge
Taylor & Francis Group

LONDON AND NEW YORK

MT

First published 2006 by Routledge
2 Park Square, Milton Park, Abingdon, Oxon OX14 4RN

Simultaneously published in the USA and Canada by Routledge
270 Madison Avenue, New York, NY 10016

Routledge is an imprint of the Taylor & Francis Group

Transferred to Digital Printing 2006

© 2006 Valerie Harwood

Typeset in Gill Sans and Times New Roman by Prepress Projects Ltd

British Library Cataloguing in Publication Data
A catalogue record for this book is available from the British Library

Library of Congress Cataloging in Publication Data

ISBN10: 0–415–34286–4 (hbk)
ISBN10: 0–415–34287–2 (pbk)

ISBN13: 9–78–0–415–34286–5 (hbk)
ISBN13: 9–78–0–415–34287–2 (pbk)

3/8/07

For LMP

Contents

Acknowledgements

This work has been supported by two grants from the University of Wollongong: URC Strategic Research Development Grant and a Faculty of Education Research Grant. My thanks to the Faculty of Education, University of Wollongong, for providing the support to complete this book, including study leave in 2004.

Earlier versions of parts of this work and some the ideas developed in it have been published elsewhere, and I thank the publishers for their permission to use this material. These publications are:

Harwood, V. (2001) Foucault, narrative and the subjugated subject: doing research with a grid of sensibility. *Australian Educational Researcher,* 28 (3), 141–66.

Harwood, V. (2003) Methodological insurrections: the strategic value of subjugated knowledges for disrupting conduct disorder. *Melbourne Studies in Education,* 44 (1), 45–61.

Harwood, V. (2004) Subject to scrutiny: taking Foucauldian genealogy to narratives of youth oppression. In M. L. Rasmussen, S. Talburt and E. Rofes (eds) *Youth and Sexualities: Pleasure, Subversion, and Insubordination In and Out of Schools.* New York: Palgrave, pp. 85–107. Copyright © Mary Rasmussen, Susan Talburt, Eric Rofes. From *Youth and Sexualities.* Edited by Mary Louise Rasmussen, Eric Rofes, Susan Talburt. Reprinted with permission of Palgrave Macmillan.

Rasmussen, M.L. and Harwood, V. (2003). Performativity, youth and injurious speech. *Teaching Education Journal,* 14 (1), 25–36.

Vinson, T. (2002). *Report of the Independent Inquiry in the Provision of Public Education in NSW, Second Report.* Sydney: Public Education Inquiry NSW.

I would also like to thank Castalia Publishing Company for permission to use the 'Vile Weed' diagram, taken from Patterson, G.R., Reid, J.B. and Dishion, T.J. (1992). *Antisocial Boys* (Vol. 4). Oregon: Castalia Publishing Company.

Chapter 1

Introduction

> She was retching and frightened. A barium X-ray of her intestine looked unremarkable, and within days the insinuations about the mental health of the little girl and her family began.
>
> (Robotham, 2004: 1)

On 31 March 2004 the front page of the *Sydney Morning Herald* newspaper carried the article titled 'Adara wasn't pretending – it was cancer' (Robotham, 2004: 1). The article describes how in September 2000 Adara, a three-year-old child who was experiencing severe and ongoing vomiting, was admitted to hospital and later diagnosed with psychiatric problems. These problems, according to Robotham, included a 'provisional diagnosis of anhedonia, which means depression', 'pervasive refusal syndrome', and 'attention-seeking and reactive depression' (ibid.). These were later proved incorrect when it was discovered that Adara had cancer, specifically a brain stem tumour. Yet when the treatment for Adara's problems drew on a psychiatric model, an interpretation persisted that viewed Adara's behaviour as attention seeking and her family's behaviour as deficient. For example, the hospital notes had '. . . orders written on September 23: "Ignore vomiting please. DO NOT TREAT vomiting as in other children. i.e. acknowledge it and continue feeding at the same rate please!! . . . Psych team to be re-involved on Monday"' (ibid.). Adara died on 12 April 2001, aged five. That this happened is shocking – not the least in terms of the distress caused to the child and family by the initial mistaken diagnosis. One of the things that this prompts us to ask is how it is that this child's illness can be diagnosed as disorderly behaviour.

This book takes a sharply critical look at the way in which the diagnosis of disorderly children has become commonplace. It examines how these ideas about children and young people have such authority and credibility in their influence over parents and caregivers, the wider community, the media and, significantly, the children themselves. In the instance of Adara, it can be argued that the proliferation of the discourses of disorderly children made it possible to diagnose a 'psychiatric' problem as an explanation for a persistently vomiting child, with symptoms such as weight loss and her 'head . . . drooping to one side' (Robotham, 2004).

Adara's story is not an isolated case. Children and young people who are considered disorderly are routinely diagnosed with a range of psychiatric disorders, including attention deficit hyperactivity disorder (ADHD) or other child disorders such as conduct disorder or oppositional defiant disorder. Such diagnoses are intimately tied up with an array of issues, and prominent amongst these is the prediction of further problems. These 'predictions' can range from poor school performance to future criminality or the risk of developing adult psychiatric disorders. For instance, the American Academy of Child and Adolescent Psychiatry (1997) maintains that 40 per cent of conduct-disordered children are likely to become adults with antisocial personality disorder[1] (APD) (a term also referred to as psychopathy or sociopathy). If it is possible to make predictions based on the diagnosis of a disorderly child, what prophecies could be made for the young child described as 'the terrorist of the 4-year-olds'? This description is included in a brief vignette of 'real life stories' on a page about 'conduct disorder' on the New York University Child Study Center website 'AboutOurKids.org'. As written on the website, 'Brandon's teachers in the daycare center report that he is the "terrorist of the 4-year-olds"' (Goodman and Gurian, 2001). If psychiatric discourses can claim to predict disordered adults based on the apparently disordered behaviour of toddlers, this description is certainly far from innocuous.

Claims about disorder and disorderly children are made with apparent ease. In the UK a thirteen-year-old boy who was involved in mugging an elderly woman was described as having 'hyper-kinetic conduct disorder which caused him difficulties at home and school' ('Graveyard mugger jailed for five years', *This is Lancashire*, 22 February 2003). Or there is the article that describes how an English court hearing the case of a 'teenage joyrider' who deliberately broke his electronic tracer tag was told that 'the boy has been diagnosed as having conduct disorder. This means he struggles to cope with stressful situations and loses his temper' ('Joyrider broke his electronic tracer tag', *Eastbourne Today*, 11 June 2004). The *Sunday Telegraph* published an article about Ben Griffiths, an eleven-year-old from Wrexham in Wales who is reported as being diagnosed with oppositional defiant disorder (ODD) and ADHD and 'banned from his local leisure centre' (Henry and Day, 2004). In January 2000 *BBC News Online* carried a story about a saliva test that 'may predict which boys will have some of the worst behaviour problems'. Citing 'Professor McBurnett' from the US, it states, 'children with persistent conduct disorder may have genes which predispose them to produce certain hormones differently, or their hormone production may have been altered before or soon after birth' ('Spit test for future criminals', *BBC News Online*, 13 January 2000).

Then there are news articles that, in their depiction of the child in psychiatric terms, report staggering injustices. Midgley (2004) in *The Times Online* describes the death of Joseph Scholes, aged 16, 'who hanged himself with a bed sheet at Stoke Heath Young Offenders Institute in Shropshire'. The article tells how Joseph's mother had to wait one year before she read the reports on his death. These reports stated that Joseph, a severely disturbed child who had self-harmed many times and was diagnosed by a psychiatrist as a depressive with a social-conduct disorder, had spent the last days of his life distressed and terrified in a strip cell wearing only a rough garment described at the inquest as like a horse blanket.

Implausibly, it appears that this young man was sent to this young offenders institute because he was involved in 'a minor street robbery'. Depictions of the psychiatrically affected child are also portrayed in *Fact Sheets for Health Professionals*, published on the World Wide Web by the Department of Human Services, State Government of Victoria, Australia (2004). This fact sheet contains a case study of a child diagnosed with conduct disorder and specific learning difficulties. An excerpt is included below:

> Dylan lives at home with his mother and only sees his father occasionally, during school holidays. His father has a history of anti-social behaviour, with a number of juvenile offences, and there was a family history of alcohol abuse. Dylan has been in child care since he was one. His mother reported a 'very normal' childhood . . . His mother's job required her to be away from home for long periods and child care arrangements were ad hoc and poorly planned. The mother initially did not see Dylan's behaviour as problematic for her and blamed the school for his behaviour problems.

The profile of Dylan, his mother and his father echoes the stereotypes frequently depicting the disorderly child and his/her family. These usually involve a single mother and parental problems such as a history of crime and alcohol abuse, and frequently include value judgements about the parental caregiving (in this case the mother's 'ad hoc' and 'poorly planned' child arrangements).

The news reports, 'fact sheets' and other publications seem to show that there is consensus regarding the legitimacy of the psychiatric depiction of children and their behaviour. But this is not the case. Take, for instance, how McLean (2004), writing in the *Times Educational Supplement,* describes the burgeoning use of the term EBD (emotional and behavioural difficulties) amongst teachers, and argues that 'we have never had an official definition or professional agreements about what constitutes "EBD"'. Or how Edwards (2004) 'as an ex-headteacher now working in the field of mental health' describes how he 'watch[es] with alarm at the ever burgeoning list of "disorders" that our young people are diagnosed as suffering from'. He also singles out the matter of *what* teachers are being taught. 'I am also concerned that many teachers, especially special needs co-ordinators, are sent on courses where they are told that ADHD . . . to give one example, is a "biologically inherited condition" as if it is an incontrovertible fact. It is nothing of the kind' (ibid.).

It is crucial to ask why the diagnosing of disorderly children is presented as having consensus. Disrupting this apparent accord is one of the purposes of this book. A second purpose is to make known how widespread and influential the discourses of diagnosing disorderly children have become. Towards this I draw on literature from Australia, the UK and the US. Although using this material, this book is not a 'comparative study' but, rather, one that deploys a Foucauldian approach to interrogating the reach of the discourses of disorderly children. This necessitates, for instance, considering some practices in the US, because a number of these influence conceptualisations of disorderly children in other countries such as Australia. The principal example that I discuss is the *Diagnostic and Statistical Manual of Mental Disorders*, arguably the most influential tome that defines the diagnostic criteria for disorderly behaviour.

With regard to the UK, seven years ago, when I was first researching these practices, it seemed to me that, unlike in Australia, the *Diagnostic and Statistical Manual of Mental Disorders* (*DSM*) was of limited consequence to the practices associated with disorderly children. However, this appears to be shifting (or, at the very least, discussion of it is more prominent). Although another classification system, the *International Classification of Diseases,* is more commonly used in the UK, there is a proliferation of discourses that draw on or are influenced by the *DSM*. For instance, whereas EBD is the commonly used label for disorderly children in the UK, associations are made with the *DSM*. For example, the *DSM-IV* is the 'most commonly cited description of ADHD' (Visser, 2003: 22). Or there are texts such *The A to Z Practical Guide to Emotional and Behavioural Difficulties* (Ayers and Prytys, 2002) that sit comfortably on the library shelves at universities such as the Institute of Education, University of London. This *A to Z Guide* provides four pages of information on conduct disorder, explaining that it is defined using 'DSM-IV or ICD-10 criteria' (ibid.: 72), and provides 'advice for teachers and parents who have children with conduct disorders'.

This brings me to an important point. Current conceptualisations of disorderly children are far-reaching. As a consequence of this, we need to reconsider just what is meant when we use the word 'diagnosis'. In short, to qualify the term 'diagnosis' as pertaining only to a formalised clinical act is to miss the effects of the wider social practices of diagnosing disorderly children. This is not to say that the formal discourses are unimportant. It is rather to argue that these discourses often have effects outside the 'formal clinical' setting. One example of this is the way in which 'non-clinicians' can 'diagnose' the disruptive child, with teachers, parents/caregivers and even other children able to propose that a child is disorderly and suggest that they 'see a doctor' or a 'specialist' or 'get help'.

Conduct disorder, oppositional defiant disorder and ADHD are behaviour disorders frequently diagnosed in young people, and often referred to in the media, by teachers, parents and caregivers, and by children and young people. This book closely examines one of these: conduct disorder. This disorder is defined in the American Psychiatric Association's (APA) (2000: 93) *Diagnostic and Statistical Manual of Mental Disorders, Fourth Edition Text Revision (DSM-IV-TR)*. According to the APA 'The essential feature of Conduct Disorder is a repetitive and persistent pattern of behavior in which the basic rights of others or major age-appropriate societal norms are violated'.

Criteria for conduct disorder also include reference to school-based problems (ibid.). With this connection to the school, conduct disorder joins the range of terms used to identify children and young people as disorderly. Some sixty years ago categories to identify young people included 'subnormal', 'mental defectives', 'retarded', 'truants' and 'problem children' (Cunningham *et al.*, 1939: 174–8). These categories describe and differentiate certain young people, primarily in relation to their attendance (or non-attendance) at school. Young people in such categories are viewed as unwanted incursions into the smooth running of the school. Such an opinion is unreservedly made by Sutton (1911: 905), a medical doctor who investigated the number of 'feebleminded' and 'very backward' children in schools in metropolitan Victoria, Australia. From his investigations Sutton concluded that the 'presence of these children in schools is a great handicap, not merely to their own education, but also to that of their normal fellows in the same class. They are so much grit in the hub of the educational machine'. Nearly a century later, with the increasing alarm about disorderly children, the schemes to include them in school or out of school, the claimed relationship between antisocial behaviour and mental disorder, the escalating use of medications, and the plethora of academic and popular literature, disorderly children continue to be a concern – and one can't help but ponder whether, despite the rebranding offered by diagnostic practices, they are still viewed as grit in the educational machine.

Drawing on Foucault

This diagnosing of disorderly children has become what could be described as a 'familiar landscape' in education (and in many other social domains such as health, criminology, welfare). Here it is crucial to bring to mind that 'It is when discourses habitually become so familiar that there is no longer any pause for re-flection and they are able to appear truthful and comfortable' (Harwood and Rasmussen, 2004: 305). As Foucault (1997a: 144) points out, 'everything perceived is only evident when surrounded by a familiar and poorly known horizon'. The task, then, is, to paraphrase Foucault, to examine this 'familiar and poorly known horizon'. In recognition of this point, my critique of the diagnosing of disorderly children draws on the Foucauldian tactic of making the familiar strange, using this tactic to literally make the familiarity noticeable and, in so doing, prompt inter-rogation of the ostensibly natural practices of diagnosing disorderly children.

To challenge this familiar landscape I pose a question designed to disrupt the familiar and poorly known horizon of the diagnosing of disorderly children: how is it that a young person can state with certitude that he or she is disordered? To respond to this question several other questions relating to conduct disorder need to be asked. These are: how does conduct disorder achieve the status of scientific knowledge? And how does conduct disorder function as an authoritative knower of young people? Lastly, the question must be posed, how do young people construct their disorderly subjectivities? Two key theoretical conceptualisations are integral for responding to these questions: first, the self is a construct of multiple subjectivities; and, second, truth, power and the self are involved in the construction and interplay of these subjectivities. Both of these rely on an understanding of the subject that sees it as produced or constructed through processes of subjectivisation. As Foucault (1996a: 472) explains, 'I would call subjectivization the process through which results the constitution of the subject, or more exactly, of a subjectivity which is obviously only one of the given possibilities of organizing a consciousness of self'. I use the term 'subject' to describe the focus of subjectivisation and consider subjectivity to be one of the many products of this process of subjectivisation. This use of subjectivity provides a means to emphasise the multiplicity of these products of subjectivisation. Therefore, the differentiation between subject and subjectivity is valuable as it enables an analysis of the construction of disorderly subjectivity in a way that permits it to be considered within the multiplicity of subjectivities any one subject may have. For example, the conduct-disordered subject (a young person diagnosed with conduct disorder) can have a multitude of subjectivities, such as 'delinquent' subjectivity.

Since the subject and subjectivity is constituted, to grasp how young people can understand themselves as disorderly we must take into account how disorderly subjectivity is constructed, which is to say, the inter-relationship between truth, relations of power and the self. Foucault (1997b: 291) explains this inter-relationship:

> I would say that if I am now interested in how the subject constitutes itself in an active fashion through the practices of self, these practices are nevertheless not something invented by the individual himself (sic). They are models that he finds in his culture and are proposed, suggested, imposed upon him by his culture, his society and his social group.

This perspective conceptualises the self as comprising multiple subjectivities, subjectivities that are produced via a process of subjectivisation. From this understanding, a young person diagnosed as disorderly can be described as having a 'disorderly subjectivity', and the diagnosis can be viewed as a process of subjectivisation.

This raises questions regarding the relationship between the scientific status of conduct disorder and the construction of disorderly subjectivity. Insight to this question can be drawn from Foucault's (1984a: 387) theorisation of the 'three elements of experience': 'the three fundamental elements of any experience [are] . . . a game of truth, relations of power, and forms of relation to oneself and others'. Because any experience involves these three elements, the supposition can be made that the process of subjectivisation must necessarily involve these three, namely games of truth, relations of power and relations of the self (or what Foucault (1988a) termed the technologies of the self). Based on this interpretation, a response can be made in terms of how each of these three elements is implicated in the 'truth' of conduct disorder and the construction of disorderly subjectivity.

These three elements of experience are deployed to form three strategic approaches for responding to my interrogation of conduct disorder and the constitution of disorderly subjectivity. The first approach employs the first element of experience, 'games of truth', to consider how the concept of disorderly children, and specifically conduct disorder, has the status of a scientific knowledge. The second approach uses relations of power to consider how conduct disorder can function as an authoritative knower of young people. The third uses relations with the self (the technologies of the self) to analyse how mentally disordered subjectivity is constituted. The analysis derived from the first two provides an understanding of how games of truth and relations of power influence the relations of the self.

When a young person is diagnosed as disorderly the diagnosis designates them as psychopathological. It is also likely to signify that much of that child's behaviour, thoughts, even intentions, can be interpreted via the discourses of mental disorder. As Edwards (2004) suggests, 'The term "disorder" is damaging in that it reinforces the notion that there is something wrong with the child, rather than something different.' One of the parents that I recently interviewed commented that, once her child had been diagnosed with ADHD, she never heard anything good about him from the school, and that there is an overall sense that 'they're just bad kids, once you get that label "bad", it stays there forever' (Parent Interview 3, 2004). A diagnosis can mean appreciably more than a mere delineation between the psychopathological young person and the non-psychopathological young person. It carries deeper and more ominous meanings in terms of the way in which being 'disorderly' influences how that child or young person is understood, both by others and by the young person him- or herself. The primary question of this book, 'how is it that a young person can state with certitude that they are disorderly?', therefore opens a way to interrogate the trend of diagnosing disorderly children. This is because, in asking how young people can understand themselves as disorderly, it must also be asked how a diagnosis of conduct disorder can have scientific credentials and how it can be diagnosed with authority.

The young people in the study

To interrogate the diagnosing of disorderly children I work with two approaches: a genealogy of conduct disorder and material from fieldwork studies into the diagnosing of disorderly children. The main fieldwork material is drawn from interviews in Australia with young people who had experienced being described as disorderly. These interviews were conducted in the late 1990s for my doctoral research and followed a semi-structured, multiple-interview format. This material comprises the stories of five young people, Rachel, Kris, Josh, Ben and Jemma, who had experienced the effects of being subjected to disorderly discourses. The names, locations and any other details that may identify the young people have been changed. At the time of the research in late 1997, Rachel was nineteen years old and working full-time for a corporation and Kris was eighteen years old and completing applications to get into university. Josh was sixteen years old, experiencing homelessness and trying to get a disability pension. Ben was eighteen years old, had almost completed a bartender's traineeship and was excited about 'finally completing a course'. Jemma was twenty and had just decided not to complete a childcare course at Technical and Further Education (TAFE) college.

These young people had an array of experiences with discourses that denoted them as disorderly. For example, Rachel had been told things about herself by her peers, her teachers and 'experts' from the psychiatric profession. She told how this began in kindergarten when her first encounter with a school counsellor caused her to be singled out from her peers. In primary school Rachel's peers told her that she had 'germs'; in high school they called her a 'red-headed rat rooter'. The name-calling did not cease when Rachel went to university, where her peers told her she was 'schizo' and 'suicidal'. By her teachers Rachel was told she was 'a problem' and 'disruptive'. Rachel's experience of being told she was disruptive began in kindergarten when she was 'aged four, turning five'. From this early start she explained, 'I got blamed for everything that went wrong in the classroom. I was labelled disruptive, it was a lovely label to have' (Rachel, Interviews).[2] Rachel met with an array of psychiatric professionals who told her she had 'behavioural problems' and 'relating problems', that she was disruptive and that she had 'depression', post-traumatic stress disorder, 'a personality disorder' and borderline personality disorder. She summed up these experiences with the comment, 'I'm just not Rachel,' remarking that this understanding had 'come from nineteen years of labels' (Rachel, Interviews). These experiences had convinced Rachel that she was problematic, but above all she knew she was not 'just Rachel', she was a person who is disorderly.

Kris had also experienced being diagnosed as disorderly, but in a way that differed from Rachel. Whilst Kris spoke of being described as disruptive, it seems that when he ceased being so he experienced being diagnosed as disorderly. He stated he was proud of his early years at high school when he was told by his teachers that he was 'naughty' and 'mischievous' and when his maths and science teachers called him a 'troublemaker'. Kris recalled being told that his class was worse than the most notoriously bad class in Sydney: 'we had one teacher that told me we were worse than the worse class in the state' (Kris, Interviews). Despite being told these things, Kris didn't think that he was 'really bad'. In comparison with later events in his school life, Kris remembered with fondness these experiences of intransigence as they represented a time when he wasn't mentally disordered.

This idea that he was 'disturbing everybody else' ended abruptly in the middle years of high school when he stopped being able to interact with his peers and his teachers. When this occurred Kris found the truth-telling changed from being 'naughty' to 'quiet' and the 'ideal student'. This change of truthfulness was accompanied by a change in how Kris felt about school. When he was 'naughty' school was fun, but when he was 'the ideal student' his memories of school were 'just ones of sadness and boredom (pause), just not knowing what to do with myself' (Kris, Interviews). As Kris explained, as he increasingly became the ideal student, he became increasingly isolated from his peers, an isolation that became complete when he was admitted to hospital and remained there for most of his middle and senior years of high school. Kris changed high schools during this period, but stayed at his new school for only two terms. 'I was sick and everything so I got into the church school and I was there for two terms – I left for my illness. And so basically I repeated year eleven again but I didn't get the pass the second time' (Kris, Interviews).

When he was in year 11, aged 15–16, Kris was placed into hospital because his parents became concerned with his weight loss. This weight loss occurred as a result of a period of dieting that Kris had embarked on because he had gained weight and hated being 'fat'. Initially he was put in an adolescent ward and was diagnosed with anorexia. Kris stated, 'I stayed up there [in the adolescent ward] for about four months and my weight just kept on getting lower' (Kris, Interviews). When Kris kept 'getting thinner and thinner' more measures were taken. As he explains, 'I got thinner and thinner and thinner and thinner to the point were I was down to sixty kilos and he [a Doctor] said well basically he put me into the too hard basket and sent me down to Dr X of the child psychiatric unit so that was the first time I was in a psychiatric hospital' (Kris, Interviews). Kris interpreted the move from the adolescent ward to the specialised Adolescent Psychiatric Hospital as meaning he was in the 'too hard basket'.

Josh was placed in what he termed a 'Special Ed' class (special education) at high school and as a result experienced significant truth-telling (in the form of harassment) from his peers. Josh explained that he went to a number of different primary schools:

> I went to about six or seven different primary schools. I've only been to two high schools. I went to lots of different primary schools because they couldn't handle me with my disability, my ADD [attention deficit disorder]. Basically the primary schools asked me to leave. And then when I went to high school they found out about my disability and then they put me in a Special Ed class . . . I had to leave my first high school because the Special Ed class closed down, so I had to move schools. I think the class closed down because of funding or something like that.
>
> (Josh, Interviews)

Particularly noticeable in this statement is Josh's confident knowledge of himself as being an individual who has ADD, referring to it as 'my ADD'. Josh was told he had ADD by a psychiatrist when he was eight years old. Josh also described himself as a 'Special Ed kid' and explained that 'a Special Ed kid is like a kid who can't sit down and handle something' (Josh, Interviews). This truth had taught Josh to know himself as an individual who can't really apply himself to tasks, a self-knowledge that underlined his belief that he has a disability. Therefore, it could be argued that being glad to be in the Special Ed class did not diminish the truth-telling effects of his 'specialness'.

Similarly to Rachel, Josh experienced the effects of what he described as harassment from his peers: 'I got called plenty of names because I was in the Special Ed class' (Josh, Interviews). Although Josh was called many names, he declared, 'It didn't affect me, they mainly teased me – I didn't bother about them, I honestly can't remember what they said' (Josh, Interviews). Despite these claims, this truth-telling from his peers caused him to be extremely sensitive to his identity as a 'Special Ed kid'. As Josh acknowledged, 'In a way you felt different [being in Special Ed]' (Josh, Interviews). The influence of this was so acute that at high school Josh restricted his relationships to those in his Special Ed class.

> At high school it was pretty shit to tell you the truth. Your only friends are your Special Ed class friends – you mixed with them all the time. Basically they were like your family. You didn't mix with the other kids. The Special Ed kids were a lot better than the high school kids.
>
> (Josh, Interviews)

In spite of this harassment, Josh believed that if he were not in the Special Ed class he 'would have left school a long time ago, I wouldn't have been able to handle it' (Josh, Interviews).

Of the young people interviewed, Ben was the only person who had been told he had conduct disorder, a diagnosis that he was told by a psychiatrist during a 'one-off' interview. Ben explained that this diagnosis didn't 'bother' him: 'I didn't really care – I never thought much of it, whatever they want to call it, that sort of thing . . . I never worried about names or any of these things, I never really got many' (Ben, Interviews). What Ben did care about with conduct disorder was that the disorder wasn't 'good enough'. Similar to Rachel, Ben would have preferred a better diagnosis:

> I wanted something better so you see I couldn't see any reason to care about conduct disorder cos I saw it as being a small insignificant little thing yeah . . . I wanted something that would really make people feel sorry for me – like I always wanted cancer and I wanted to die just so that people'd feel sorry for me. I wanted something like severe manic depression.
>
> (Ben, Interviews)

Although Ben wanted a more severe mental disorder, he did not want something like 'schizophrenia', which he thought was 'too severe'. Ben was aware of the different way people with 'severe' mental disorders were treated: 'then they don't want to know you cos you – they just feel sorry for you they want to help you' (Ben, Interviews). Later in our interviews Ben stated he was very concerned by one of the truths he had been told that was associated with conduct disorder, the truth that he could become a psychopath (antisocial personality disorder is the term used in the *DSM-IV-TR*).

Unlike Rachel, Kris and Josh, Ben did not discuss being told truths at school.

He described school as 'just a waste of my time . . . they weren't teaching me anything new' (Ben, Interviews). This opinion influenced his decisions to attend school: 'yeah well basically sometimes I'd turn up at school and if the work was really challenging then yeah I'd do it but usually I'd just show up at school and say I already know this and so I'd be out the door as fast as I can' (Ben, Interviews). When Ben wasn't attending school he said he just hung out with his friends at the local mall 'and that sort of thing'. Although it seems that from the school's perspective Ben was behaving in a manner that was a problem (not attending school), from his perspective school just wasn't a problem: it was boring; he 'just couldn't be bothered going there so it didn't affect me' (Ben, Interviews).

At the time of the interviews with Jemma, she had only begun to start using this name and new identity for herself. Prior to this she had been called 'Kathy'. Jemma was told many truths about herself by both adults and her peers, including 'slow', 'dumb', 'stupid', 'slut', 'no good at anything and useless', a 'fat heifer', that she had 'dyslexia', 'depression', and that she was a 'black mamma'. Jemma was the only young person who identified as black, describing how her peers teased her about the 'the colour of my skin'. She explained that these truths 'made me believe that I was a good for nothing and useless child' (Jemma, Interviews). Whilst this racial harassment troubled Jemma, she described the most distressing actions as when she was told she belonged in the 'slowest class'. Jemma described how she was put in the 'slow class' in primary school and remained in the 'slow classes' throughout high school. She concluded that she was in this class because she couldn't learn, and explained that the effects of this truth had been 'definitely dreadful' (Jemma, Interviews).

Notes on methodology

The key methodological perspectives that I draw on in my discussion are Foucauldian genealogy and a Foucauldian approach to narrative research. Foucauldian genealogy can be understood as a 'history of the present' in which, as Foucault (1988b: 262) explains, 'I set out from a problem expressed in the terms current today and I try to work out its genealogy'. Through this questioning of the present, genealogy can be used to antagonise the familiarity of diagnosing disorderly children and, in particular, the ways in which conduct disorder is made 'scientific'. Here genealogy is conceived as neither a method nor a system (Ransom, 1997; Tamboukou, 1999), but a strategy that responds to specific questions focused on the diagnosing of disorderly children and the construction of the disorderly child. Responding to this need for creativity, I deploy a genealogical strategy that draws on Foucault's 'three axes of genealogy':

> Three domains of genealogy are possible. First a historical ontology of ourselves in relation to truth through which we constitute ourselves as subjects of knowledge; second, a historical ontology of ourselves in relation to a field of power through which we constitute ourselves as subjects acting on others;

third, a historical ontology in relation to ethics through which we constitute ourselves as moral agents. So three axes are possible for genealogy.

(Foucault, 1983a: 237)

Drawing on this statement I suggest that each axis performs a vital role in the constitution of the disorderly child subject. The first refers to how truth is implicated in the production of disorderly children. This includes the fields of psychiatry and education. The second axis focuses on the relations of power that enable the diagnosing of disorderliness. These power relations, to quote Simons (1995: 30), include 'political structures, systems of rules and norms, techniques and apparatuses of government, dividing practices, and strategic relations between subjects who act upon each other'. To consider relations of power Foucault's (1980a) suggestion of a 'grid of analysis' is taken up and used to analyse the ways in which the relations of power function to make behaviour disorders an authoritative knowledge of young people. The third axis concerns the self, and considers the way in which a young person is involved in the constitution of him- or herself as disordered. This involves analysing the fieldwork data from the young people in relation to truth, power and self.

My analysis of the three axes of truth, relations of power and technologies of the self is made using what I term the 'four angles of scrutiny' (Harwood, 2004). These angles of scrutiny comprise discontinuity, contingency, emergences and subjugated knowledges. The first three angles, discontinuity, contingency and emergence, are specifically used for the genealogy of conduct disorder. The fourth, subjugated knowledge, includes two types, subjugated erudite knowledge and subjugated disqualified knowledge. The first, subjugated erudite knowledge, is applied to the genealogy of conduct disorder. The second, subjugated disqualified knowledge, is used to consider the construction of disorderedly subjectivities. These angles of scrutiny provide 'ways in' for conducting a genealogical analysis that can interrogate the diagnosing of disorderly children.

Genealogical 'histories of the present' demand that one think very differently about 'history'. In so doing the genealogist 'finds that there is "something altogether different" behind things: not a timeless and essential secret, but the secret that they have no essence or that their essence was fabricated in a piecemeal fashion from alien forms' (Foucault, 1977: 142). In doing this the genealogist strives to create a jagged and discontinuous 'history of the present', a task that is the opposite of a smooth and continuous history. This use of discontinuity is a tactic to unsettle familiar truths of the disorderly child and, more specifically, a diagnosis such as conduct disorder. The objective is to locate specific breaks and ruptures in the truth of conduct disorder and diagnosing disorderly children, and to destabilise, for instance, the assertion that conduct disorder occurs as the result of scientific development. In Chapter 3 I discuss several discontinuities, including the differing notions of conduct disorder and the varying classifications of conduct disorder in the *DSM*.

The difference between contingency and discontinuity can be illustrated in terms of what the genealogist investigates. For discontinuity, the genealogist is looking for points of rupture and difference in the apparently continuous truth of the disorderly child and of conduct disorder. To consider contingency, the genealogist asks questions such as 'on what conditions or occurrences was the creation of conduct disorder contingent?' This style of question implies that truths such as conduct disorder *are* necessarily contingent on something and therefore were 'created' at certain points. This point is clear in the following quotation: 'the things which seem most evident to us are always formed in the confluence of encounters and chances, during the course of a precarious and fragile history' (Foucault, 1988c: 37). Contingency brings to the surface the contingent nature of 'self-evident' truths such as the familiar practice of diagnosing disorderly children. Ransom (1997: 88) suggests that two aspects of contingency need to be considered by the genealogist. First, the genealogist needs to be aware that things 'which present themselves as natural end products of a comprehensible and progressive history are revealed as a cobbled patchwork of heterogenous elements'. Second, these things do not come together in some regulated fashion, but 'respond to haphazard conflicts' (ibid., citing Foucault, 1977: 154).

A way to use these points is to apply Foucault's suggestion of taking up tactical questions, such as 'Why did that work? How did that hold up?' (Foucault, 1980a: 209). Using these types of questions provokes a different interpretation of the conduct disorder, for, instead of taking conduct disorder (or disorderly children) as a given, one is prompted to ask, 'on what factors is the truth of conduct disorder contingent?' Or on what factors is the diagnosis of disorderly children contingent? In Chapter 3 I examine contingencies such as how conduct disorder is contingent on a notion of mental disorder, and the contingent relationship between conduct disorder and delinquency.

Considering truth in terms of discontinuity and contingency supports an interpretation of truths as 'emergences'. In discussing contingency, Foucault referred to emergence, stating: 'What reason perceives as *its* necessity, or rather, what different forms of rationality offer as their necessary being, can perfectly well be shown to have a history; and the network of contingencies from which it emerges can be traced' (Foucault, 1988c: 37, emphasis in original). Emergences are also mentioned by Butler (1999: 15), who explains: '"Genealogy" is not the history of events, but the enquiry into the conditions of the emergence (*Entstehung*) of what is called history, a moment of emergence that is not finally distinguishable from fabrication'. Considering the disorderly child as an emergence indicates that it did indeed emerge, and thereby places an emphasis on its 'creation'. Since it was constituted, it is possible to look for its discontinuities and contingencies. Discontinuity, contingency and emergence can be harnessed to interrogate the 'science' of conduct disorder and the construction of disorderly subjectivities. Discontinuity can be deployed to ask whether conduct disorder has remained the same, contingency can ask upon what the truth of conduct disorder is contingent, and emergence prompts posing the question 'When and how did this mental disorder emerge?'.

Subjugated knowledges are the fourth angle of scrutiny. These knowledges are what Foucault (1980b: 82) describes as 'those blocs of historical knowledge which were present but disguised within the body of functionalist and systematising theory and which criticism – which obviously draws upon scholarship – has been able to reveal'. These knowledges are valuable tools for the genealogist since from these it is possible to create 'something one might call a genealogy, or rather a multiplicity of genealogical researches, a painstaking rediscovery of struggles together with the rude memory of their conflicts' (ibid.: 83). Foucault describes two types of subjugated knowledges: erudite knowledges and local memories or disqualified knowledges. By contrast, subjugated erudite knowledges are those 'historical contents that have been buried and disguised in a functionalist coherence or formal systematisation' (ibid.: 81). This implies that the systematisation of a truth such as conduct disorder necessitated the 'burial' of certain erudite knowledges.

Genealogy can be described in terms of this interplay between domination and subjection. In so doing, genealogy 'seeks to re-establish the various systems of subjection: not the anticipatory power of meaning, but the hazardous play of dominations' (Foucault, 1977: 148). Thus, by finding a play of dominations, a system of subjection can be located in the apparent unity of the discourses of disorderly children. Through identifying points of domination, subjugated erudite knowledges signify moments of discontinuity in the accumulation of the so-called scientific knowledge of disorderly children. It is precisely through locating such subjections that this discourse can be made fragile. To use these subjugated erudite knowledges the genealogist must painstakingly search for 'historical traces of this play of dominations'. For a genealogy of conduct disorder this demands attention to the presence of subjugated erudite knowledges, such as that of Edwards (2004), the 'ex-headteacher now working in the field of mental health', who critiques the practices of disordering children.

Whilst erudite knowledges can be understood as expert or qualified knowledges that have been buried in the formulation of dominating systems of knowledge, subjugated disqualified knowledges are those that by contrast are considered bereft of expertise and qualification. These are 'a whole set of knowledges that have been disqualified as inadequate to their task or insufficiently elaborated: naive knowledges located low down on the hierarchy, beneath the required level of cognition or scientificity' (Foucault, 1980b: 82). The young people's stories of being diagnosed as disorderly included earlier in this chapter are examples of knowledges that have been excluded and are considered 'beneath the . . . level of . . . scientificity'. Subjugated disqualified knowledges are valuable to the genealogist and the criticism that genealogy hopes to establish, since 'it is through the re-appearance of this knowledge, of these local popular knowledges, these disqualified knowledges, that criticism performs its work' (ibid.: 82). By employing subjugated disqualified knowledges, genealogy can be used to 'entertain the claims . . . against the claims of a unitary body of theory which would filter, hierarchise and order them in the name of some true knowledge and some arbitrary idea of what constitutes a science and its objects' (ibid.: 83). Subjugated disqualified knowledges of young people such as Rachel, Ben, Josh, Kris and Jemma offer the possibility of going against the 'unitary body' of knowledge that diagnoses disorderly children.

In addition to genealogy, the research in this book draws on perspectives from narrative research to develop an approach for telling the interview participants' stories. I work with the idea that the narrative research notion of 'story' can be manipulated to suit the Foucauldian strategy of subjugated disqualified knowledges (for further discussion, see Harwood, 2001). As Barone (1992a: 20) points out, 'Great stories enable readers to gaze in fresh astonishment upon a part of their world they thought they had already seen. They also allow readers to get better acquainted with people they thought they had already known'. In drawing on subjugated disqualified knowledges, it can be argued that the stories of young people may be vital to re-thinking assumptions about the so-called disorderly child. The telling of such stories is thus the stuff of what Barone (1992b: 143) terms the 'critical educational storyteller', who is 'out to prick the consciences of readers by inviting a re-examination of the values and interests undergirding certain discourses, practices, and institutional arrangements found in today's schools'. In so doing the aim is to 'entice some readers into reconsidering comfortable attitudes and values and others into affirming latent perspectives not sanctioned by the dominant culture' (Barone, 1995: 66). An important aspect of such an aim is writing the story of the interview participants in a way that is believable. This draws on a point made by Sandelowski (1994: 61), who writes:

> When you talk to me about my research, do not ask me what I found; I found nothing. Ask me what I invented, what I made up from and out of my data. But know that in asking you ask me this, I am not confessing to telling any lies about the people or events in my studies/stories. I have told the truth. The proof for you is in the things I have made – how they look to your mind's eye, whether they satisfy your sense of style and craftsmanship, whether you believe them, and whether they appeal to your heart.

Writing the participant stories necessarily involves interpretation on the part of the researcher/writer. The unavoidability of this influence and, indeed, the logic for acknowledging its necessity is aptly described in Rosaldo's (1987) analogy of the making of research with the making of a photograph. An analogy such as this makes it clear that, as with the photograph, the researcher/writer is similarly implicated in composition of the research (Harwood, 2001). One way to work with this issue is to directly state that what is written is the *researcher's* version of events. I represent the participant stories in such a way as to create a persuasive account of subjugation, or what Barone calls 'an artfully persuasive *educational story*' (1995: 66, emphasis in original). The composition of the young people's stories in Chapters 6 and 7 strives for what Sandelowski (1994: 60) describes as a 'readable research report', 'a research report that reads like a novel: one that tells a good story that is coherent, consistent and believable but that is also aesthetically and intellectually satisfying'. Added to these points I have also endeavoured to aim for what Barone (1992a; 1992b) describes as accessibility, compellingness and moral persuasiveness. It also pertinent to note that in accessing the young people I am not attempting to 'give them voice', I am attempting to write stories of their subjugation and disqualification, to craft accounts of subjugated disqualified knowledges that can support a genealogical criticism of the diagnosing of disorderly children. This emphasis on story is explicitly drawn on as a means to take up Foucault's (1984b) challenge to make genealogy something that stirs us from 'what we think'.

The fieldwork with the five young people was located in a youth centre in metropolitan Sydney, Australia. All of the young people who participated in this study had experienced being diagnosed with a mental disorder (and some more than one). Each of the young people's stories focuses on their experiences of being told that they were 'disorderly', a 'disorderliness' that includes being described both as mentally disordered and/or as a 'problem'. This focus is deliberately broader than a diagnosis of 'conduct disorder' because I am interested in how the young people were described as disorderly and how school experiences and diagnosis were implicated in this. This meant that, from the perspective of subjugated disqualified knowledges, a range of stories could be told about the practices of diagnosing disorderly children.

The number of participants for this study was restricted to five because of the emphasis on in-depth multiple interviews. This process involved a flexible semi-structured approach that was based on eight open-ended questions and enabled the interviewer to respond and adapt to each of the young people. For example, the plan was to have two to three interviews of between forty-five and sixty minutes' duration. However, in the field this was modified, and for one of the young people only one interview was conducted, whereas with another participant it was decided to have four interviews.

An important point to note is how the multiple interviews supported the development of a rapport with the young person, which proved to be especially important for this topic. The young people tended to talk widely about their experiences of being told they were mentally disordered or that they were 'a problem'. The questions were therefore not restrictive but served to prompt a wide discussion of practices of 'disordering' and the making of young people into 'disorderly problems'. The discussion of these interviews in Chapters 6 and 7 focuses on how mentally disordered and 'problem' subjectivities of the young people were constructed, and how school and psychiatric expertise were involved in these constructions. This discussion is organised into a layered analysis and does not adhere to temporal order; rather their stories are discussed in non-linear and sometimes cyclical ways.

Qualitative research from two small fieldwork studies is drawn on to build on my analysis. The first is from a study (2003–05) into parents and caregivers who have been told that their child is disruptive. This study involves semi-structured in-depth interviews with parents and caregivers in metropolitan Sydney and regional New South Wales (NSW). The data that are reported in this book are drawn from three interviews from regional NSW. These participants were recruited via newspaper advertisement in local papers and via contact with parent support groups. The second is a small study of young people's attitudes towards prescription and over-the-counter medications conducted in 2004. Three focus groups were run with young people ranging in age from 14 to 17, with participants recruited from youth organisations in a location in regional NSW. This fieldwork was designed to further investigate a study of young people and prescription and over-the-counter medications completed in 2001 by the NSW Commission for Children and Young People (2002).

Approval from appropriate Human Ethics Research Committees was granted for each of these studies. All of the studies required consideration of how the nature of the topic might impact on the participants. Particular care was required to manage the ethical issues of interviewing the five young people, who had experienced stigmatisation and difficult life circumstances such as homelessness, unemployment or health issues. Added to these considerations, these participants had also experienced considerable intervention by authority in their lives (for example, from school counsellors, government welfare workers, police, psychologists and psychiatrists). It was therefore vital to ensure that a distinction was made between the research interview and these other experiences. Awareness of the relations of power between the researcher and the participants in all three studies was therefore imperative, and especially for the in-depth, multiple interviews with the five young people. This involved being alert to the positioning of the researcher as expert and deliberately attempting to disrupt this status. This disruption is of consequence because it is not possible to access subjugated disqualified knowledges by replicating the relations of power that make them 'subjugated'.

Audio recordings of interviews were transcribed and the transcriptions were made available to the five young people prior to the commencement of the next interview. This provided the opportunity for material to be scrutinised and altered by the participants. This process resulted in some material being altered or deleted at the direction of the young person. 'Recording through writing', whereby the young person dictated their interview responses and I typed them, proved to be another practical strategy for the young people to monitor and make adjustments to the material to maintain their confidentiality. During both the interviews for the main study and the interviews with the parents/caregivers, provision was also made for information to be altered during the interviews. For example, when participants decided there was something they didn't want recorded, the audio recording was paused. For all three studies, any material that may identify the participants has been changed. The details altered include the names of participants and any other people who were discussed (such as teachers, psychiatrists, children, partners), names of schools, hospitals and psychiatric units, geographic locations and certain specific experiences.

The structure of the book

The organisation of the chapters closely corresponds with the analysis of the three Foucauldian elements of experience: truth, power and the self. In the next chapter, 'Disorderly children', I discuss the problem of young people being diagnosed as disorderly and explain how I draw on Foucault to formulate a means to analyse the emergence of conduct disorder and, more broadly, the construction of mentally disordered subjectivity. In Chapter 3, 'Disorderly conduct and the truth of the disorderly child', I use a genealogical approach to analyse the 'truth' of conduct disorder. From this discussion of 'truth', in Chapter 4, I consider the way relations of power are implicated in the fabrication of conduct disorder. In Chapter 5, I continue this line of interrogation by focusing specifically on how power is involved in the diagnosing of disorderly children. This chapter discusses the administration of diagnosis and how the school is implicated in practices of diagnosing disorderly children. The emphasis of this discussion is on a study of schools in NSW, and this is extended to consider the implications in school education in countries such as the UK and the US.

In Chapters 6 and 7, I move to the third element of experience, the self. It is in these chapters that I work with the stories of the five young people to consider how the technologies of the self are implicated in the construction of disorderly subjectivities. Although both Chapters 6 and 7 focus on the self, I incorporate an analysis of truth and power in relation to the self into each of the stories from the five young people. These stories are thus organised into several layers of analysis corresponding to each of the axes – truth, power and the self. The analysis of conduct disorder made in Chapters 3, 4 and 5 is drawn on to consider how truth and power influence technologies of the self. Chapter 6 begins with a discussion of the young people's stories of the truths that were told of being 'disorderly' or 'a problem'. From these stories of 'truth-telling', power, the second layer of analysis, is added. The technologies of the self form the third layer of analysis. Using this last layer of analysis enables me to consider how the self is involved with truth and power in the formation of disorderly subjectivities. This structure is repeated in Chapter 7, but with a focus on how to question the diagnosing of disorderly children. To do this I consider how the self (and the relation to truth and power) is involved in challenging disorderly subjectivities.

Chapter 2

Disorderly children

References to behaviour disorders and the diagnosing of children as disorderly have become increasingly common in countries such as Australia, the UK and the US. Descriptions of children are made from a vocabulary that includes behaviour problems, behaviour difficulties, emotional and behavioural difficulties (EBD), behaviour disorders, emotional and behavioural disorders, conduct disorders (CD), oppositional defiant disorders (ODD) and attention deficit hyperactivity disorders (ADHD). At times when reference is made to behaviour problems or behaviour difficulties, it seems that reference is not being made to a mental disorder. At other times this seems less than clear, the lines seemed blurred and behavioural difficulties seems to connote psychiatric disorder. Poulou and Norwich (2002: 112) capture this confusion in relation to EBD, stating it is a 'broad and vague term which is used mainly in the education service to refer to a pupil's difficulties in behaviour, emotions and relationships which are severe and persistent such that they interfere with their learning and development'. They then make the point that EBD 'is a term which overlaps with psychiatric disorder at one end and disruptive behaviour or behaviour problems at the other' (ibid.).

Although these authors note an overlap in defining EBD, they appear to suggest that there is a continuum that has psychiatric disorders at one end and behaviour problems at the other. It is a tenuous proposition to claim such a linear distinction, since it assumes that one can simply refer to behaviour problems without invoking the spectre of mental disorders. For example, we need to ask, is it possible to speak of a boy with behaviour difficulties and do so without the invocation of disorders such as ADHD or conduct disorder? So pervasive are the discourses of psychiatric disorder that it is difficult to imagine how behaviour problems can be conceived without its influence, even if it is only to repudiate the possibility of a diagnosis.

The psychiatric diagnostic criteria for disruptive behaviour disorders are detailed in the APA's (2000) *Diagnostic and Statistical Manual of Mental Disorders Text Revision* (*DSM IV-TR*), a recently published 'text revision' of the revised 1994 edition, *DSM-IV*. Within the *DSM-IV-TR*, criteria for disruptive behaviour disorders are found in axis one, 'Disorders Usually First Diagnosed in Infancy, Childhood and Adolescence'. This broad heading includes ten categories: 'Mental Retardation', 'Learning Disorders', 'Motor Skills Disorder', 'Communication Disorders', 'Pervasive Developmental Disorders', 'Attention-Deficit and Disruptive Behavior Disorders', 'Feeding and Eating Disorders of Infancy or Early Childhood', 'Tic Disorders', 'Elimination Disorders', and 'Other Disorders of Infancy, Childhood, or Adolescence' (APA, 2000). The disruptive behaviour disorders are detailed under the sixth category, 'Attention-Deficit and Disruptive Behavior Disorders'. The disorders in this category are, 'Attention-Deficit/Hyperactivity Disorder', 'Attention-Deficit/Hyperactivity Disorder Not Otherwise Specified', 'Conduct Disorder', 'Oppositional Defiant Disorder', 'Disruptive Behavior Disorder Not Otherwise Specified' (APA, 2000). Amongst these, conduct disorder and oppositional defiant disorder are claimed by Hinshaw and Zupan (1997: 36, citing APA, 1994) to be 'the two mainstays of the disruptive behavior disorders'.

Each of these disorders has precise criteria. The *DSM-IV-TR* criteria for conduct disorder state:

> The essential feature of Conduct Disorder is a repetitive and persistent pattern of behavior in which the basic rights of others or major age-appropriate societal norms or rules are violated (Criteria A). These behaviors fall into four main groupings: aggressive conduct that causes or threatens harm to other people or animals (Criteria A1–A7), nonaggressive conduct that causes property loss or damage (Criteria A8–A9), deceitfulness or theft (Criteria A10–A12), and serious violations of rules (Criteria A13–A15). Three (or more) of these characteristic behaviors must have been present during the past 12 months, with at least one behavior present in the past 6 months. The disturbance in behavior causes clinically significant impairment in social, academic, or occupational functioning (Criteria B). Conduct Disorder may be diagnosed in individuals who are older than age 18 years, but only if the criteria for Antisocial Personality Disorder are not met (Criteria C). The behavior pattern is usually present in a variety of settings such as home, school, or the community. Because individuals with Conduct Disorder are likely to minimize their conduct problems, the clinician often must rely on additional informants. However, the informant's knowledge of the child's conduct problems may be limited by inadequate supervision or by the child's not having revealed them.
>
> (APA, 2000: 93–4)

This definition is influential because it is located within the *DSM*, which is an extremely powerful and influential compendium of psychopathology, one that has a significant authority in contemporary discourses of disorderly children. For example, in his chapter in the *Handbook of Child Psychopathology* (Ollendick and Herson, 1998), Frick (1998: 216) emphasises that 'Criteria in the fourth edition of the Diagnostic and Statistical Manual of Mental Disorders (APA, 1994) for the Disruptive Behavior Disorders are one of the most influential and widely used systems for classifying children with conduct disorders'. There are methods other than the *DSM-IV-TR* to diagnose childhood behavioural disorders, but, based on the widespread reference to the *DSM*, it can be argued that this manual is the most dominant.

The dominance is apparent in the many media reports about children and behaviour disorders, including those that tell dramatic accounts of the alleged predictive potential of the disorderly diagnosis. An apposite example is *A Dangerous Mind*, a story from the Australian Broadcasting Commission's *Four Corners* programme, televised nationally in Australia (with the exception of Tasmania) on 1 July 1996 (Moncrieff, 1996). This story discussed the background of Martin Bryant, the man responsible for the murder of thirty-five people at Port Arthur, Tasmania, Australia. Drawing on discourses of disorderly children, *A Dangerous Mind* focused on the search for predictive clues for Bryant's behaviour. The story included a compelling scene of children playing whilst a voice-over described some of the *DSM* diagnostic criteria of conduct disorder. At the story's close the narrator made this alarming remark:

> Scientists continue to debate the interaction between our genes and our upbringing, but they all agree on one thing, that most of the factors which make up the next potential Martin Bryant can be identified early. Many of them were there in the young Martin. The question is whether we have the commitment to act. Otherwise those like Martin Bryant will always remain invisible until another bloody Sunday when it's too late.
>
> (Moncrieff, 1996)[1]

Media accounts such as this extend the diagnosing of disorderly children to include practices that can identify the potentially murderous adult. The pursuit of prediction is similarly apparent in the newspaper article on Bryant, 'Inside the mind of a killer' (Jones and Patterson, 2000). The article discusses a psychiatric report on Bryant that details connections between the alleged bullying he experienced at school and the killing of the thirty-five people and describes how Bryant had several mental disorders, including conduct disorder, attention deficit hyperactivity and Asperger's syndrome.

Although Bryant's story is a shocking example, it is not the case that predictions of danger are reserved for the 'out of the ordinary' instance of extremely violent behaviour. It is plainly stated in the *DSM-IV-TR* that those with childhood-onset types of conduct disorder have an increased likelihood risk of antisocial personality disorder as adults (APA, 2000). As I stated in Chapter 1, a percentage is provided by the American Academy of Child and Adolescent Psychiatry (1997), which declares that 'Approximately 40% of children and adolescents with CD go on to develop Antisocial Personality Disorder (APD), with the prevalence of APD in the general population of adults estimated to be 2.6%'. Such predictions are echoed in the peculiarly titled journal article, 'Early identification of the fledgling psychopath: locating the psychopathic child in the current nomenclature', which makes the startling claim that adolescent boys who have 'hyperactivity, impulsivity, and attention problems concurrent with conduct problems . . . most closely resembled psychopathic adults' (Lynam, 1998: 566).

In addition to antisocial personality disorder there are a range of other grave outcomes predicted for disorderly children diagnosed with conduct disorder, such as 'criminality' and 'alcoholism', and '5% develop schizophrenia' (Tonge, 1998: 67). Galli *et al.* (1999) propose that conduct disorder (and other mental disorders) can be found amongst 'adolescent child molesters'. Todd and Gesten (1999) also write of the 'child-abuse potential in at-risk adolescents'. These predictions of ominous outcomes seem to be tied up with the notion that the disorderly child is unlikely to change for the better. Such is the claim made in an Australian study by Rey *et al.* (1995) that looked for 'continuities between psychiatric disorders in adolescents and personality disorders in young adults'. These researchers report that there 'is currently little evidence showing that disruptive adolescents respond to intervention' and that 'disruptive adolescents appear to have particularly negative personality outcome . . . Because of their severe impairment, this group is a major public health problem' (ibid.: 899).

The concern with conduct disorder

If the research, government surveys and media reports are to be believed, there are increasing numbers of children and young people with behavioural problems. This is reflected in the claims that conduct disorder is amongst the most prevalent of the child psychiatric disorders, with, for example, Australian authors maintaining that it is 'very common among children and adolescents in our society' (Braithwaite *et al.*, 1999). Writing in the *British Journal of Psychiatry*, Simonoff *et al.* (2004: 118) similarly state 'conduct disorder is the most common child psychiatric disorder'. An article in the British newspaper the *Guardian* claims 'The mental health of teenagers has sharply declined in the last 25 years, and the chances that 15-year-olds will have behavioural problems such as lying, stealing and being disobedient have more than doubled' (Bunting, 2004). Two years earlier, the *Guardian* carried a story reporting that 750,000 children had 'clinically significant conduct disorders' (Carvel, 2002).

The estimates of the prevalence of conduct disorder vary. In Australia, the report *Mental Health of Young People in Australia*, which draws on the *DSM-IV* definition of conduct disorder, maintains that 3.0 per cent of all children and adolescents have conduct disorder (Sawyer *et al.*, 2000). In the UK, 'The British child and adolescent mental health survey 1999' (Ford *et al.*, 2003) measured the prevalence of *DSM-IV* disorders, reporting that 9.5 per cent of children and adolescents have a *DSM-IV* disorder and 6 per cent have any disruptive disorder, with 1.5 per cent having conduct disorder. By contrast, *Mental Health of Children and Adolescents in Great Britain*, which used the *International Classification of Diseases-10 (ICD-10)* criteria for mental disorders, reports that 5 per cent of children have conduct disorder (Meltzer *et al.*, 2000). A figure of 3.2 per cent prevalence for conduct disorder is listed in the UK report *The Health of Children and Young People* (Maughan *et al.*, 2004). Research by Collishaw *et al.* (2004) notes the issues of the varying studies of prevalence (including problems with divergent definitions), yet still concludes that there has been a large increase in conduct problems in young people over the last twenty-five years in Britain.

In the US the American Academy of Child and Adolescent Psychiatry (1997) estimates that the prevalence of conduct disorder is between 1.5 and 3.4 per cent. Similarly, *Mental Health: A Report of the Surgeon General* claims that the prevalence of conduct disorder among '9–17-year-olds in the community varies from 1 to 4 percent depending on how the disorder is defined' (US Department of Health and Human Services, 1999). A report from British Columbia, Canada (Waddell *et al.*, 2004), cites an overall estimate that draws on epidemiological research from the UK, US and Canada to arrive at a figure of 4.2 per cent. It then applies this percentage to the population of children in British Columbia, drawing the conclusion that around 42,000 children have conduct disorder.

This variation in estimates of prevalence is even larger when disorderly children are defined according to categories such as 'behaviour disorders', 'disruptive behaviours', 'severe behaviour disorders', 'behaviour problems', 'emotional and behaviour disturbance' and 'emotional and behaviour disorders'. In the state of Victoria, Australia, 5.1 per cent of students in state-run primary and high schools in 2001 are reported as having severe behaviour disorder (17,000 students from a total of 535,412 students) (Victorian Government, 2002). Similarly large estimates are described in the UK. *Special Educational Needs in England, January 2004* (SFR 44/2004) reports that, among students at maintained primary and secondary schools, behaviour, emotional and social difficulties accounted for 26.8 per cent of School Action Plus students and 13.8 per cent of Special Educational Need students (Department for Education and Skills, 2004). In this reference, 'School Action Plus' refers to students for whom the school has sought specialist outside advice, and 'Special Educational Need' refers to students who have been 'legally statemented' as having 'special educational needs' (SEN) by their local education authority.

In the US a range of prevalence estimates are cited for the loose category of behaviour problems, with this variation seeming to depend on how the 'problem' is defined (Narrow *et al.*, 1998). Despite these definitional issues, there appears to be consensus that the prevalence of disorderly children is 'alarmingly high' (Huang *et al.*, 2004). An estimate reported by Pottick (2002) claims that 31 per cent of youths admitted to mental health services in the US in 1997 had a psychiatric diagnosis belonging to the category of disruptive behaviour disorders (which includes conduct disorder). Ruffolo *et al.* (2003: 431) cite research by Cohen *et al.* (1996) that 'during any year, approximately one-fifth of youths have diagnosable emotional or behavior problems that cause at least temporary interference with functioning in family, school or community settings'. The supposed increasing numbers have drawn speculation on the costs of disorderly children with, for example, Scott *et al.* (2001: 4) estimating that, in relation to public services, 'individuals with conduct disorders cost 10 times as much as those without conduct problems'.

Diagnoses of conduct disorder are applied across a range of ages, up to the age of eighteen, with some researchers, such as Keenan and Wakschlag (2004), arguing that it can be suitable for preschoolers. In terms of location, disorderly children are apparently 'more common in cities than in rural areas' (US Department of Health and Human Services, 1999). There is also discussion (and debate) regarding disorderly children from ethnic minority groups. Research by Lau *et al.* (2004) in the US examined differences between teacher, parent and youth reports of student behaviour, contending that racial issues are implicated in the high numbers of African American young people reported as having problem behaviours. Citing Pigott and Cowen's (2000) research, they state 'studies have shown that teachers judge African American children as having more disruptive or hyperactive symptoms, poorer educational progress' (Lau *et al.*, 2004: 146).

Uncertainty regarding the application of *DSM* diagnostic criteria to minority groups even prompts some researchers to evaluate whether *DSM* criteria can be 'validly used' in relation to children from these groups. Keenan and Wakschlag (2004: 358) made such an 'investigation' in relation to preschoolers, and claim conduct disorder and oppositional defiant disorder diagnoses can be 'applied to African American children living in urban poverty, a group who have often been underrepresented in the literature on diagnostic validity'. Conversely, a 2003 survey by Meltzer *et al.* (2003: 27), which examined the persistence of childhood mental disorders in Britain, reported that 'Age, sex, ethnicity, and physical illness were not significant correlates of persistent conduct disorder', but that it was affected by low family income.

This debate over the representation of ethnic groups in mental disorder prevalence data is evident in a letter to the editor of the *American Journal of Psychiatry* that comments on recent surveys of prevalence of ADHD in the US and Britain (Evans, 2004). These surveys reported lower treatment rates for black children in the US and lower rates of ADHD diagnosis of black children in the UK (Evans, 2004). Yet, as Evans surmises, in the UK 'the overall rate of mental disorder in black children was higher than in any other ethnic group, with conduct disorder making the biggest contribution to the difference' (Evans, 2004: 932). This prompted Evans to ask whether

> we are therefore more likely to attribute behavioral disturbances to ADHD in whites and to conduct disorder in blacks? Given the less-certain illness status of conduct disorder, this reveals important differences in our attitudes to personal responsibility and treatability in different ethnic groups: in short, that black is bad and white is mad.
>
> (ibid.)

The distinction that Evans alleges between 'bad' and 'mad' is questionable, given that conduct disorder is defined as a mental disorder. These differences should give pause for thought – but not to a consideration that endeavours to find what the 'real' disorders are but rather to ask why certain children and young people are more at risk of the diagnostic gaze. As Desai (2003: 100) argues, 'whilst it is important to include ethnicity as a variable in order to "root out" covert racism, over-focusing on this has led to explanations which do no more than pathologise black people and black communities'. These debates draw attention to the alarming problems with notions of disorderliness and the racialised assumptions that appear implicit in practices of diagnosing disorderly children.

Although there is much debate over questions of prevalence and 'race', it appears that there are fewer disputes when the focus is placed on the 'factor' of low income. Echoing the above claim by Meltzer *et al.* (2003), a story in the *Guardian* states 'Children of poor families are three times more likely to suffer a mental disorder than those brought up in well-off households' (Brindle, 1999). Similar issues are raised in the UK Office of National Statistics (2001: 131) survey *Prevalence of Mental Disorders among Children*, which reported that 'Children from households with lower gross weekly incomes were more likely than those from households with higher incomes to display a mental disorder of some kind'. Australian reports cite an increased prevalence of conduct disorder in lower income families (Sawyer *et al.*, 2000). US researchers Costello *et al.* (2003: 2028) describe a relationship between poverty and conduct disorder, noting that 'The effect of poverty was strongest for behavioral symptoms (those included in the DSM-IV diagnoses of conduct and oppositional disorder)'. Incredibly, one psychoanalytic view of the relationship between socio-economic status (SES) and conduct disorder states that 'Children with severe conduct disorders from lower SES and abusive backgrounds simply do not have the containing and holding environment that other children have to develop adult ego functions to survive' (Twemlow *et al.*, 2002: 227). This is an unashamedly moral interpretation of poverty and mental illness – a moralistic leaning that is not so distinct from the moral imperatives of the mental sciences some hundred years ago. Conceptualisations of disorderly children must be scrutinised with a critical attentiveness to racial and socio-economic considerations.

Likewise, other high 'representations', such as the number of boys who are allegedly disorderly, must be scrutinised. It appears that research literature from the UK and the US agrees that there is greater prevalence of conduct disorder amongst boys (Scott *et al.*, 2001; US Department of Health and Human Services, 1999). There are reports of 'a ratio of between 4:1 to 12:1' (Ayers and Prytys, 2002: 73) and in Australia a percentage for boys of 4.4 per cent of the population and 1.6 per cent for girls (Sawyer *et al.*, 2000). The reportedly high number of boys with mental health problems is the lead story for the media release for the 'mental health' section of the British publication *The Health of Children and Young People* (Maughan *et al.*, 2004). There are researchers, such as Keenan *et al.* (1999), who argue that 'conduct disorder is a relatively common disorder' and that, in addition to the risk of developing antisocial personality disorder, CD girls are likely to 'get pregnant'. These researchers, not surprisingly, go on to cite 'sexual activity as one of the primary public health concerns associated with CD in girls' (ibid.: 12).

Other researchers have claimed that gay, lesbian and bisexual (GLB) young people are at increased risk of developing conduct disorder (Fergusson *et al.*, 1999). Elze (2002: 97) suggests an 'association between sexual minority youths' perceptions of a negative community environment for gay, lesbian, and bisexual people and their externalising problems'. Similarly, Lock and Steiner (1999) point to experiences of 'social intolerance' and 'externalising behaviour' and 'conduct' problems in GLB youth. Whilst Anhalt and Morris (1998) review the issue of psychopathology in GLB young people, they do point to flaws in the methodology used for much of the research (such as low samples). See Harwood (2004), where I discuss this problem of psychopathologising sexual minority young people.

Schools are often depicted as having to manage 'large numbers' of disorderly children. Whilst school responses to these disorderly children may vary across different school districts, states and countries, what seems common is the conviction that these students 'have long been regarded as the most difficult group of children with special needs to integrate into the regular classroom' (Bradshaw, 1998: 115). Young people who are considered to be not 'functioning' at school are likely to have encounters with mental health services (Campbell, 1998). For instance, Porter, a school counsellor from a regional Australian high school, emphasised psychiatric knowledge and diagnosis (including input from a clinical psychologist) as fundamental to assessing students for an 'ED/BD' (emotional disorders/behavioural disorders) class. Increased attention to the issue of disorderly students covers a range of ages, with a mounting focus on the 'early years'. In Australia, for example, programmes such as APEEL (A Partnership Encouraging Effective Learning) are designed for children who are at the beginning of their schooling and who are considered at 'high risk of developing conduct disorders' (National Crime Prevention, 1999: 55).

The burgeoning fixation on behaviour disorders also invokes some quite surprising analogies, such as that proposed by Patterson *et al.* (1992) (Figure 2.1). As can be seen in this diagram, the model is illustrated using the 'vile weed', a plant that, as Harris and Simmonds (2002: 2) explain, 'grows rampant in Oregon'.

Patterson *et al.* (1992) depict the vile weed as growing from the ground of 'antisocial parents', 'unskilled grandparents', 'stressors', 'parent substance abuse' and 'child temperament' and reaching its conclusion in 'chaotic employment career', 'institutionalization' and 'disrupted marriage'. Although the analogy of an antisocial child with a vile weed must surely seem extraordinary to most, it is employed by other researchers to study disorderly children. For example, Harris and Simmonds (2002) use it in their discussion of the 'Youth Horizons Trust Programme'. The use (and demand) for this model is described by Bogenschneider and Gross (2004: 20), who, referring to the uptake of theory in policy development, explain how 'following one Wisconsin Family Impact Seminar, we received multiple requests from policy makers for Patterson's "Vile Weed," a visual portrayal of the Oregon Social Learning Center's theory of the etiology of violent juvenile crime'. They also add that 'one state legislator used this analogy – which illustrates the importance of early family intervention – in a debate on the floor of the senate' (ibid.: 20).

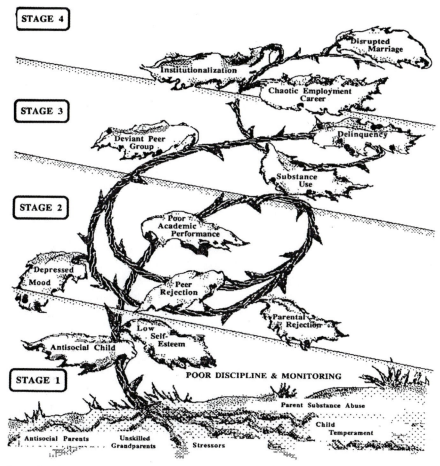

STAGE 4

STAGE 3

STAGE 2

STAGE 1

Disrupted Marriage

Institutionalization

Chaotic Employment Career

Deviant Peer Group

Delinquency

Substance Use

Poor Academic Performance

Depressed Mood

Peer Rejection

Parental Rejection

Low Self-Esteem

Antisocial Child

POOR DISCIPLINE & MONITORING

Parent Substance Abuse

Child Temperament

Antisocial Parents   Unskilled Grandparents   Stressors

Figure 2.1 The vile weed: stages in the coercion model. Reproduced with permission from Patterson *et al.* (1992: 13).

With the increasing rates of disorderly children, increasing diagnoses, increasing costs and the alleged spiralling social issues, it would seem that disorderly children must be on the increase and diagnostic attention is warranted. But perhaps we should be asking different and far more critical questions of this phenomenon. With analogies such as a vile weed being used to characterise the antisocial child, serious questions need to be asked of the practices that diagnose disorderly children. Perhaps we should be asking not *who is at risk of behavioural problems*, but, rather, *who is at risk of being diagnosed as disorderly*?

Getting critical

Compared with the literature that advances behaviour disorders and the diagnosing of disorderly children, there is limited available literature that is critical of these practices. The shelves of many bookstores in countries such as Australia, the UK and the US customarily contain popular texts on 'troubled kids'. Books such as *100 Questions and Answers about Your Child's Attention Deficit Hyper-activity Disorder* (Nass and Leventhal, 2005), *Emotional and Behavioral Prob-lems of Young Children* (Gimpel and Holland, 2003), *The Difficult Child* (Turecki and Tonner, 2000), *The Defiant Child: A Parent's Guide to Oppositional Defiant Disorder* (Riley, 1997) and *It's Nobody's Fault: New Hope and Help for Difficult Children and their Parents* (Koplewicz, 1996) explain the disorders and generally use the professional background of the author (for example, 'a psychiatrist and father') to give it authenticity. Such books endorse behaviour disorders and often the medicalisation of children, and need to be treated warily.

By drawing on Foucault, who was particularly critical of the 'science' of psychology and psychiatry, a powerful form of critique can be levelled at behaviour disorders and the practices of diagnosing disorderly children. Foucault has been utilised by several authors to mount arguments against the scientificity of psychiatry, mental disorder or the application of this knowledge in areas such as education. For example Hultqvist (1998) uses Foucault to examine the emergence of 'developmental psychology' as a means to govern the preschool child in Sweden. Critics of psychiatric and psychological nomenclature who use Foucault include Donzelot (1979), Harper (1996), Henriques *et al.* (1984), Laurence and McCallum (1998a; 1998b; 2003), McCallum (1997; 1998; 2001), Rose (1985; 1989) and Slee (1995).

Several critiques of behaviour disorders have been published by Laurence and McCallum, including one of conduct disorder and the notion of 'comorbidity' (1998a) and a genealogical critique of attention deficit disorder (1998b). In the latter they argue that the *DSM* is intrinsic to creating attention deficit disorder, and provide a discussion that unsettles the idea that there is a biological aetiology of ADD or ADHD that can be located in the brain. In a more recent article, 'Conduct disorder: the achievement of a diagnosis', Laurence and McCallum (2003) analyse the emergence of conduct disorder and its relation to the government of the population. McCallum's (1998; 2001) analysis of antisocial personality disorder uses a genealogical approach to develop a critical perspective on this disorder and discusses how it is associated with the law and tied to mechanisms that seek to govern the individual. Other critical work that examines conduct disorder includes an article by Richters and Cicchetti (1993) interestingly titled 'Mark Twain meets DSM-III-R: conduct disorder, development, and the concept of harmful dysfunction'. This article scrutinises the assumption that the behaviours associated with conduct disorder signify an underlying mental disorder, raising questions including how the 'usage of the label is widely perceived to be tantamount to an endorsement and perpetuation of the underlying assumption [that there is a mental disorder]' (ibid.: 24). In another example, the Canadian doctoral dissertation by Bogardus (1997) takes a critical perspective of conduct disorder – but uncritically allies the term to deviance.

There is a larger critical (and non-critical) literature on ADHD. The critical work includes Bennett (2004), Danforth and Navarro (2001), Laurence and McCallum (1998b), Miller and Leger (2003), Monk (2000) and Tait (2001; 2005). Tait (2005: 36) provides a discussion that examines different perspectives on 'truth' of ADHD, and in particular makes the comment that 'the production of truth is inexorably tied to the right to produce truth, and whereas this right once belonged to religion, it now belongs to science'. In relation to ADHD, Miller and Leger (2003) examine the drug Ritalin in terms of the 'risk society', providing an analysis of the construction of both ADHD and the *DSM*. Monk (2000) examines education, law and the 'construction of the ideal pupil'. Commenting on ADHD and the increasing diagnoses of Ritalin in Britain, Monk (2000: 361) argues that 'medical knowledge and expertise operate as a technique of modern government that serve to legitimise the problematisation of child behaviour that deviates from the norm'. Also with reference to the UK, Bennett (2004) drew on a Foucauldian analysis to examine the issues mothers face in relation to 'mothering a child with ADHD'. In the US, Danforth and Navarro (2001: 186) analysed the language of laypersons when speaking about ADHD, emphasising that these 'language users draw heavily from dominant cultural discourses that pose moral problems of child activity as individual phenomena subject to medical diagnosis and intervention'. This take-up of scientific discourses of disorderly children is a pressing issue, especially when these discourses are so frequently presented as indisputable scientific facts in the media.

Slee (1995: 75) contends that ascribing attention deficit disorder to children 'transforms the child from bad to sick'. Drawing on Tomlinson (1982), he argues that the notion of deficit within the child has benefits for the school:

> Educational psychology ... has provided educational policy-makers with ways of explaining disruptive student behaviour which delimit pedagogical and organizational culpability. Moreover, the responses to their analyses promote an expanding raft of diagnostic, counselling and remedial practices which serve the professional interests of the psychological and special educational fraternities.
>
> (Slee, 1995: 169–70)

Such diagnostic practices are habitually implicated in the exclusion of young people from education on the premise that, as a mental disorder, the problem resides within that young person. This issue of exclusion is taken up by Cooper (2002), who uses Foucault to examine the issue of the removal of young people from British high schools, arguing that the practices of exclusion form part of a disciplinary regime that dominates and regulates in order to produce the 'docile' student. Practices of 'docility' similarly occur to students subjected to disciplines within the school. One such practice, 'special sport', is discussed by Saltmarsh and Youdell (2004), who note the panoptic control enforced on a group of male students considered to have 'behaviour problems'.

Foucault is also drawn on by Lewis (2003) to critique the use of surveillance measures by schools to screen for homicidal youth. These practices of 'surveillance' can range from the watchful eye of the teacher and the diagnostic tests of psychologists to the literal surveillance of closed circuit television. Surveillance tactics can also include documents such as *The School Shooter: A Threat Assessment Perspective* (O'Toole, 2000). This is a 'threat assessment' produced by the US Federal Bureau of Investigations (FBI). As Janet Reno, the US Attorney General, explains, this document 'presents a model procedure for threat assessment and intervention – including a chapter on key indicators that should be regarded as warning signs in evaluating threats' (ibid.: iii). *The School Shooter* draws on the US Institute of Medicine's (1999) *Report on Adolescents*, to pronounce that 'Twenty percent have a diagnosable mental health disorder at sometime during adolescence, the highest rate for any age group through the life-span' (ibid.: 12).

In relation to the issue of surveillance (of which the FBI's *The School Shooter* seems an administrative extreme), an apposite remark is provide by Baker (2002: 685) in her observation:

> If the degree of surveillance that is directed at children who are so labelled were to be turned on the adults in the school, then perhaps there would emerge many teachers, administrators, and psychologists whose observed behavior might be thought of as disturbing and emotional.

It is disquieting to consider that, if the focus of the surveillance measures were thus shifted, the adults might well qualify as disorderly. Aside from a few authors, it seems the debate concerning disorderly children is largely restricted to discussion of diagnosis, treatment and prediction. These are discussions that seek to improve 'scientific knowledge' of disorderly children and their disorders, and do not question how these disorders are constructed – or the way that they construct the disorderly child.

Foucault's work on truth, power and the self provides a means to consider how mental disorders such as conduct disorder are made authoritative and, secondly, how disorderly subjectivity is constructed. To do this involves considering what Foucault described as three 'traditional problems'. These are:

> (1) What are the relations we have to truth through scientific knowledge, to those "truth games" which are so important in civilization and in which we are both subject and object? (2) What are the relationships we have to others through those strange strategies and power relationships? And (3) what are the relationships between truth, power, and self?
>
> (Foucault, 1988d: 15)

These three problems are expanded upon in Foucault's (1990) introduction to Volume 2 of the *History of Sexuality*, in which he explains how he worked with these in order to construct a 'genealogy of sexuality'. To conduct this genealogy of sexuality and the relations with the self, Foucault proposed three axes of investigation: '(1) the formation of sciences (*savoirs*) that refer to it, (2) the systems of power that regulate its practice, (3) the forms within which individuals are able, are obliged, to recognize themselves as subjects of this sexuality' (ibid.: 4). These axes of investigation are associated with Foucault's 'three traditional problems' and are linked to Foucault's (1984a) 'three fundamentals of experience'. As Foucault (ibid.: 387) states with regard to his enquiries into the areas of madness, delinquency and sexuality:

> each time I also tried to point out the place occupied here by the other two components necessary for constituting a field of experience. It is basically a matter of different examples in which the three fundamental elements of any experience are implicated: a game of truth, relations of power, and forms of relation to oneself and to others.

Here the fundamentals of experience, truth, power and the self, form the problems for Foucauldian analysis and the three axes of investigation form a means to analyse each problem. My approach draws on this, working with truth, power and the self to analyse the practices that diagnose disorderly children.

The emphasis that Foucault (1978: 4) placed on truth is especially tangible in his comment that 'ours is a society which produces and circulates discourse with a truth-function, discourse which passes for the truth and thus holds specific powers'. This can be taken to mean that diagnosing disorderly children circulates in such a way that it has a truth function. But how does this truth function operate? A means to ponder this question can be found in the following:

> Each society has its régime of truth, its 'general politics' of truth – that is, the types of discourse which it accepts and makes function as true; the mechanisms and instances that enable one to distinguish true and false statements; the means by which each is sanctioned; the techniques and procedures accorded value in the acquisition of truth; the status of those who are charged with saying what counts as true.
>
> (Foucault, 2000: 131)

Each of these statements, the mechanisms, the means of sanction, the techniques and, importantly, those who get to say 'what counts as true', are points that can be considered in an analysis of the construction of disorderly children. This style of analysis is important – but it is not suggestive of finding a means to escape truth. Rather, it is about ways to work with the obligation to truth and to move about *within* this relationship to truth (Foucault, 1997b: 295). From this perspective it is not necessary to find a means to 'escape' a regime of truth in order to challenge or change its influence, what can be done is to 'play the game differently'. As Foucault states, 'one escaped from a domination of truth not by playing a game that was totally different from the game of truth but by playing the same game differently, or playing another game, another hand, with other trump cards' (ibid.).

For Foucault, 'truth' is intricately linked with power, which implies that analysing power is therefore integral to examining the truth. Foucault (1988e) provides a description of power, using four points to explain his conceptualisation. Firstly he states '1. Power is not a substance. Neither is it a mysterious property whose origin must be delved into. Power is only a certain type of relation between individuals' (ibid.: 83). The second point refers to rationalisation: '2. As for all relations among men, many factors determine power. Yet rationalization is also constantly working away at it' (ibid.).[2] With regard to rationalisation and, in particular, political rationality, Foucault provides the third and fourth points:

> 3. What has to be questioned is the form of rationality at stake. The criticism of power wielded over the mentally sick or mad cannot be restricted to psychiatric institutions; nor can those questioning the power to punish be content with denouncing prisons as total institutions. The question is: how are such relations of power rationalized? Asking it is the only way to avoid other institutions, with the same objectives and the same effects, from taking their stead.

> 4. Political rationality has grown and imposed itself all throughout the history of Western societies. It first took its stand on the idea of pastoral power then on that of reason of state. Its inevitable effects are both individualization and totalization. Liberation can only come from attacking, not just one of these two effects, but political rationality's very roots.
>
> (ibid.: 83–4)

This conceptualisation of power underlines the role of rationality in the wielding of power. Analysing the diagnosing of disorderly children thus requires an examination that extends to the practices of power and how these practices are rationalised. This means that, although I focus on the *DSM* and its effects, I am doing this as a practice that occurs via certain rationalisations. This is not to suggest that the *DSM* is *the* practice, and to do away with it will simultaneously do away with diagnosis. Rather, it is to consider the *DSM* as a practice that, via its capacity to designate mental disorder, is an exemplar of the way in which diagnosing disorderly children is rationalised.

The third experience, the self, is the focus of Foucault's (1984c; 1986; 1990) three volumes of *The History of Sexuality*. The last two volumes departed significantly from the plan mapped out in the first volume, which was to examine the history of desire. These two volumes were organised 'around the slow formation, in antiquity, of a hermeneutics of the self' (Foucault, 1990: 6). This change in focus is reflected in the interviews and seminars given by Foucault in the early 1980s (for example, the interviews Truth, Power, Self: An Interview with Michel Foucault (1988d), conducted in 1982, The ethics of the concern for the self as a practice of freedom (1997b), conducted in 1984, and the seminar Technologies of the Self (1988a), presented in 1982). This interest in the 'technologies of the self' is especially relevant to an analysis that seeks to consider how the young person is involved in the construction of a disorderly subjectivity.

Foucault's articulation of the constituted nature of the subject is a key point to this consideration of disorderly children and the constitution of disorderly child. This rejection of the unified subject is articulated by Foucault (1996b: 452) in the following quotation from an interview in April 1984:

> I don't think there is actually a sovereign, founding subject, a universal form of subject that one could find everywhere. I am very sceptical and very hostile toward this conception of the subject. I think on the contrary that the subject is constituted through practices of subjection, or, in a more anonymous way, through practices of liberation, of freedom.

Borrowing from this perspective, it can be argued that the subjectivity labelled 'disorderedly child' does not exist in any unified way. The disorderedly subjectivity occurs via certain practices of subjection and practices that function through regimes of truth and relations of power. Significantly, this means that practices of freedom are implicated in the very practices that create disorderedly subjectivity. This is possible because the self, or more precisely the relation the self has to the self, is at the heart of the creation of subjectivity. The essence here is that in Foucault's view, the relation one has with oneself is vital. As he explains:

> another side to the moral prescriptions, which most of the time is not isolated as such but is, I think, very important: the kind of relationship you ought to have with yourself, *rapport a soi*, which I call ethics, and which determines how the individual is supposed to constitute himself as a moral subject of his own action.
>
> (Fooucault, 1983a: 237–8)

This perspective suggests that the type of relation a young person chooses to have with themself[3] is of great importance to the way in which subjectivity is constructed. This implies that a young person's subjectivities are intricately tied up in the manner in which that individual has constituted themself. Based on this view it is then possible to grasp how these subjectivities are constructed by considering regimes of truth, relations of power and technologies of the self. Since these subjectivities are formed through multiple relations, the notion that disorderedly subjectivity is 'fixed' can be immediately problematised.

In repudiating the notion of a unitary subject, and taking on a consideration of the mechanisms of games of truth, relations of power and technologies of the self, it is possible to analyse how the disorderly subject is produced. This hinges on taking a particular view of the problem. It is not, as Foucault (1996a: 472) comments, to 'define the moment from which something like the subject appeared, but rather the set of processes through which the subject exists with his different problems and obstacles and through forms that are far from being exhausted'. To paraphrase Foucault, it could be asked 'what set of processes enable the disorderly child to exist'? The next chapter begins to respond to this question by focusing on truth to analyse the diagnosing of disorderly children.

Chapter 3

Disorderly conduct and the truth of the disorderly child

'Words and things' is the . . . ironic title of a work that modifies its own form, displaces its own data, and reveals at the end of the day, a quite different task. A task that consists not – of no longer – treating discourses as groups of signs (signifying elements, referring to contents of representations) *but as practices that systematically form the objects of which they speak.*

(Foucault, 1972: 49, emphasis added)

The above quote provides a tantalising invitation to think differently about conduct disorder. To paraphrase Foucault, what would it mean to think of truths such as conduct disorder not as signifiers of mental disorder but, to draw on Foucault, 'as practices that systematically form the objects of which they speak'? Such an analysis would paint a quite different picture of conduct disorder: rather than a definitively scientific truth, it could be grasped as something made possible via certain discursively constituted practices.

The four angles of scrutiny – contingencies, discontinuities, emergence and subjugated knowledges – provide a means to interrogate these practices. Several contingencies for the truth of conduct disorder can be considered: the need for a flexible definition of mental disorder; the 'child' object; the concern with delinquency and its relation to psychopathology; and the classification of disordered truths. This is not an exhaustive list of contingencies for conduct disorder; indeed, another that could be examined closely (but is not in this discussion) is the media as a contingency in the production of the disorderly child. Discontinuity serves two strategic functions in interrogating the truth of conduct disorder. First, discontinuity can expose the construction and internal workings of conduct disorder. This tactic is valuable since it enables a view of conduct disorder not as authoritative, but as an arbitrary form of classification brought to life via specific practices. Second, discontinuity can be used to articulate the emergences of associated truths and relations of power. These truths and relations of power are integral to the persuasive 'truthfulness' of conduct disorder. The analysis of the emergence of conduct disorder and reference to subjugated erudite knowledge are interwoven in the discussion of contingency and discontinuity in this chapter (the genealogical tactic of subjugated disqualified knowledges is used to consider the construction of disorderly subjectivity in Chapters 6 and 7). By emphasising these contingencies, discontinuities and emergences, it becomes possible to grasp how conduct disorder, and especially its appearance as scientific, authoritative and legitimate, is made possible. The challenge of this chapter is to draw on this conceptualisation of discourse to unsettle the notion that a diagnosis of conduct disorder is made on the basis of 'signs' of 'conduct disorderedness' within the 'disorderly' child.

Contingencies and the emergence of conduct disorder

Given that a diagnosis of conduct disorder is taken to denote a mental disorder, it seems logical to ask 'What is mental disorder?' This is not a straightforward question. One would assume it would be appropriate that a definition of 'mental disorder' be located in the manual that defines conduct disorder, the *Diagnostic and Statistical Manual of Mental Disorders, Fourth Edition, Text Revision (DSM-IV-TR)* (2000). However, this proves to be something of an assumption. Take, for example, the announcement made in the introduction that, 'although this manual provides a classification of mental disorders, it must be admitted that no defini-tion adequately specifies precise boundaries for the concept of "mental disorder"' (APA, 2000: xxx). This difficulty with definition was also noted by Frances, when he was Chair of the *DSM-IV* Task Force[1] in the 1994 edition of the *DSM-IV* (the version preceding the 2000 text revision).

> DSM-IV is a manual of *mental disorders*, but it is by no means clear just what *is* a mental disorder and whether one can develop a set of definitional criteria to guide inclusionary and exclusionary decisions for the manual. Although many have tried (including the authors of the DSM-IIIR), no one has ever succeeded in developing a list of infallible criteria to define a mental disorder.
>
> (Frances, 1994: vii, emphases in original)

The definition from earlier editions of the *DSM* referred to by Frances (1994) is as follows:

> In DSM-III each of the mental disorders is conceptualized as a clinically significant behavioral or psychological syndrome or pattern that occurs in an individual and that is typically associated with either a painful symptom (distress) or impairment in one or more important areas of functioning (disability). In addition, there is an inference that there is a behavioral, psychological, or biological dysfunction, and that the disturbance is not only in the relationship between the individual and society. (When the disturbance is *limited* to a conflict between an individual and society, this may represent social deviance, which may or may not be commendable, but is not by itself a mental disorder.)
>
> (APA, 1980: 6)

In commenting on this definition, two senior authors of the *DSM-II* – Spitzer, Chair of the *DSM-III* Task Force on Nomenclature and Statistics, and Williams, Text Editor of the *DSM-III* and Coordinator of the *DSM-III* field trials – declare 'The DSM-III definition of mental disorder makes no assumption that each mental disorder is a discrete entity with sharp boundaries between it and other mental disorders or between it and no mental disorder' (Spitzer and Williams, 1982: 22). It is perplexing that people are assigned diagnosis of mental disorder, such as conduct disorder, yet it is 'by no means clear just what *is* a mental disorder' (Frances, 1994: vii). How is it there can be such confusion over what might be the most elemental of details? It could be imagined that the crux of diagnosing conduct disorder, and thus diagnosing a disorderly child, is being able to define 'mental disorder', or at least differentiating between mental disorder and non-mental disorder.

Although this is apparently contradictory, this very absence of definition is a contingency in the formulation of the truth of conduct disorder. This is because the ongoing design and redesign of mental disorders such as conduct disorder can proceed with less restriction because this definition of mental disorder is inexact. As will be argued later in this chapter, the APA's (1980; 1987; 1994; 2000) definitions of conduct disorder vary over the three versions of the *DSM-III, DSM-III-R* and *DSM-IV* (the *DSM-IV-TR* is a text revision of the *DSM-IV* and is not a full revision such as between the *DSM-III-R* and the *DSM-IV*). This variation would arguably be difficult if it were located within the confines of a well-defined notion of mental disorder. Hence this indefinableness of mental disorder is contingent to creating, changing and deleting mental disorders.

The contingency of the 'child'

In addition to this indefinableness of mental disorder, another contingency of conduct disorder is having an *object to define*: the child that needs diagnosis. Since conduct disorder belongs to the category 'Disorders Usually First Diagnosed in Infancy, Childhood and Adolescence' and primarily refers to those under the age of eighteen (with a small exception made for individuals over eighteen and who do not meet antisocial personality disorder criteria) this object must necessarily be the non-adult or the child. For this to function, a formulation of 'child' is necessary, one that is a knowable, diagnosable and treatable entity, an entity in need of being known. This entity is the child or, more precisely, the child as an object of psychiatric truth.

There is much difference of opinion as to the 'origin' of the child as the object of psychiatric truth – a difference that is quite apparent when several psychiatric texts are surveyed. For Kazdin (1996: ix), 'Until quite recently, emotional, behavioral, and learning problems of children and adolescents have been neglected in the mental health and related professions'. In this statement the meaning of 'quite recently' is unclear. The time frame for this 'origin' is better specified by Blau (1996: 65), who makes the claim, 'Adolescent behavior problems have been studied for the past three to four decades'. Yet, according to Kanner (1972: 26), 'until about 1930 . . . psychiatrists did not know children, and pediatricians did not know psychiatry'. It appears this may have been said with some 'authority' since, according to Stone (1997: 164), Kanner 'published the first textbook in English on child psychiatry'. However, contrary to Kanner, Wallace (1994: 36) places child psychiatry as emerging in the early twentieth century, something 'arising from interactions between pediatricians and social welfare workers. It overcame the longstanding myth that mental illness does not occur in children'. This last opinion situates the origins of child psychiatry some sixty years before Kazdin's (1996) estimate, fifty years prior to Blau's (1996) and thirty years before Kanner (1972).

As can be seen, these historical particulars from psychiatric texts are inconsistent. This irregularity is further demonstrated in examples of the early medical interest in the mind of the child. For instance, included amongst the 'half yearly reports' in the *Dublin Journal of Medical Sciences* there is a summary by Atkins of the observations drawn by Martin Cohn, a medical doctor, that 'Mental diseases are more common among children than was formerly supposed' (Atkins, 1884: 245). Cohn goes on to explain that 'An explanation of this may be found in the fact that only lately the diseases of childhood have been more thoroughly studied' (Atkins, 1884: 245). At a similar time, Maudsley 'devoted a long chapter to the "insanity of early life" in *The Pathology of Mind* published in 1879' (Stone, 1997: 115). Forty years prior to Maudsley's (1879) publication, in France in 1838 Esquirol published *Maladies Mentales,* in which he 'differentiated the mentally defective from the psychotic child . . . and reported several interesting case histories of children with homicidal impulses' (Alexander and Selesnick, 1967: 373). In the later part of the nineteenth century Emminghaus urged delineation between child and adult 'mental diseases', and urged that there be 'a clear-cut separation of scientific study in the two fields' (Harms, 1960: 187).

Earlier still, in France in 1806, Pinel (1962), the head of Bicêtre, a 'mental hospital', published data on the ages of 'Maniacs received at Bicêtre'. In the data published by Pinel the ages are clearly broken into groups, beginning with the ages '15–20' (Pinel, 1962: 112), an age that is now known as 'adolescence'. Pinel's data detail the number of maniacs received at Bicêtre during the period 1784–92. For example, in 1784 five maniacs aged fifteen to twenty were received, and in 1787 this number increased to twelve (Pinel, 1962). From these data it is unambiguous that individuals aged fifteen to twenty were not precluded from being received at Bicêtre, nor from examination and treatment. The way in which these young individuals were conceptualised may well have varied in the two hundred years separating Pinel's (1962) data, first published in 1806, and those of Kazdin (1996). It is not the case that medically orientated interest in the mind of young individuals is a new phenomenon. What *is* significant is that it was not until the twentieth century that a science concerned with the 'child-as-psychiatric-object' formulated itself into the subdiscipline termed 'child psychiatry'.

In view of these examples, it must be questioned why it is necessary to assert that the child as a psychiatric object is of recent origin. If we draw on the perspective that these psychiatric sciences produce the objects of which they speak, then this child object would need to emerge as much with Kazdin (1996) as it did for Kanner in the 1930s. From this standpoint, these emerging child objects can be considered as distinctive as the practices of child psychiatry 'speaking them into existence'. Thus, accompanying the specific gaze of Pinel (1962) emerges an equally specific fifteen- to twenty-year-old object. Similarly, accompanying the 'science of child psychiatry' is its specific object, the 'child as psychiatric object'. Subsequently, accompanying discourses of disorderly children is its object – disorderly children. This knower–object relation is thus a mutually dependent relationship: without the psychiatric science of the child, there is no 'child as psychiatric object', and without its object there is no child psychiatric science.

This psychiatric science of the child has endeavoured to know its object well; identifying it, treating it and even seeking to prevent it from becoming disorderly. Frequently, the rationale used for these practices has been linked to protection of the community, since it is not just the mentally disordered child that poses risk; the potential adult within this child poses a capacity for even greater risk. Thus the quest for prevention is concerned not simply with the child as a 'child unit', but with the estimated future adult. In the following quote taken from an article published in 1928, this quest is unmistakably paramount:

> Far be it for me to even think that this world can be set free from criminals as a result of the physicians' efforts alone. We can change neither human nature nor social nor economic conditions, *but we can do very much in the way of shaping character of the children of today, the men and women of tomorrow.*
>
> (Jahr, 1928: 495, emphasis added)

This fear of the dangerous implicates the psychiatric science of the child in the 'shaping' of children's characters. When Jahr (1928) makes the child an object that can be shaped by the physician and connects the child of today 'to the men and women of tomorrow', he inserts the future into the present of the child-object. Jahr uses the terms 'psychiatrist' and 'mental hygienist' interchangeably and, notably, makes a distinction between these specialists and the paediatrician. He remarks that 'these workers seem more diligent than the pediatricians, for almost out of a clear sky there has developed a vast literature on child psychology and its kindred subjects' (ibid.: 492). This proliferation of interest in the child shares a close relationship with the notion of the child as psychiatric object that is seen as harbouring the potential of future danger. In a similar way, then, it can be argued that the practices that render children disorderly share an equally interdependent relationship with the disorderly child object.

The contingency of delinquency and psychopathology

Another contingency of conduct disorder is the concern with delinquency and the connection of conduct disorder to psychopathology. The beliefs that the delinquent harbours the potential criminal are similar to the assumptions that the child as psychiatric object contains a potentially dangerous adult. As such, the delinquent forms a social concern that requires investigation and demands remediation. Current practices of disordering children cannot be easily separated from notions of delinquency and the portent of the future criminal.

That delinquency has prominent status as a social concern can be deduced from the efforts to categorise the delinquent, to understand the delinquent, to treat the delinquent, to predict the delinquent and to prevent the delinquent. Indeed, writing in 1938 in the *Edinburgh Medical Journal*, Gordon (1938: 44) notes that 'A good deal has been written and still more spoken in recent years about conduct disorder, juvenile crime and the difficult child'. Earlier still, large numbers of children were being studied in the US by Healy and Bronner (1926). According to White (1996: 185), between 1909 and 1915 Healy and Bronner examined '2000 offenders who came before the Chicago Juvenile Courts', and this was followed by a similar study between 1917 and 1923 of '2000 offenders who came before the Boston courts'. In another scheme in the US that dates from 1946, no fewer than '5000 child guidance cases' were studied, with the investigation yielding the 'discovery' of certain traits for the 'Syndrome of Socialized Delinquency' and the 'Syndrome of Unsocialized Aggressive Behavior' (Jenkins, 1960).

This importance placed on studying the delinquent is made explicit in a statement made in 1908 by the Honorable B. B. Lindsey, Judge of the Denver Juvenile Court, US. This prominent figure said, 'The growth of the juvenile or children's courts, in the last seven years, not only emphasizes the importance of the subject of juvenile delinquency, but the necessity for a better understanding concerning it' (Lindsey, 1908: ix). Concern with delinquency was also evident in Australia, with a report published in the *Medical Journal of Australia* stating that delinquency is 'at once discreditable to the Commonwealth, deplorable and irresponsible' ('Mental defect and delinquency', 1923: 479).[2] Although these social concerns instigate intense practices of knowing, it must be noted that this interest has not decreased the threat of youth.

In the late twentieth and early twenty-first centuries, practices of knowing delinquents are tied to those sciences affiliated with knowledge of the mind. An example of this is the argument made by Breggin and Breggin (1994) that the US government has invested in biological psychiatry as a means to know and control violent individuals. Earlier in the twentieth century medically orientated explanations were also made of delinquency. Take for example this comment by Salmon, a medical doctor:

> We think of the greatest woes of childhood as destitution and disease, but delinquency, of a degree requiring the attention of courts and officers of the peace, shadows the lives of more children than do some of the most prevalent and serious diseases, and the danger of entering upon criminal careers is a more threatening one than is hunger or bodily neglect. If this great burden rests now upon childhood and youth and later will be borne by society in

general can be even partly lifted, the task is one of the most pressing duties of the day.

(Anderson, 1923: 418)

Here delinquency is not only an issue of social concern, it is something that has a relation with disease. This is a significant connection because situating pathology with crime opens a space for diagnoses such as conduct disorder to occupy.

The linking of pathology to delinquency is remarkably explicit in this statement taken from a 1923 issue of the *Medical Journal of Australia*: 'It is possible for well trained medical psychologists and psychiatrists to detect masked forms of mental deficiency likely to lead to moral delinquencies while the child is young' ('Mental defect and delinquency', 1923: 480). Associating criminal tendencies with the 'masked forms of mental deficiency likely to lead to mental defect' creates the need for a suitably potential criminal *and*, significantly, a mentally aberrant child object. From this association various delinquent objects can emerge. In the US, amongst these objects were the 'defective delinquent', the 'moral imbecile,' 'psychopathic inferiority' and 'constitutional inferiority', as well as 'imbecile' and 'feeble-minded' (Stearns, 1916: 430). There is also the 'psychopathic delinquent', a term described by Vogt (1947), and in the UK 'juvenile delinquency' (Rhodes, 1939) and 'juvenile offenders'. Popular terms used in Australia in the 1920s included 'moral delinquents', 'mentally defective' and 'psychopathic child' ('Mental defect and delinquency', 1923).

The emergence of these objects (the psychopathic child and the defective delinquent) depended on psychiatry taking an interest in the delinquent. Extrapolating from the following comment by Anderson, it would seem that delinquency was one of the domains of interest: 'A noticeable swing of the pendulum is taking place in the application of psychiatry to social problems . . . until recently, the conception of psychiatry's position in delinquency was limited to the classification of the mentally handicapped' (Anderson, 1923: 414). Early formations of a relationship between delinquency and psychiatry are also apparent in the emergence in the US of Healy's research clinic, the 'Juvenile Psychopathic Institute in 1909' (Alexander and Selesnick, 1967: 377) and in the child guidance clinics. At the time of their use in the early twentieth century, child guidance clinics were extremely popular, gaining international attention, including that of Australia. In Victoria, Australia, in the 1930s and 1940s 'clinics were established in connection with the Department of Health and the children's courts' (Williams, 1949: 675). Similarly, a child guidance clinic was established in NSW 'in November 1936, as part of the School Medical Service. The staff consisted of a psychiatrist, psychologist and a social worker, all full-time' (Cunningham *et al.*, 1939: 174).

Mental hygiene was another area that had displayed interest in bringing the delinquent into a relation with mental disorders. This is made explicit in two of the eight aims of the New South Wales Council for Mental Hygiene:[3] Aim 4 reads 'To promote the study and treatment of nervous manifestations in childhood with the object of preventing more severe development in later years and the instruction of parents and others in the handling of difficult and "problem" children' (Noble, 1929: 301). Aim 6 states 'To investigate the problems of social maladjustment such as dependency and criminality in relation to congenital and acquired mental disorders' (ibid.). What seems apparent is that, through the rubric of mental hygiene, psychiatry could come into contact with a greater number of young individuals, based on their 'disturbing social behaviours'. Curiously, this increased focus on delinquent and disturbing children did not necessarily result in a better definition of delinquency. Indeed, it seems that defining delinquency is a difficult undertaking (Clarizio and McCoy, 1970). This difficulty is summed up by Vogt (1947: 19–20): 'Where does normal mischief end and delinquency begin in childhood and adolescence? I confess to not knowing where the line of demarcation is or where it should be'.

Considering the problems in defining delinquency, it is not surprising that the distinction between delinquency and conduct disorder is unclear. For authors such as Gelder *et al.* (1989: 792), differentiation pivots on a legal aspect: 'Delinquency is not a psychiatric diagnosis but a legal category'. Hinshaw and Anderson (1996) appear to concur with this legal emphasis, viewing delinquency as a 'legal' term and conduct disorder as a psychiatric one. These two groups of authors seem in agreement, except that Gelder *et al.* (ibid.) qualify their legally orientated differentiation by stating 'juvenile delinquency may be associated with psychiatric disorder, especially conduct disorder'. This differentiation is given further clarification by Gelder *et al.* (ibid.), who explain 'Delinquency is often equated with conduct disorder. This is wrong, for although the two categories overlap, they are not the same. Many delinquents do not have conduct disorders or any other psychological disorder. Equally, many of those with conduct disorder do not offend'. So conduct disorder and delinquency may be considered both as separate categories and as categories that can overlap.

As stated above, differentiation between conduct disorder and delinquency is frequently based upon the distinction between psychiatric mental disorder and legal definition. Nevertheless, notions of *what* constitutes the mental disorder conduct disorder and *what* constitutes delinquency are certainly not consistent. Whilst the terminology remains similar, the definitions vacillate. For example, some criteria for delinquency in 1908 (such as truancy) exist in the *DSM-IV-TR* criteria for conduct disorder. Other 1908 predictors of truancy, such as 'cigarette smoking' (New York Juvenile Asylum, cited in Travis, 1908),[4] are not considered to be delinquent or conduct disordered – although it must be noted that, curiously, more recent research makes the claim that maternal smoking may be related to conduct disorder in boys (Wakschlag *et al.*, 1997).

Another definition is offered by the American Beyers, a 'Superintendent of the House of Refuge' (Travis, 1908). As reported by Travis, Beyers 'observes two classes' of delinquents: '(1) those due to neglect or incompetence of the home; (2) those due to incompetence of the State' (ibid.: 50). It is worthwhile to pause and consider how this view would reconfigure the currently popular conceptualisation of the disorderly child from an individual with some type of mental deficit to one who is a signifier of 'state' or 'home' incompetence – although the latter description of 'incompetence of the home' has resonance with the prevailing characterisations of disorderly child as from a 'single-parent home'. Quite distinct from this idea of incompetence, Lindsey (1908: x) advocates that juvenile delinquency 'pertains to all children', 'for all children are delinquent at some time or other . . . at least ninety-five per cent of children who are dealt with as delinquents are no different from the average child'. Then, in another effort to define the delinquent, Travis provides a somewhat prolific classification:

(1) The delinquent by occasion, stumbling, or chance (an isolated act).
(2) The delinquent by misfortune or destitution (in grave danger of delinquency).
(3) The delinquent by parental incompetency (ignorant, tactless, or vicious parents).
(4) The delinquent by contracted habit (junk pickers, etc.).
(5) The delinquent by unequal economic struggles (negro *vs.* white; immigrant *vs.* native; poor class *vs.* well equipped).
(6) The delinquent by effective environment (poor associates; poor over-sight).
(7) The delinquent by effective heredity (in narrow sense of neurotic tendencies).
(8) The delinquent by congenital defect (accident of birth etc.).
(9) The delinquent by physical defect acquired (disease or mal-development).
(10) The delinquent by mental defect acquired (disease, no training, mal-development).

(ibid.: 51)

The categories in this classification are either an external causation or shifted to the locus of the body, a physical or mental defect. In this scheme of delinquent knowledge, 'all of the first six classes are normal . . . some of those of the last four classes are morbid, degenerate, some insane, and perhaps some of these are atavistic and criminal by nature' (ibid.: 51–2). Thus there is a 'normal delinquent' and one that is 'other' than the 'normal delinquent'. This 'non-normal', 'other' or 'non-average' is a potential space for the mentally defective or defective delinquent to emerge.

The prevalence of this entity, the 'non-average' or 'aberrant' delinquent, multiplied as crime was increasingly placed in relation to mental dysfunction. There are numerous examples of this relation. For example, in *Crime and Insanity* Mercier (1911: x) makes the statement, 'Crime is . . . a disorder of conduct'. Another, drawn from 'a survey of delinquents', asserts a very detailed delinquent aetiology:

> To the trained observer the class of boys and girls in truant schools and in
> industrial and reform schools includes a rather large proportion of defectives
> where the intellectual defect is relatively slight and is overshadowed by the
> moral deficiency . . . They may be idle, thievish, cruel to animals or smaller
> children, wantonly and senselessly destructive and lawless generally . . . These
> children are not simply bad and incorrigible, but they are irresponsible by
> reason of the *underlying mental defect*. The mental defect and the moral lack
> are alike and visible effects of *incurable affection of the cerebral cortex*.
>
>   (Fernald, 1904, cited in Stearns, 1916: 427–8, emphasis added)

In this quote Fernald (1904) unites delinquency and 'underlying mental defect',
a defect that assumes form as an aberration located in 'the cerebral cortex'. In
this statement there is a conflation of notions of crime, lawlessness, senseless
destructiveness and cruelty. This conflation is collapsed into the notion of mental
defect. This is then collapsed into the aberrations of certain cells in the 'cerebral
cortex'.

Despite all these aberrations and faulty cerebral cortices, there remains a degree
of uncertainty about the precise nature of this relation. I illustrate this with two
quotations from quite distinct 'periods'. Raine makes this observation: 'Not only
is it impossible to conclusively demonstrate that crime is a psychopathology, but
also it is equally difficult to demonstrate that it is *not* a psychopathology' (1993:
3, emphasis in original). Eighty years earlier a decidedly similar conclusion was
reached by Mercier (1911: 11): 'Every one knows that there is a certain relation
or connection between insanity and crime: few have any clear notion what the
relation or connection precisely is'. Notwithstanding these inconsistencies, it
seems that, as certain peripheries of crime became the concern of psychiatry, a
special type of aberrant child emerged as an object of psychiatric jurisprudence.
Linked with these notions, a disorderly child emerges, one who is intimately
linked to both mental disorder and the sciences of the mind. The question is, how
is it that such a disorderly child can emerge, and how can these diagnoses appear
so legitimate?

The contingency of classification

Measures for knowing the individual are, as critics of the psychiatric and psychological disciplines such as Foucault (1988f) and Rose (1989) have argued, the
dividing practices 'par excellence' of western culture. They are therefore powerful devices that warrant critical attention. The classification of mental disorder
is currently dominated by two systems, the APA's (2000) *DSM-IV-TR* and the
mental disorder section of the World Health Organization's (WHO) (1992; 2003)
International Classification of Diseases ICD-10. Although these systems appear
distinct, the APA was involved in the authorship of the mental disorder section of
ICD-10 (Kirk and Kutchins, 1992). In the more recent edition, the *DSM-IV-TR*,

it is explained that 'those preparing ICD-10 and DSM-IV have worked closely to coordinate their efforts, resulting in mutual influence' (APA, 2000: xxix).

Although at present these dominate, classification of mental aberration has not always been a domain governed by one or two classification systems. For example, in the appendix of *Psychopathological Disorders in Childhood: Theoretical Considerations and a Proposed Classification* (Group for the Advancement in Psychiatry (GAP), Committee on Child Psychiatry, 1974), no fewer than twenty-four different child disorder classifications are listed, the earliest from 1920. Whilst conduct disorder is contingent on a classification system, the refinement supposedly represented by the *DSM-IV-TR* can be genealogically reinterpreted as dominance, and those classification systems 'left behind' understood as fragments of discontinuity.

More than thirty years ago Clarizio and McCoy (1970: 63) reported 'A review of the literature reveals more than two dozen attempts from 1920 to 1966 at formal classifications of the totality of behavior problems occurring during childhood and adolescence'. These different methods of classification almost all date from the first half of the twentieth century. Notwithstanding these varied attempts, there was early scepticism as to the practicability of classification. Reporting on children studied in psychiatric demonstration clinics under the auspices of the Commonwealth Fund of New York City in the 1920s, Anderson (1923: 426, emphasis added) notes that, with regard to 'mental classification', 'We appreciate fully *how impossible it is to include, under one artificial classification scheme,* all the wealth of the valuable information gathered by the psychiatrists and psychologists in analyzing and searching the mental life of these children'.

In spite of opinions such as Anderson's, systems of classification are posited, and these systems can change. One explanation proposed for such changes is that the new systems represent the culmination and improvement of previous attempts. Against this interpretation it can be argued that these assortment of classifications attest to an ongoing attempt by psychiatry to posit itself as a science. In their critique of the *DSM*, Kirk and Kutchins note this importance, asserting 'The development of the *DSM-III* by the APA was a major public effort to defend psychiatry by making diagnosis appear to conform more closely with the image of technical rationality' (1992: 222–3). The degree to which classification is vital to the science of psychiatry was indicated by Drapes (1906) in the British publication the *Journal of Mental Science* (the article was reviewed in 1907 in the *American Journal of Nervous and Mental Diseases*, 34: 274). For Drapes, if the study of insanity is to be scientific, it must have its own definitive classification system. A system of classification was similarly important for the 'science' of child psychiatry. This is a point noted by Jenkins (1973: 28): 'Scientific progress in child psychiatry depends, as in other fields, upon reducing the infinite variety of problems through some broad categorisation'. In this way notions of science can be called upon to validate changes to classification systems and, at the same time, notions of science can be the very reason for compiling such systems.

Statistical and research purposes are also cited as rationales for honing classification schemata (Husain and Cantwell, 1991). Indeed, the emergence of the first *Diagnostic and Statistical Manual of Mental Disorders* is associated with the US government collection of statistics on the 'mentally ill'. According to Kramer (1968: xi) these statistics have been collected 'since the decennial census of 1840'. Forty years after the first US governmental actions to know the mentally aberrant, effort was made to classify these 'mentally ill' for statistical purposes. For this function a seven-division classification of the insane was devised and this was created by the US Census Office in 'consultation with the members of the New England Psychological Association and with other "expert alienists"' (Census Office, 1888, cited in Kramer, 1968: xii).[5]

This process again occurred in 1923, when a classification system was developed in response to a 'special census of patients in hospitals for mental disease'. Notably, this classification was 'developed collaboratively by the American Psychiatric Association (then the American Medico-Psychological Association) and the former National Committee for Mental Health' (Kramer, 1968: xii). As can be deduced, there was a relationship between the then American Medico-Psychological Association and the US government. To illustrate the extent of this relationship it is worthwhile quoting the following passage from the foreword to the first edition of the *Diagnostic and Statistical Manual of Mental Disorders*:

> The collection of statistics on mental illness morbidity has long been a stepchild of Federal Government. Delegated from year to year on a fiscal basis to the Bureau of the Census, morbidity statistics in this most important area perhaps would never have been collected had it not been for the untiring efforts of former Committees on Statistics of the American Psychiatric Association and the National Committee on Mental Hygiene. It has therefore been most important in the past that this manual devote most of its attention to statistics, as was indicated by its name.
>
> (American Psychiatric Association Committee on Nomenclature and
> Statistics, 1952: x)

The name *Diagnostic and Statistical Manual of Mental Disorders* unambiguously reflects its relation to the governance of individuals, and this relation between psychiatry and statistics demonstrates the prominent role of the APA in the procedures of governing the individual.

'Communication' is another rationale used for classification: it is argued to be a pressing necessity because it is essential for the successful communication of knowledge about mental disorders. As Cameron (1955: 67) emphasises, 'the means by which experience and knowledge can be exchanged is equally lacking without some classification of the manifestations of disturbance'. Husain and Cantwell (1991: 55) offer a similar explanation: 'A comprehensive diagnostic classification system of childhood psychiatric disorders enables clinicians and researchers from different backgrounds to communicate effectively about the disorders'. Thirty years before that, Robinson *et al.* (1961: 808) stated 'categories are useful in communicating among clinical staff members', and Foxe (1947: 29) concluded that 'With psychiatric classification, trained men find it easy to communicate with one another in their description of individuals'.

In spite of the claims that it is only 'a means of communication', classification is no simple matter, and it is surprising that 'communication' continues as a rationale for classifying. This convolutedness is indicated by differing approaches to classification such as the two divisions 'categorical' and 'dimensional'. The categorical system (the *DSM* is an example of this) 'consist[s] of a list of disorders, with specific clinical criteria for the diagnosis of each disorder' (Husain and Cantwell, 1991: 56). By contrast, the dimensional approach 'utilize[s] mathematical and statistical models to define factors or dimensions of behaviors. A behavior profile results from rating a child on several dimensions of behavior. Mathematically derived syndromes of behavior can be predicted by clustering the individual profiles of several patients' (ibid.). In categorical schemes such as the *DSM-IV-TR*, the presence of mental disorder is 'defined by inclusionary and exclusionary criteria – [that] are held to be "present" versus "absent" and to be distinct from other diagnoses' (Hinshaw and Anderson, 1996: 117). However, according to Hempel (1965: 151), these strict criteria can be flawed: 'Classification, strictly speaking, is a yes-or-no, an either-or affair . . . In scientific research, however, the objects under study are often found to resist a tidy pigeonholing of this kind'.

However, as Hempel (ibid.) argues, people are not 'pigeons'. Given this incompatibility, it is remarkable that a classification scheme like the *DSM-IV-TR* is successful at speaking the truth of mental disorder and plays such a fundamental role in the diagnosing of disorderly children. This dominance by the *DSM* prompts one to ask, how is it that these varying attempts at classification stopped (or paused) with the later versions of the APA's (1980; 1987; 1994) *Diagnostic and Statistical Manual of Mental Disorders*? To respond requires analysing this manual of mental disorders from both the perspectives of truth and power. I begin by analysing in terms of truth, and in the following chapter examine how relations of power are implicated in the construction of this system of classifying mental disorders.

The first edition of *Diagnostic and Statistical Manual of Mental Disorders* was published in 1952 and reprinted fourteen times (APA, 1952). Since this, three more editions, a revised edition and a text revision have appeared. In 1968, the second edition, the *Diagnostic and Statistical Manual of Mental Disorders (DSM-II)*, was published. Twelve years later the third edition of the *Diagnostic and Statistical Manual of Mental Disorders (DSM-III)* was published. Citing Cooksey and Brown (1998), Miller and Leger (2003: 15) argue 'the shift from DSM-II to DSM-III marked an important moment in the history of psychiatry, as the biopsychiatric model came to dominate over the psychoanalytic model'. The *DSM-III* was followed seven years later by a revised edition, known as the *Diagnostic and Statistical Manual of Mental Disorders, Third Edition, Revised (DSM-III-R)*. The next edition, the *Diagnostic and Statistical Manual of Mental*

Disorders, Fourth Edition (DSM-IV), was published in 1994. It has a recent 'text revision' published in 2000, the *Diagnostic and Statistical Manual of Mental Disorders, Fourth Edition, Text Revision (DSM-IV-TR)*. As its authors explain, the purpose of this revision was to correct any 'factual errors', check 'information was up-to-date' and make changes to the text to 'reflect new information available since the DSM-IV literature reviews completed in 1992', make 'improvements that will enhance the educational value of DSM-IV' and 'update ICD-CM codes' (APA, 2000: xxix). It also states that 'no substantive changes in the criteria sets were considered, nor were any proposals entertained for new disorders, new subtypes, or changes in the status of the DSM-IV appendix categories' (APA, 2000: xxix).

The *DSM-IV-TR* contains 943 pages. The first edition of the *Diagnostic and Statistical Manual of Mental Disorders* was published in 1952 and is considerably smaller, containing 132 pages. This is a difference of 811 pages in thirty-two years. The question to be put is whether the recent edition with its sevenfold increase in size represents advancement in psychiatric science. Or is it rather that this latter edition represents a more organised practice of knowing and speaking its objects into existence?

The creation of the first *DSM* provides a telling contrast to the fourth edition, *DSM-IV*. This first edition was created by a seven-member 'Committee on Nomenclature and Statistics' (APA, 1952: XII). To build this new nomenclature this committee drew on the *Standard Nomenclature of Disease* by the National Conference on Medical Nomenclature (1942). According to the APA, feedback was sought on the proposed revision through the distribution of 'a nine-page questionnaire' (APA, 1952: ix), with responses coming from 'approximately 10% of the membership of the American Psychiatric Association' (APA, 1952: viii). This canvassing included organisations such as the 'American Neurological Association, American Psychoanalytic Association, Academy of Neurology, American Psychopathological Association' (APA, 1952: viii). Altogether, of '520 questionnaires distributed; 241 were returned in time for consideration by the Committee. Of these, 224 (93%) expressed general approval' (APA, 1952: ix).

Although these questionnaires achieved a high approval rating, of the members of the APA canvassed, only half responded. Thus, the construction of the first *DSM* was made by a seven-member committee with very limited input from the members of the APA! Subsequent to this input, three more steps made this edition official. There was a brief process of revision, there was approval by the 'Editor of the Standard Nomenclature' and, lastly, approval by the 'Council of the American Psychiatric Association' (APA, 1952).

The making of this first edition of the *Diagnostic and Statistical Manual of Mental Disorders* appears uncomplicated compared with the procedures used to create the *DSM-IV*. Unlike the 'seven member committee' of the first *DSM*, the creation of the *DSM-IV* required a thirty-seven-member *DSM-IV* Task Force, thirteen separate disorder workgroups (comprising a total of ninety-eight members) and two separate committees (comprising a total of sixteen members). This information is presented in the opening pages of the *DSM-IV*, conveying in detail the credentials (and therefore authority) of those involved in the construction of this classification system. It would seem this extensive reference to authoritative contributors is particularly necessary given what Caplan (1995: 31) describes as the limited numbers of individuals who *actually* make *the* decisions about the content of the *DSM-IV*. She maintains that 'in practice, decisions about who is normal begin with at most a few dozen people – mostly male, mostly white, mostly wealthy, mostly American psychiatrists'. This need to substantiate the contributors from the outset indicates how vital legitimation is to making mental disorders and their classification truthful and scientific.

Despite the grand influence of the later versions, the first edition of the *DSM* was considerably humbler. In fact, according to Jenkins, this first edition met with scant regard:

> its categories were recognized by no organisation except the American Psychiatric Association. The National Institute of Mental Health had to translate the diagnostic categories into those of the International Classification of Diseases before reporting them to the World Health Organization. Even the American Medical Association utilized the categories of this International Classification rather than those of the American Psychiatric Association.
>
> (Jenkins, 1973: 23)

Additionally, this first edition met with criticism for its 'negligence' of child mental disorders (Clarizio and McCoy, 1970). By contrast, the most recent edition, the *DSM-IV-TR*, devotes approximately one hundred pages to the mental disorders of 'infancy, childhood and adolescence'. The construction of the second edition, the *DSM-II*, appears to have had just such an agenda, since 'there was an organized effort to bridge this gap and build an acceptable compromise' (Jenkins, 1973: 23). This attention to the mental disorders of children again occurred in the third edition, the *DSM-III*, which had the 'largest increase in diagnostic categories' (Kirk and Kutchins, 1992: 101).

Intensification of diagnostic categories applicable to children and adolescents is regularly substantiated as 'scientific progress'. Justification of such changes is offered by Rapoport and Ismond, who inform readers that categorisation 'by nature . . . will tend to encourage an ongoing process of definition and refinement' (1996: xvii). This rationalisation seems to support the argument that an ill-defined concept of mental disorder is contingent to creating and altering the definitions of conduct disorder. The grounds for diagnostic specification need to be as persuasive as the scientific rhetoric legitimating its disorderly metamorphoses. For conduct disorder to be truthful and effective as one of the designators of the disorderly child, what is required is a secure infrastructure that pays careful attention to practices of legitimation. Just such an infrastructure is provided by the *DSM-IV-TR*.

Discontinuity and the emergence of conduct disorder

Behind the backdrop of 'historical developments', the *DSM* field trials and research, one finds an array of conduct disorders. It is not that *DSM-IV-TR* conduct disorder is a scientifically superior understanding of conduct disorder. It is more that it is a successful knower of young people that shares with other conduct disorders an interest in the behavioural transgressions of the young. One of the points of discontinuity of conduct disorder is the variation in how it is conceptualised as a transgression linked to the disorder of the mind. Another is the discontinuity in the way conduct disorder is classified. This discontinuity refers not just to differences between classification systems, but also to variations within the *DSM* itself.

Discontinuity and transgression

Not all conduct disorders obey the rule of equating a child's transgression with mental aberration. This is a significant difference since it renders distinct two actions merged in the *DSM-IV* conduct disorder: the act of knowing transgression and the act of knowing mental disorder. For instance, conduct disorder is not always considered to be a transgression that belongs to mental disorder, and, significantly, conduct disorder is not always considered to be something an individual cannot control. In addition, there are a variety of transgressions that have been considered to be conduct disorders. What these irregular transgressions seem to share is the way they are subjectively perceived as disturbances.

Hamill (1929), in an article titled 'Enuresis' published in the *Journal of the American Medical Association*, conceptualises conduct disorder as something the individual can control and change. At the commencement of this article Hamill (1929: 254) states: 'At the Children's Memorial Hospital enuresis is referred to the psychiatric clinic. There it is handled on the theory that the condition is a conduct disorder; this is done because of certain conceptions of the state of consciousness of sleep'. Two points require consideration in this quote. First, in Hamill's view, bedwetting is considered a problem for psychiatry and is accordingly 'referred to the psychiatric clinic'. The second point is that enuresis is considered a conduct disorder. The significance of this categorisation lies in Hamill's rationale for this diagnosis. Enuresis, for Hamill, is nominated as a conduct disorder because it is considered to be a 'functional disorder' (ibid.: 255). 'Functional disorders' are a type of disorder the individual can control or change. For example, Hamill (ibid.) states: 'recovery from which [enuresis] was to be expected only when the child was ready to assume responsibility for itself'. Here, the term 'conduct disorder' is used to delineate that the child has responsibility for his or her actions.

In making conduct disorder a category in which the child has responsibility for its actions Hamill (1938: 55) is critical of the organic explanation of conduct disorder popular at the time. For example, his view contradicts explanations for conduct disorder such as that proposed by Gordon, who contends that when 'certain emotional disturbances which affected the sacral centres through the diencephalic control were operative, the reflex broke down completely'. Hamill (1929: 255) is similarly critical of organically orientated treatments, such as 'belladonna, bromides . . . circumcisions and tonsillectomies employed to treat enuresis'. By contrast, conduct disorder for Hamill is a classification denoting an aberration the child can choose to control, as distinct from an organic aberration the child cannot control. This differs markedly from the opinion of Koplewicz (1996: 236): 'Neuropsychological testing has shown that children and adolescents with CD seem to have an impairment in the frontal lobe of the brain, the area that affects their ability to plan, to avoid harm, and to learn from negative consequences'. This account regards conduct disorder as something quite beyond the child's control, an aberration whereby behaviour and frontal lobe malfunctioning have manifested a special kind of relationship, where transgression and mental disorder are coalesced.

In addition to the notion of the frontal lobe malfunction, a profusion of diverse behaviours have been ascribed as a conduct disorder. This abundance is emphasised by Gordon, who says:

> Under the heading of conduct disorder it is permissible to describe all behaviour which is not in accordance with the accepted code of the community in which the individual lives. Such a definition casts a wide net . . . [to] include . . . such a universally detested crime as murder, behaviour such as indulgence in sexual intercourse . . . and such a private and domestic delinquency as bedwetting.
>
> (Gordon, 1938: 43)

Neither murder nor 'indulgence in sexual intercourse' is listed amongst the criteria for conduct disorder in the *DSM-IV-TR*. Perhaps the difference between the apparent specificity of diagnostic criteria in the *DSM-IV-TR* and Gordon's (1938) expansive list of transgressions could be attributed to the sixty-year time gap. This, however, does not appear to be the case. At a time contemporaneous with Gordon, Thom (1940: 188–259) places some limitation on the transgressions envisaged as constituting conduct disorder by excluding 'alcoholism', but including problems such as 'bedwetting', 'fault-finding', 'daydreaming', 'unhappiness', 'weeping', 'delinquency', 'cheating', 'running away', 'stealing', and 'unmanageableness'. A definition by Miller quotes a range of 'bad habits', including 'masturbation, fidgeting, nose picking, thumb-sucking, nail biting, and clothes picking; temper tantrums, destructiveness, cruelty, rebellion and delinquencies such as lying, stealing, wandering and truancy, sexual offences against others; and succumbing to sexual stimulation by others' (Miller, 1936 cited in GAP 1974: 144).

A different description is provided by Strecker, who lists in order of frequency the traits displayed by children with behaviour disorders or conduct deviations:

disobedience, tantrums, marked restlessness, stealing, running away, truancy, homicidal trends, teasing, lying, impudence, quarrelling, cruelty to children, destructiveness, nocturnal wandering about the house, 'showing off', marked profanity, sexual deviation, constant talking, filthiness of person, street begging, 'fighting', sleeping in parks, riding freight trains, setting fire to houses, setting fire to clothing, sex perversion, alcoholism, cruelty to animals, irritability, writing obscene letters, forgery, screaming, wandering about the country, boastfulness, turning in fire alarms, sullenness and slyness.

(Strecker, 1928: 139)[6]

That conduct disorder can include 'riding freight trains' or 'constant talking' for Strecker (1928) but not for Miller (1936) or Gordon (1938) demonstrates a differing of opinion during this period. This suggests it would be unwise to explain the differences between current conceptualisations of conduct disorder as defined in the *DSM* and earlier conceptualisations as being simply due to a difference in time.

This difficulty in definition has been raised by several authors, with some pointing out the influence that opinion plays in deciding what is, indeed, conduct-disordered. Davidson (1996: 433, emphasis in original) declares this characteristic in the following statement: 'Clearly, moral judgements are inherent in our conception of disorder, for the very term *conduct* carries with it the connotation of good or bad'. This is an influence acknowledged by Gelder *et al.* (1989: 789), who conclude, 'The prevalence of Conduct Disorders is difficult to estimate because the dividing line between them and normal rebelliousness is arbitrary'. It is impossible to detach this 'science' from the social. As much can be drawn from Burdick's (1928: 457) announcement in the American *Psychiatric Quarterly* that 'Crime as we understand it is a conduct disorder measured in terms of social customs and usages'. It is also not dissimilar to the observation made by Barkley, that 'behavior rating scales are "simply quantifications of adult opinions. As a result they are subject to the same sources of unreliability as those opinions . . ."' (Reid *et al.*, 2000, citing Barkley, 1987: 219). It would seem then that, amongst the discontinuities in the concept of conduct disorder, what does present as continuous is the influence of moral judgements. Whereas we could say that social customs and mores do influence conceptualisations of conduct disorder, it would be mistaken to assume that these obey some kind of unitary social code. What is indicated by this array of behavioural concerns is not a prevailing obsession with a particular behaviour but rather an increasing preoccupation with the differentiation of children on the basis of vacillating conditions of transgression.

This discontinuity can be further demonstrated by considering the variation in what transgressions were used to define conduct disorder. For instance, a range of transgressions was tabulated by Healy (1920), a medical doctor, in 'Nervous signs and symptoms as related to certain causations of conduct disorder'.[7] In this paper Healy considers conduct disorder in terms of disordered conduct and misbehaviour and states that the term 'conduct disorder' designates a disorder of conduct, an outward manifestation of misbehaviour. In this scheme Healy assigns an array of misbehaviours as conduct disorders. These include:

> violent temper, sometimes with assaults on property or person, cruelties or definite sadism, various sorts of extreme meannesses, exhibitionism, fetich collecting, deliberate moral contamination of others, to say nothing of other forms of sex misconduct, persistent school truancy, running away from home, desertion, miserliness, malicious treatment of property, setting fires.
>
> (ibid.: 680)

In noting these misbehaviours Healy (ibid.: 690) is careful to qualify the amount of mental disturbance in children with conduct disorder. 'Intensive study of a large number of young delinquents has led to the conclusion that about 10 per cent are sufferers from inner turmoil that we call mental conflict'. This means that for the conduct disorder of Healy, *not all have 'inner conflict'*, or not all disorderly transgressions are *mixed with mental disorder*.

In the early 1920s in the US, disorderly conducts became the focus of a unique psychiatric exercise, the 'demonstration clinic'. In a report on the 'St Louis Demonstration Clinic', Anderson (1923: 419) explains that its purpose was to demonstrate 'the value of psychiatric services in the study and treatment of "conduct disorders" in children' and, in particular, to teach the value of psychiatric practices to health workers and others involved in the training or education of children'. At the 'St. Louis Demonstration Clinic' the conduct disorders of 250 children were 'given intensive clinical study':

> 154 children were charged with stealing (ranging all the way from simple thefts in the home to the stealing of automobiles); 25 children were charged with burglary; 79 with truancy; 82 with frequent running away from home; 66 with sex delinquencies; 98 with being unmanageable and staying out late at night; 16 with fighting and other conduct disorders. Seventy-four percent were actual court cases, being referred to the clinic by either the judge or a probation officer. Twenty-six per cent were not charged with any offense and were not under arrest. Nevertheless, the great majority had histories of marked behavior difficulties and conduct disorders.
>
> (ibid.: 426)[8]

Consequently, by way of these psychiatric demonstration clinics a range of children's behaviours were entering psychiatric jurisdiction. The disorderly conducts born through an increasing interest in delinquency are therefore integral to an emerging science of knowing and classifying the child. This interest in disorderly conducts combined with moral judgements has had important implications for the construction of conduct disorders and, therefore, the disorderly child. The degree to which *certain* adults in *certain* professional positions found unacceptable *certain* forms of behaviour becomes a crucial formula for the constitution of what is considered disorderly and, accordingly, who is a disorderly child.

The discontinuity in classifying conduct disorder

There has been a range of attempts to classify conduct disorder, with many of these using 'cause' as a basis of distinction. These 'causes' seem to vacillate between 'biological' and 'environmental'. For the biological emphasis, it seems that an ongoing imperative is somehow to link conduct disorder with a biologically based abnormality. Gordon (1938: 46) reasons that conduct disorder is caused by either 'static irreversible lesions' or the 'alterations of functions'. In this view 'an important factor in determining conduct disorder is a failure of that inhibition and regulation which is demanded by our social code' (ibid.: 52), with the explanation for this being the varying 'irradiation of excitation and inhibition' in the cortex (ibid.: 53). Although he proposes a neuropsychological basis for conduct disorder, this is only in a minority of cases, as 'the greater number of these cases of conduct disorder in children are due to psychological and environmental causes' (ibid.: 54). This said, Gordon (ibid.: 55) does seem to take the position that organic factors exert some influence on individuals and their self-control, claiming that 'in most cases of conduct disorder . . . more than one factor is operative, certain influences weakening control and disturbing integration, while others fire off the unchecked emotional disturbance which determines homicide, assault, theft or whatever it may be'. This suggests that on the one hand few conduct disorders are due to neuropsychological causes, whilst on the other regulation or control is determined by neuropsychological factors.

One of the entry points for psychiatric intrusion into the domain of children's disorderly conducts was via the science of encephalitis (the inflammation of the brain). The connection between the two can be suggested by considering the published speculations of two researchers in the period of the 1920s. Strecker (1928) investigated encephalitis and head trauma as a precipitator of behaviour changes in children, and hypothesised a causative link between encephalitis and behaviour. The idea of such a connection was also explored by Kasanin, who inferred that other cerebral trauma may act in a manner similar to encephalitis and cause behaviour disorder. Specifically, he observed: 'Besides the problem of the relation of cerebral injury to personality disorders there is the very interesting point of whether a severe concussion of the brain sets up a pathological process essentially of the same character as epidemic encephalitis' (Kasanin, 1929: 385). In making this observation, Kasanin cites an example of a child whose head had been stepped on by a horse, making the proposition that a relation between alteration of brain and behaviour disorders makes possible other structural aetiological hypotheses.

What I term the 'biological' view of conduct disorder has become arguably one of the most persuasive (Breggin, 1994). Biological causative links for *DSM-IV* conduct disorder include brain chemistry (Koplewicz, 1996), maternal smoking (Wakschlag *et al.*, 1997) and genetics (Comings, 1997). Although these are influential, they are not undisputed, and there is much discontinuity in what is represented as a united front. Such discontinuity is perceptible in arguments that assert a relationship between genetics and conduct disorder. The notion of a 'genetic influence' on psychiatric conditions is disputed by Kendler (1992), 'one of psychiatry's most active gene researchers' (Breggin and Breggin, 1994: 60).[9] These authors quote this gene researcher as stating that 'the amount of actual, rigorous data that we have is really very modest and is limited mostly to a couple of adoption studies' (Kendler 1992, cited in Breggin and Breggin, 1994: 60). Not surprisingly, this contentiousness is ignored by many pro-genetic writers of psychiatric literature, with authors such as Koplewicz (1996) advancing seemingly irrefutable proclamations about genetic causation with no reference to the debate. For example Koplewicz (ibid.: 236) asserts that 'certain children have a genetic vulnerability to this disorder' and 'The role of genetics in CD is less than crystal-clear. We do know that a vulnerability to the disorder is inherited'. Similarly, Cadoret *et al.* (1995) claim with regard to their research that 'The findings of genetic–environmental interaction in these studies confirm the importance of such interactions in the genesis of conduct disorder and aggressivity'. Genetic causation of conduct disorder has also been researched in Australia by Slutske *et al.* (1997: 274), using twin research with '2,682 adult twin pairs' and concluding that there is 'a substantial genetic influence on risk for Conduct Disorder (CD)'. These misleadingly definitive views contrast with Blau (1996: 68), who concludes 'No specific genetic evidence has been found for ODD in research'. Given the intimate nosological relationship between oppositional defiant disorder and conduct disorder, the lack of genetic evidence for ODD raises questions regarding the ostensibly straightforward claims of a genetic causation for conduct disorder.

Classifying conduct disorder and locating it as mental disorder does not necessarily depend on a biologically oriented emphasis. There are classifications where the importance may be on the effect on others, as in Miller's (1936), or those like Cameron's (1955), with its 'concept divisions'. This scheme is organised into 'three basic concepts' – 'developmental', 'reactive' and 'individual' – with six 'developmental', six 'reactive' and seven 'individual' symptoms. In this system conduct disorder is situated in the 'reactive concept', a division based upon the 'child adapting and reacting to the environment' (ibid.: 69). This conduct disorder is categorised amongst quite diverse symptoms: 'Primary habit disturbance – of eating, elimination, sleeping; Secondary habit disorders – gratification habits, tension habits; Motor symptomatology – speech disturbance; Disturbance in personal relationships – dependence, jealousy reactions; Conduct disorders – delinquency and educational or work disturbance' (ibid.). Compared with other classifications containing conduct disorder, it is unusual to notice conduct disorders included alongside 'speech disturbance' or 'primary habit disturbances' such as 'elimination'.

The unlikeness of these associations is recognised by Cameron (ibid.) and explained, 'At first glance the classification of such diverse symptom entities as response to environment appears to have little to commend it. Justification lies only in clinical experience'. This clinically justified conduct disorder is defined in this manner:

> Conduct disorder implies disturbed behavior of a sort that invokes social or moral condemnation, and in general is applied to children who have at least reached school age. Both in its origins and results it is readily seen as a reaction of the child with the environment. A particular set of circumstances places some behavior of this kind as delinquent.
>
> (ibid.: 70)

Four points can be drawn from this definition. First, the function of disturbance and 'social or moral' condemnation is both explicit and necessary for this conduct disorder. Second, the term 'conduct disorder' is applied to children who have 'at least reached school age'. This prerequisite is not necessarily observed in current practice: 'the onset of Conduct Disorder may occur as early as the preschool years, but the first significant symptoms usually emerge during the period from middle childhood through middle adolescence' (APA, 2000). Children aged as young as four were surveyed for conduct disorder in the *Ontario Child Health Study* (Offord, 1997). The third point concerns Cameron's reference to the way in which 'particular circumstance' can place some conduct-disordered behaviour as delinquent behaviour. The fourth point is that Cameron conceptualises both the 'origins and results' of conduct disorder in terms of the relation of the child with the environment. This preference for 'environmental cause' would be extremely difficult to promulgate in the current biologically orientated aetiology of the *DSM-IV-TR*.

The emphasis on prediction in the conduct disorder literature is another point where the genealogist can locate discontinuity. Take for example Canavan and Clark (1923: 775), who list behaviours from their study of children of non-psychotic parents including 'trespass', 'minor misbehavior', 'truant', 'crime against property' and 'trespass; immoral' as conduct disorders. These transgressions are not remarkable when compared with other conduct disorders. What is noteworthy in this version of conduct disorder is the pronouncement made about the possible futures of the conduct-disordered children. For Canavan and Clark (ibid.: 777), 'The psychotic, the feebleminded, and the backward children in this group are probably definitely on a level from which they will not rise, but the nervous children and those who have conduct disorders may develop into good citizens'. This prediction of 'good citizenry' is certainly different from the expectations of the APA's (2000) conduct-disordered child, which promises menacing portents such as antisocial personality disorder. Perhaps the key to understanding how antisocial personality disorder (also referred to as psychopathy) is implicit with the *DSM-IV-TR* conduct disorder is in the location of psychopathology to internal origins. Here a point by Gordon (1938: 46) can be used to illustrate this point: 'the majority of examples of conduct disorder are reversible, that is to say do not present a permanent change of character, and that we are therefore dealing with alterations of functions and not of structure'. This opinion brings an altogether different conceptualisation of the biologically determined conduct-disordered object, where Gordon's view enables the creation of a conduct-disordered object which is reversible, that is, it has the potential of 'non-conduct-disorderedness'. By contrast, if a conduct disorder becomes enmeshed in biologically derived rationale, especially one of structural abnormalities, there is little hope of change and every chance of future pathology.

The discontinuity in the DSM classification of conduct disorder

Despite the varieties of conduct disorder, the concept described in the *Diagnostic and Statistical Manual of Mental Disorders* prevails as the 'most influential and widely used systems for classifying children with conduct disorders' (Frick, 1998: 216). Yet conduct disorder did not exist as a category of mental disorder in the *Diagnostic and Statistical Manual of Mental Disorders* until the third edition, published in 1980 (Lahey *et al.*, 1994). Since this initial appearance, conduct disorder has undergone a metamorphosis with each edition of the *DSM*. This metamorphosis is evident in the changing criteria used to diagnose conduct disorder. In the *DSM-III* there are 'four specific subtypes' of conduct disorder, 'Undersocialised, Aggressive; Undersocialised, Nonaggressive; Socialised, Aggressive; and Socialised, Nonaggressive' (APA, 1980: 45). Seven years later, in the *DSM-III-R* 'three types' of conduct disorder are proposed: 'group type', 'solitary aggressive type' and 'undifferentiated type' (APA, 1987). Another stretch of seven years yields further changes in the *DSM-IV* (APA, 1994). In the *DSM-IV* the 'three types' have disappeared and three 'subtypes' have appeared, the 'Childhood-Onset type', 'Adolescent-Onset type' and 'Unspecified Onset', with the explanation that the last 'subtype is used if the age at onset of Conduct Disorder is unknown' (APA, 1994: 95). Each change in definition redesigns the truth of conduct disorder and, by proxy, realigns its object, the disorderly child. The effect of this changing of categorisation on the categorised object is unmistakable in this observation:

> Many of the diagnostic categories for childhood disorders have changed from DSM-III, to DSM III-R and again to DSM-IV ... categories that retained the same name from one edition to another underwent important changes in criteria. As a result, children who received a particular diagnosis, such as conduct disorder (CD), according to one edition, often failed to qualify for that diagnosis in the next edition and vice versa.
>
> (Achenbach, 1998: 70, citing Lahey *et al.*, 1990)

Discontinuity is conspicuous in this shift in definition and in the consequent changes to the object of definition, especially in the way a previously disorderly child could fail to qualify for the diagnosis of conduct disorder between these editions of the *Diagnostic and Statistical Manual of Mental Disorders*. This point is demonstrated by Lahey and Loeber (1994), who comment, with reference to Lahey *et al.* (1990), on the changes in the 'diagnostic definitions' of ADHD, conduct disorder and oppositional defiant disorder 'across editions of the [DSM]'. Their next statement points out the consequences of this variation: 'Although these evolving diagnostic definitions have included the same core characteristics in each version, they have changed considerably at their boundaries, sometimes resulting in sizeable changes in the prevalence of the disorders' (ibid.: 52). What is extraordinary is that these changes and the associated consequences can occur, and all the while an air of prominent scientificity is maintained. The sustained scientificity of conduct disorder amongst the 'sizeable changes of prevalence rates' and altered disorderly objects demonstrate the influence and legitimation of this truth. This being so, it is even more pressing to consider the alterations of conduct disorder in the *DSM*.

Despite the sweeping changes, there are claims of an origin of the *DSM-IV* conduct disorder. That there are differing conduct disorders for which an origin is required attests to the discontinuity in this superficially unified truth. Referring to Jenkins and Hewitt (1944) and Hewitt and Jenkins (1946), Henn *et al.* (1980: 1160) suggest that the *DSM-III* subtypes 'arose from a series of studies beginning with the analysis by Hewitt and Jenkins of referrals to a child guidance clinic in 1944'. Husain and Cantwell (1991: 87) similarly point to Jenkins and Hewitt (1944) as the researchers who did 'the first empirical work on conduct disorder'. But what is confusing is that Jenkins and Hewitt (1944) in *Types of Personality Structure Encountered in Child Guidance Clinics* do not use the term 'conduct disorder'. It seems both Henn *et al.* (1980) and Husain and Cantwell (1991) interpret *DSM-IV* conduct disorder in the work by Jenkins and Hewitt (1944). The interpretive quality of these claims is further evidenced by Husain and Cantwell's (1991: 88, emphasis in original) statement that whilst the work of Jenkins and Hewitt (1944) was 'the basis for inclusion in DSM-II of a whole category of behavior disorders . . . DSM-III changed the term from *behavior disorders* to *conduct disorders*' .

Similar discrepancies can be seen in the claims of a broader origin for conduct disorder. Robins, for example, maintains that the 'first official definition' of conduct disorder appeared in the 1974 'WHO glossary for mental disorders in the *International Classification of Diseases (8th ed. [ICD-8])*' (Robins, 1999: 37). In this edition, the category 'conduct disorder' is explained as being included for 'informal use' as a means to 'remedy the deficiency' in the 'inadequate provision for the classification of the disorders of childhood' (WHO, 1974: 54). Robins's view seems to suggest that any other use of the term such as by Cameron (1955) or Gordon (1938) or Healey (1920) was not 'official'. Differing again, Lorei and Vestre (1969: 185) propose 'The label conduct disorder was suggested by Buss's (1966) use of the term as a broad category that includes psychopathy, drinking problems, and sexual deviations'.[10] These inconsistencies in opinion indicate the difficulty in pinning down an 'origin' of conduct disorder. Most tellingly, the disparities attest to the importance placed on notions of a linear scientific development in the knowledge of conduct disorder. From a Foucauldian perspective, the question is one not of 'origin', but of the lines of emergences and possible spaces where the *DSM-IV-TR* conduct-disordered object could manifest. By questioning this notion of origin we not only disrupt the scientific lineage that would claim conduct disorder as an evolvement in understanding, we can also bring to light the debates and disagreements about this category and its diagnosing of the disorderly child.

The first two editions of the *DSM* contain reference to conduct-oriented problems, but these references are as subcategories of other 'disorders'. Additionally, although conduct disorder is a mental disorder of 'the child', the first edition of the *DSM* (APA, 1952) has no explicit section on children. By contrast, the *DSM-IV-TR* (and *DSM-IV*) has a specific section, located on 'Axis One, Disorders Usually First Diagnosed in Infancy, Childhood and Adolescence'. The first edition of the *DSM* describes a subcategory 'Adjustment reaction of childhood', and this is listed in the 'Personality Disorders' category under the title 'Transient Situational Personality Disorders' (APA, 1952). This subcategory, 'Adjustment reaction of childhood', is divided into '000-x841 Habit disturbance, 000-x842 Conduct disturbance and 000x843 Neurotic traits' (APA, 1952: 41–2).[11] This is the definition provided for '000-x842 Conduct disturbance':

> When the transient reaction manifests itself primarily as a disturbance in social conduct or behavior, it will be classified here. Manifestations may occur chiefly in the home, in the school, or in the community, or may occur in all three. Conduct disturbances are to be regarded as secondary phenomena when seen in cases of mental deficiency, epilepsy, epidemic encephalitis, and other well-recognized organic diseases. Indicate symptomatic manifestations under this diagnosis; for example, truancy, stealing, destructiveness, cruelty, sexual offences, use of alcohol etc.
>
> (APA, 1952: 41–2)

The term 'disorder' is not used in the title of '000-x842 Conduct disturbance', only in the title of the section 'Personality Disorder'. In the *DSM-II*, published sixteen years later, the dysfunction 'Conduct disturbance' disappears and there is no mention of the term 'conduct' in the section 'Behavior Disorders of Childhood and Adolescence'. Described in this section of the *DSM-II* are seven types of 'behaviour disorder':

.0 Hyperkinetic reaction of childhood (or adolescence)
.1 Withdrawing reaction of childhood (or adolescence)
.2 Overanxious reaction of childhood (or adolescence)
.3 Runaway reaction of childhood (or adolescence)
.4 Unsocialized aggressive reaction of childhood (or adolescence)
.5 Group delinquent reaction of childhood (or adolescence)
.9 Other reaction of childhood (or adolescence).

(APA, Committee on Nomenclature and Statistics, 1968: 12)

Twelve years later the *DSM-III* emerged with its own conduct disorder. Henn *et al.* offer an explanation for the transformation of the 'reactions' of the *DSM-II* to the conduct disorder of the *DSM-III*. They explain that 'In the proposed DSM-III classification scheme, group delinquent reaction becomes socialized conduct disorder; undersocialized aggressive reaction becomes undersocialized conduct disorder, aggressive type; and runaway reaction is broadened to the undersocialized conduct disorder, unaggressive type' (Henn *et al.*, 1980: 1161). Thus, according to this system of continuing evolution, conduct disorder did exist in the *DSM-II*, albeit under different names and descriptions. To accept this style of thinking, 'change' must be viewed as a semantic shift that accompanies the 'scientific' honing of this mental disorder.

The proposal that this decisive change represents little more than a 'broadening' of definitions is a justification deserving scrutiny. To do this I consider the claim that the conduct disorder subtype 'Undersocialised, Nonaggressive' from the *DSM-III* is a broadened form of 'Runaway Reaction of Childhood' from the *DSM-II*. The definition of 'Runaway Reaction of Childhood' in the *DSM-II* is numbered '308.3' and states, 'Individuals with this disorder characteristically escape from threatening situations by running away from home for a day or more without permission. Typically they are immature and timid, and feel rejected at home, inadequate, and friendless. They often steal furtively' (APA, 1968: 50). By contrast, this is the 'broadened' form that appears in the *DSM-III*:

312.10 Conduct Disorder, Undersocialised, Nonaggressive
Diagnostic Criteria
A. A repetitive and persistent pattern of nonaggressive conduct in which either the basic rights of others or major age-appropriate societal norms or rules are violated, as manifested by any of the following:
(1) chronic violations of a variety of important rules (that are reasonable and age-appropriate for the child) at home or at school (e.g. persistent truancy, substance abuse)
(2) repeated running away from home overnight
(3) persistent serious lying in and out of home
(4) stealing not involving confrontation with a victim
B. Failure to establish a normal degree of affection, empathy, or bond with others as evidenced in *no more than one* of the following indications of social attachment:
(1) has one or more peer-group friendships that have lasted over six months
(2) extends himself or herself for others even when no immediate advantage is likely
(3) apparently feels guilt or remorse when such a reaction is appropriate (not just when caught or in difficulty)
(4) avoids blaming or informing on companions
(5) shows concern for the welfare of friends or companions
C. Duration of pattern of nonaggressive conduct of at least six months

D. If 18 or older, does not meet the criteria for Antisocial Personality Disorder.

(APA, 1980: 48)

To suggest that 'Runaway Reaction of Childhood' has simply been 'broadened' is misleading. Knowledge about the mental state of those who 'run away' may be sourced by eclectic means. Jenkins (1969) draws on the research of Maier (1949), who

> has demonstrated that in rats, at a certain level of frustration, adaptive behavior is replaced by what he calls frustration behavior. Frustration behavior is maladaptive, stereotyped, repetitive, and is typically increased by punishment. *All of these characteristics are evident in the behavior of the unsocialised aggressive child.*
>
> (Jenkins, 1969: 1036, emphasis added)

It is an intriguing phenomenon that rodents can be employed in the production of truths about children, truths that can in the presence of certain contingent formations become persuasive mental disorders.

Contingencies and discontinuities enable conduct disorder to function as a truth that has the capacity to bring into being the 'objects of which it speaks'. To the assertion that conduct disorder is a phenomenon that has patiently awaited 'scientific' recognition we can reply that it is a truth that is equally in need of its phenomena as its phenomena are in need of it. This reciprocal relation is dependent on numerous contingencies including the indefinableness of mental disorder, the child as psychiatric object, the delinquent and its pathology and the substantiation provided by classification. What is crucial to grasp is that the *DSM-IV-TR* conduct disorder does not manifest from some linear heritage of conduct disorders. Rather, the 'history' of conduct disorder, to borrow from Foucault (1998a: 429), 'appears then not as a great continuity underneath an apparent discontinuity, but as a tangle of superimposed discontinuities'. What can be recognised in this array of conduct disorder is a tangle of discontinuities superimposed so that, at specific moments, they seem to be one. The contingencies and discontinuities enable conduct disorder to emerge because they have very precise effects that contribute to the construction of conduct disorder as *dominating knowledge*. This dominating knowledge masks the discontinuities of conduct disorder. This requires further consideration in terms of how this truth is manufactured so successfully and how it is administered to create its 'inviolable objects'. It is to this task that I now turn.

Chapter 4

Interrogating the power to diagnose disorderly children

In forty minutes we had a label and a script for some medication
(Parent Interview #1, 2003)

In the above quote a parent describes her experience of having a paediatrician diagnose her five-year-old son Brad with ADHD. From that diagnosis the young child experienced being 'officially' known as disorderly. It seems that to be known as disorderly is a clear-cut process: you get diagnosed. But to accept this is to miss the complexities of the diagnostic practices, and risks failing to question just why such a diagnosis can define a child as disorderly. The crucial question to ask is how is it that a young person can be made a disorderly subject and, further, how is it that the person understands him- or herself as disorderly? These questions require a consideration of power – which is not simply to pose the question 'Who has the power to diagnose?' but rather to ask what relations of power enable the diagnosis to occur. To refine this question I turn to this statement by Foucault:

> In studying these power relations, I in no way construct a theory of power. But I wish to know how the reflexivity of the subject and the discourse of truth are linked – 'How can the subject tell the truth about itself?' – and I think that relations of power exerting themselves upon one another constitute one of the determining elements in this relation I am trying to analyze.
>
> (Foucault, 1998b: 451)

Following this formulation, the question can be structured in this way: How is a young person's reflexivity linked with the discourse of disorderliness? Or to put it another way: How can the young person tell disorderly truths about him- or herself? This linkage can be delved into from the perspective of power relations, where it can be asked how power is implicated in the means by which a young person understands him- or herself as disorderly.

I have adapted two of Foucault's tactics in order to create a 'structure' for this consideration of power relations. The first of these is what Foucault (1980a: 199) calls a 'grid of analysis': 'if power is in reality an open, more-or-less coordinated (in the event, no doubt ill-coordinated) cluster of relations, then the only problem is to provide oneself with a grid of analysis which makes possible an analytic of relations of power'. The 'grid of analysis' used in this discussion is informed by the second tactic, Foucault's five-point analysis of power:

> the analysis of power relations demands that a certain number of points be established: 1. The system of differentiations which permits one to act upon the actions of others . . . 2. The types of objectives pursued by those who act upon the actions of others . . . 3. The means of bringing power relations into being . . . 4. Forms of institutionalisation . . . 5. The degrees of rationalization'.
>
> (Foucault, 1983b: 223)

This 'five-point analysis of power' provokes specific questions regarding the functioning of the relations of power involved in the production of conduct disorder – and the diagnosing of disorderly children.

The first point of Foucault's (1983b) analysis of power is used to reinterpret the *Diagnostic and Statistical Manual of Mental Disorders* as a 'system of differentiations'. The second point prompts the questioning of the types of objectives pursued in this relation of power. This style of question can be utilised to disturb the scientificity of the relations of power making conduct disorder, a ruse that twists the notion of the objectivity of the expert. The third point both provides the principal structure for this analysis of power relations and draws attention to the means through which the actions producing conduct disorder are brought into being. The fourth point raises awareness of the multiple levels at which the relations of power function. This includes the way action can be made on a young person via the school and by institutions such as the juvenile justice system, the police and the health system. The last point highlights the rationality of power relations, or the principles that substantiate the actions made on the actions of young people. The third point of Foucault's analysis, 'the means of bringing power relations into being', forms a rationale for organising the analysis of power into a discussion in this chapter of the tectonics (or making) of conduct disorder, and a discussion of the next chapter on the administration of conduct disorder.

By focusing on power I am not attempting to delineate power as a *separate* actor in the realm of subjectivisation. My intention is to ask how power is implicated in the means by which a subject tells the truth about itself. More specifically, I am asking how power is implicated in the way a young person speaks of disorderly truths about him- or herself. Importantly, I am not suggesting that there is a specific 'power' involved in producing these mentally disordered subjectivities, but rather that, via an analysis in terms of power relations, the relationships between subjectivisation and truth can be made more explicit. As Foucault (1998b: 451) emphasises, power relations 'is a field of analysis and not at all a reference to any unique instance'. Thus, in this chapter power is employed as means to analyse the linkage between the discourses of conduct-disordered truth and the disorderly subject.

Although I am nominating truth as distinct from power, it is a fictitious conceptualisation performed for the benefit of this analysis. Truth and power are not disparate entities. They are, to corrupt a colloquialism, two sides of an awkward coin. This is a point made clear by Foucault in the interview 'Truth and power':

> The important thing here, I believe, is that truth isn't outside power or lacking in power: contrary to a myth whose history and functions would repay further study, truth isn't the reward of free spirits, the child of protracted solitude, nor the privilege of those who have succeeded in liberating themselves. Truth is a thing of this world: it is produced only by virtue of multiple forms of constraint. And it induces regular effects of power.
>
> (Foucault, 2000: 131)

Diagrammatically, power and truth can be considered separately. However, in so doing it is vital to remain attentive to the relationship each has to the other. That is to say, without the effects of power the truth of conduct disorder could not be produced and through the truth of conduct disorder certain effects of power can manifest. From this perspective, demarcating truth and power is problematic. Certainly, envisaging them as independent entities is tantamount to missing the subtle, yet inescapable relation between the two. As Foucault (ibid.) states, truth 'is produced by virtue of multiple forms of constraint' and this truth 'induces regular effects of power'. Thus, one induces the effects of the other.

This effect is most obvious in the moments when a conduct-disordered truth persuades a young person to construct a disordered subjectivity. Here there is a relation between the young person and the purveyor of truth. As Foucault (1983b: 217) suggests, 'what characterizes the power we are analyzing is that it brings into play relations between individuals (or between groups). However, this relation is not restricted to the individuals who appear directly involved in the subjugation (the school counsellor, the psychiatrist). Relations of power reach to the depths of truth-making (at once producing truths and the effects of truth). To consider power relations as operating only in the moments of diagnosis is to adopt a superficial view, one ignorant of the cacophony of competing actions to exert power over others and the counter-responses of intransigence. For conduct disorder, considering the relations of power includes not just the moment when a category is bestowed on a child or young person, it is tied to the levels of truth-making that produce such diagnostic terms, to the organisations that make these terms, and to those that endorse them.

That said, the question remains of just 'What is power?' or perhaps 'How do we imagine power to work, to exist?' We could, following Foucault, consider power as an 'action' or more precisely, 'a way in which certain actions modify others . . . Power exists only when it is put into action, even if, of course, it is integrated into a disparate field of possibilities brought to bear upon permanent structures' (Foucault, 1983b: 219). Here I draw out two points important to this conceptualisation of power: first, 'power exists only when it is put into action' and, second, one instance of an effect or an action such as a person being diagnosed as conduct-disordered is not a single instance of power. Rather, the presence of such an action implies multitudinous relations or, as Foucault (ibid.) states, relations of power are 'integrated into a disparate field of possibilities'. Foucault (ibid.: 220) further clarifies this concept of 'action':

> In effect, what defines a relationship of power is that it is a mode of action, which does not act directly, and immediately on others. Instead it acts on their actions: an action upon an action, on existing actions or on those which may arise in the present or the future ... It is a total structure of actions brought to bear on possible actions; it incites, it induces, it seduces, it makes easier or more difficult; in the extreme it constrains or forbids absolutely; it is nevertheless always a way of acting upon an acting subject or acting subjects by virtue of their acting or being capable of action. A set of actions upon other actions.

After Foucault, the question could be asked, 'How do the actions of the truth of conduct disorder modify others?' This description by Foucault provides a means to envisage power in an active sense. As an action that acts on another action, power is an entity that can exist only through a relationship. Integral to this relationship are two other 'Foucauldian factors': the individual and their technologies of the self and the discourses of truth.

Important to this conception of power is the way in which questions about power are formulated. The very structure of the question can imply that power exists as an entity as opposed to being a creature of action. This understanding is the premise for Foucault's use of the 'how' question:

> To put it bluntly, I would say that to begin the analysis with a 'how' is to suggest that power as such does not exist. At the very least it is to ask oneself what contents one has in mind when using this all-embracing and reifying term; it is to suspect that an extremely complex configuration of realities is allowed to escape when one treads endlessly in the double question: What is power? and Where does power come from?
>
> (ibid.: 217)

These are crucial points, for to ask where *is* power in the making of mentally disordered subjectivity is to suggest that, somewhere, there is a source of power. This further suggests that if this is 'discovered' and altered (or stopped) the effects of this power can be eliminated. This notion, however, is erroneous, and such remedial actions will not achieve their goals. In this configuration the term 'power' is easily reduced to an almost singular simplistic concept. Adopting this view takes a position contrary to the conceptualisation of power as a relation. Consequently, considering power as an 'action acting on the actions of others' not only denies the possibility of a 'place where power exists', it simultaneously posits power as multilayered and multifunctional. This style of questioning and the impacts it can make on how power is conceptualised is made clear in the following quotation from Foucault:

> To approach the theme of power by an analysis of 'how' is therefore to introduce several critical shifts in relation to the supposition of a fundamental power. It is to give oneself as the object of analysis power relations and not power itself – power relations which are distinct from objective abilities as well as from relations of communication. This is as much as saying that power relations can be grasped in the diversity of their logical sequence, their abilities, and their interrelationships.
>
> (ibid.: 219)

This style of reasoning is behind the question, 'How are the reflexivity of the young person and the discourses of conduct-disordered truth linked?' This question could be reframed as 'How is it that there is this power relationship whereupon the action of diagnosing conduct disorder can be made upon the actions of certain young people?' In addition to providing a means to access the relations of power, the 'how' question also provides a means of access to the diverse relationships of power implicated in the action of disordering a child.

Responding to the question of how power is implicated in the making of conduct disorder involves considering power from two perspectives: in terms of how conduct disorder is made truthful, and in terms of how this truth makes a young person disorderly. To examine the first perspective the discussion is organised into three sections. In the first section, 'Nosology, power and truth', I focus on the power relations implicit to constructing the *DSM*. In the second section, 'Expert knowledge, psychiatric expertise and the medical necessity', I consider the power relations that facilitate 'psychiatric expertise'. And in the last section, 'Expert knowledge, schools and education', I examine the power relations that enable this expertise to permeate the school.

Nosology, power and truth

Using Foucauldian terms, psychiatry's standing as a science can be described as being premised on its system of differentiation – the classification system. The import of such a system was not lost on clinicians such as Drapes, who stated in 1906 that:

> In any department of knowledge worthy of the name of science I think it will be admitted that one of the most important elements is terminology. I doubt if

any branch of science has suffered more than our own from the disability of an imperfect terminology, a point which it is hardly necessary to argue.

(Drapes, 1906: 75)

Almost one hundred years since this admission of the 'disability of an imperfect terminology', it could be contended that psychiatry's scientific liability is remedied via terminological apparatus such as the *Diagnostic and Statistical Manual of Mental Disorders*. The *DSM*, then, is a system that not only provides a structural grid of demarcation for action on the actions of others, but also substantiates the science of psychiatry.

In order to validate psychiatry as a science, the system of differentiations must be known as scientific. For the *DSM* this translates to it being considered 'medically scientific', a process that involves the merging of mental disorders with medicine. Just as Drapes commented on the need for a classification system in 1906, so too there were calls for associations between mental disease and medicine. Noble, an Australian psychiatrist, recognised that such a relationship to medicine is critical to mental disorder: 'In the past, the science of mental hygiene has had little opportunity of development, because until the present century mental diseases were looked upon quite apart from general medicine' (Noble, 1929: 300). To achieve this relationship, various means were found such as linking psychiatry with the cells of biology. For example, Henderson explains that:

At the commencement of the twentieth century psychiatry experienced a fresh impetus. A possible underlying physical basis for all mental ills was strongly advocated, and strenuous and ingenious attempts were made to forge a link between clinical signs and symptoms and pathological findings. Bacteriological investigation was in the forefront, the opsonic index and the proper form of autogenous vaccine was carefully determined, leucocytes were counted with particular reference to eosinophilia, and thyroid extract was exhibited in courageous doses.

(Henderson, 1939: 9)[1]

Instilling these biological phenomena enables mental disorders to be construed through cells and chemical imbalances, a conceptualisation that infuses an impression of scientificity into psychiatry.

This installation of the biological into mental disorders is reflected in the realignment of psychiatric nosology to fit biological schemata, a realignment demonstrated by comparing *DSM-IV-TR* (APA, 1994) with earlier versions. Jenkins (1973: 21, emphasis added) outlines that in the first edition, *DSM-I*, the major division in the classification was between diagnoses 'caused by or associated with impairment of brain tissue function and those which are not . . . the primary distinction is between those disorders which are known or *presumed* to be organic, and those which are known or *assumed* to be functional'. In the *DSM-IV-TR*, however, the majority of mental disorders either have a biological underpinning or, as Breggin and Breggin (1994) argue with regard to the *DSM-IV*, are the subject of research endeavours to establish one. It is significant that the first edition of the *DSM* had, as previously discussed, little of the influence of the later versions. It could be suggested that a key factor in the success of the later versions is the authority of medical science gained via a conceptualisation of biological factors in mental disorders. These biological theorisations of mental disorder are extremely influential. A case in point is that in the US biologically orientated research on mental disorder attracts significantly more funding than other theoretical perspectives (ibid.).

The *DSM-IV-TR* is an authoritative reference text that is widely used for the diagnosis of mental disorders – or, at the very least, is influential in the formulation of notions of disorderly children. The *DSM-IV* has been translated into several languages, including 'Chinese, Danish, Dutch, Finnish, French, German, Greek, Hungarian, Italian, Japanese, Norwegian, Portuguese, Russian, Spanish, Swedish, Turkish and Ukrainian' (Caplan, 1995: xix). In the US and Australia, the *DSM* is the prevailing classification, and in the UK it is generally stated that reference is to the *ICD-10*. The UK government website Wired for Health states that the *ICD-10* 'is predominantly used in the UK and Europe' and that the *DSM* is predominantly used in the USA, but is also used across the world (Department of Health and Department for Education and Skills, 2005). Although the *ICD-10* is more commonly used in the UK, the growing reference to the *DSM-IV* cannot be ignored. *DSM* diagnostic categories are being increasingly taken up in the UK with it being cited, for example, in the Lords Hansard Text in the discussion of the Mental Health Bill (House of Lords Debate, 2002, 23 July). It is also referred to on the website of the Royal College of Psychiatrists, which includes, for example, a text by Richardson and Joughin (2002) that cites the *DSM-IV* when defining conduct disorder. This influence must also be grasped in terms of the association between the *ICD-10* and the *DSM-IV/DSM-IV-TR*. The *DSM* has a degree of influence over the *ICD*. This is evident in the writing of the *ICD-10*, with, as Husain and Cantwell (1991: 53) note, the APA being 'asked by WHO to contribute to development of the mental disorder chapter of ICD-10'.

Despite being a 'de facto international standard', there is substantial criticism of the *DSM* (Caplan, 1995; Kirk and Kutchins, 1992; Sadler, 2004). Caplan describes herself as a 'former consultant to those who construct the world's most influential manual of alleged mental illnesses: the APA *Diagnostic and Statistical Manual of Mental Disorders*' (1995: xv). With this 'insider perspective' Caplan makes it clear that:

> I got an inside look at how this august body decides who is normal, and what I saw disturbed me deeply. I was shocked to realize how little I, as a mental health professional, had known about how authorities in my own field went about choosing whom to classify as mentally ill.
>
> (ibid.: 8)

She then refers to the debate over 'masochistic personality disorder' to illustrate this 'choosing' as opposed to 'scientific' quality of the construction of mental disorder. She explains '. . . I knew that the label had been used unofficially to heap unjustifiable blame on so many people (mostly women and members of racialized and other devalued groups) by claiming that they brought their problems on themselves and enjoyed suffering' (ibid.: 85). Masochistic personality disorder was subsequently changed to 'self defeating personality disorder' and included in the *DSM-III-R*; then, seven years later, in the *DSM-IV* the disorder was not listed.

Caplan's 'insider gaze' provides a suggested rationale for the omission of this mental disorder in the *DSM-IV* (it is also not in the *DSM-IV-TR*). Here she describes how 'Lynne Rosewater reported that, during the hearings, "[T]hey were having a discussion for a criterion" [about masochistic personality disorder] and Bob Spitzer's wife [a social worker and the only woman on Spitzer's side at that meeting] says, "I do that sometimes" and he says, "Okay, take it out" '(ibid.: 91). The Bob Spitzer referred to in this quote is Robert Spitzer, a psychiatrist and the head of the *DSM-III-R* Task Force. This account reveals how, contrary to the claim of objectivity, subjective decision-making is unmistakably involved in the construction of the *DSM*. This 'insider's gaze' also illustrates how well such subjective decision-making can be camouflaged by the rhetoric of 'science'.

The promulgation of information attesting scientificity is therefore crucial to establishing the authority of the *DSM*. Later versions of the *DSM, DSM-III, DSM-IIIR, DSM-IV, DSM-IV-TR*, each include numerous reports of research substantiating the diagnostic categories, and detailed lists of expert 'contributors'. One outcome of these claims to scientificity is that conduct disorder can be understood as a valid mental disorder, with the *DSM* providing an expert scientific view. According to this stance, the considerable changes in the definition of conduct disorder in versions of the *DSM* from *DSM-III* to *DSM-IV* (Southam-Gerow and Kendall, 1997) can be explained as results of the development or honing of scientific knowledge. This is a persuasive explanation, and certainly one that draws on connections to science and scientific authority. Leaving aside this tangle of scientific claims, we could take a critical perspective on these changes and understand them in terms of the varying attitudes of the authors who construct the *DSM*. This view suggests that the manual is an arbitrarily constructed nosological apparatus. From this standpoint, the relations of power necessary to create conduct disorder are precisely those relations that can imbue subjective interpretations with scientific rigor.

Expert knowledge: psychiatric wisdom and the medical necessity

Making the subjective appear scientifically rigorous lends authority to psychiatric categories and, of course, onto those who administer the diagnosis. Claims regarding the standing of psychiatry can be read in statements such as the following by Macpherson:

> When it is considered that the general population is permeated by mental disorders, that many forms of bodily disease are of mental origin and that there are few acute physical diseases which do not exhibit mental correlative symptoms, any assumption of a superiority to a knowledge of psychiatry is a confession of ignorance.
>
> (Macpherson, 1926: 176)

This quote indicates the emphasis placed on the psychiatrist as the expert, the specialist who has the primary responsibility for the administration of the system of differentiations demarcated in the *DSM*. Although other 'experts' can be involved or implicated in the diagnosing of disorderly children (the paediatrician, the clinical psychologist, the general practitioner), the psychiatric role is the one vested with the ultimate authority. It is the case that this classification system is, after all, a product of psychiatry. Psychiatric knowledge of nosology is thus crucial to substantiating the position of the expert. From this perspective, not only is nosology a means through which to create and categorise psychopathological aberration, it simultaneously becomes a means to create the expert 'knower' of these categories. Thus, as disorderly conducts are made conduct disorders, and conduct disorders become diagnoses of disorderly children, so too must there necessarily be an expert knower of these categories – and of the disorderly child.

Considering the administration of conduct disorder and disorderly children from this perspective appears to respond to the question of 'who exercises power'. However it is vital to avoid the pursuit of this type of question, because, as Foucault (1988g: 103) states, 'I don't believe that this question of "who exercises power" can be resolved unless the question "how does it happen?" is resolved at the same time'. From this viewpoint it is preferable to ask 'How does this power of the expert happen?' or 'How is it that the expert *is* an expert?' or 'How do certain individuals come to have this status?' In the discussion that follows two angles are taken to delve into this question. The first is 'the consolidation of expertise' and the second is 'the institutionalisation of expertise'. The consolidation of psychiatric expertise can be understood as requiring three processes. First, psychiatry needed to embed itself in the field of medicine. Second, psychiatric knowledge needed to be elevated above that of the physician. Lastly, to be successful as the expert of the mind of the child, child specialisation had to be privileged within psychiatry. For the second angle, the institutionalisation of expertise of conduct disorder, I place the focus on three aspects: the expert and the care of the public; the expert, the delinquent and the criminal; and, lastly, the school, the delinquent and the expert.

The first angle, consolidation of expertise, is concerned with the demarcation of 'expert', where the expert is one who owns certain knowledge and, because of this ownership, is authorised to take certain actions. Just as mental disorder needed to be infused with biological meaning, so too the expert on the mentally disordered requires the prestige of medical science. The importance of medicine and its foremost symbol, the doctor, is salient in the following excerpt, taken from one of the interviews I conducted with a parent:

I was brought up, you went to see the doctor and you did what the doctor told you and you took what the doctor gave you and no questions asked. But this was different. I mean the whole visit was different. I felt really strange being there; I felt the doctor himself was a bit strange. So I had all these niggling doubts and even though he had given me a label to use and especially the word dexamphetamine and I've got this little five-year-old and I just couldn't get my mind around giving a child this drug, probably because of all the rumours and everything and it was all negative stuff that I'd heard. So we weren't about to start giving him this. But that was when he was in kindergarten and then . . . [in] year 4 he became really difficult. So we decided to put him on the medication.

(Parent Interview #1, 2003)

This parent describes the influence of the doctor, and the difficulty in resisting the directive to medicate her young son with dexamphetamine, a psychostimulant frequently used for the treatement of ADHD (Ritalin – methylphenidate – is another) (Kaplan and Sadock, 1998). Although she did resist, the consequence of having what the school recognised as a 'disorderly child' resulted in her complying with the mandate to medicate.

Psychiatry could be characterised as grappling to find a medical basis in much the same manner as Drapes (1906) sought terminology to verify psychiatry as science, or as biology is apparently needed to make the *DSM* scientific. Such movement towards the medical is proclaimed by Farrar, who notes the great importance of implicating the humble cell in the matters of the mind:

The contributions of the microscope to psychiatry during the past twenty years have indeed been great, and the hopes for the future can be no less. By the combination of various elective staining methods through which definite constituents of the cortex can be isolated and studied separately as well as in their mutual relations, a collective appreciation of the character of the *disease process* has been attained in certain pathological conditions with an accuracy to detail before undreamed of.

(Farrar, 1905: 453, emphasis in original)

This use of cells and chemicals opened up the possibility of scientific affiliations other than medicine. One of these possibilities was the discipline of 'agriculture'. A case in point are the 'Fitter Families contests' run during the 1920s in the US – which were held in the 'human stock' sections' of state fairs (Kevles, 1985: 62). These Fitter Families contests were associated with the American Eugenics Society, which had links to the Eugenics Education Society, which had 'branches . . . in Birmingham, Cambridge, Manchester, Southampton, Liverpool, Glasgow, and Sydney, Australia' (ibid.: 59). To enter a Fitter Families contest, 'All family members had to submit to a medical examination – including a Wassermann test and a psychiatric assessment – and take an intelligence test' (ibid.: 62). The connection to agriculture was made explicit in the Fitter Families brochure, which states: 'The time has come when the science of *human husbandry* must be developed, based on the principles now followed by scientific agriculture, if the better elements of our civilization are to dominate or even survive' (ibid.).[2] The 'better elements' of civilization would have referred to notions of the better 'race' and better 'minds' and 'bodies'. Mitchell and Snyder (2003) term the circulation of eugenic ideas the 'Eugenic Atlantic', and argue that both disability and 'race' are lines of inquiry that need to be brought to bear on the practices that deployed supposed physiological markers to demarcate the 'feebleminded' or 'deficient'. Who then, we must ask, was permitted to compete in these Fitter Families competitions? What families were welcome and what families were not – and what families won?

The positioning of agricultural analogies alongside medical ones suggests the science of the mind at a crossroads in its affiliations, and one influenced by the practices of eugenics. Perhaps the choice of medicine was taken because of concerns such as the low prestige afforded by agriculture. Assimilation with medicine was not, however, without difficulty, a major issue being that of demarcating the mind as the preserve of the psychiatrist. For example, Jahr (1928: 496) contends that, in matters of 'disorders of conduct', 'It is true that a number of these behavior problems need the advice of the psychiatrist, but a large majority of the milder disorders of conduct can be handled by conscientious physicians with advantage'. This comment indicates that it is possible that, contrary to the contemporary domination of the field by psychiatry, a less dominant approach could have occurred. Perhaps medicine could have remained the expert on the child and its behaviour or, at the very least, the expert on almost all of its behaviours.

The tensions between medicine and psychiatry are significant in that they represent archaeological fragments of an emerging technology of expertise. Promoting madness as having a medical base was crucial to legitimising the asylums (and those in charge of them) of Victorian Britain. The tense relationship between medicine and psychiatry is recognisable in Macpherson's (1926: 176) comments on medicine's scepticism about placing 'so-called mental disorders . . . in clinical medicine'. As Macpherson laments, '[I]t is common to hear medical men say that they know nothing of psychiatry and in a tone that implies that they are quite content with their ignorance' (ibid.). As is clear in this statement, Macpherson was in favour of the insertion of mental disorders into medicine and aghast at the 'ignorance' of the 'medical men'. To validate psychiatry, Macpherson placed much effort into the establishment of psychiatric clinics in NSW, Australia. Take this quote for example:

> If we sum up these results we must come to the conclusion that the establishment of psychiatric clinics confers a boon on the public, on the medical profession and on the psychiatrist. Psychiatry has too long been divorced from clinical medicine and its practitioners have been forced to occupy a circumscribed

and unenviable position while a wider field of work was urgently awaiting their services.

(ibid.: 178)

But the move to legitimisation was far more than just making madness medical: it needed to make psychiatry something that was more than medicine. The issue of being forced into 'circumscribed' and 'unenviable positions' is taken up twenty years later by Williams in the *Medical Journal of Australia,* where it is argued that 'The leadership in this field by our profession is often disputed' (Williams, 1949: 678). This leadership disputation is exemplified in Williams's fear that workers other than the psychiatrist may take in interest in this area, '*whether we like it or not*' (ibid.: 676, emphasis added). This issue had also been raised some years prior at a meeting of the New South Wales Branch of the British Medical Association, 31 August 1933, by Dawson, a Professor of Psychiatry at Sydney University (Dawson, 1933). Dawson warned that 'The general public is beginning to seek advice regarding the nervous child, and unless we as a profession meet the need, treatment will be *sought elsewhere*' (ibid.: 545, emphasis added).

Although psychiatry later did become established as the expert knowledge of the mind, further ground had to be covered to secure psychiatry as the expert on children's minds. Similar to psychiatry, the subspecialty child psychiatry had difficulty being accepted as an authoritative medical knower. This difficulty is noticeable in the timing of the allocation of prestige to child psychiatry. Schowalter (2003) points to some suggestions that child psychiatry began in the US with the formation of child guidance clinics in Chicago in 1899. There is also the suggestion that the

> movement toward subspecialization picked up speed in 1943 when the American Psychiatric Association converted its section on Mental Deficiency to the Section on Child Psychiatry. Six years later, the Section was elevated in status to the Standing Committee on Child Psychiatry. In 1947, the Group for the Advancement of Psychiatry appointed a Committee on Child Psychiatry.
>
> (Schowalter, 2003: 44)

There is quite a spread of time between 1899 and 1947, and presumably the establishment of 'official' groups such as the American Academy of Child Psychiatry in 1953 seems to make the 1899 claim for the formation of child psychiatry unconvincing. If we posed the question differently, instead of searching out an origin of child psychiatry, we could instead inspect the various emergences of practices that sought to speak authoritatively about the child's mind.

The attention to the establishment of child psychiatry reveals much about the need for authority and verification. This is unmistakable in Lipton's comments on the lack of 'academic departments of child psychiatry in Australia and no full professors in the field' (Lipton, 1978: 158). This is because, 'from a secure and fertile base, with *scientific and medical credibility*, the child psychiatrist will be able to collaborate with departments of adult or general psychiatry to contribute to the development of the truly general psychiatrist of the future' (ibid.: 160, emphasis added). Academic and medical credentials were crucial for Lipton because they meant *scientific credibility*. The importance of this medical association is also unambiguous in the recommended terminology for the guidance clinic: 'where possible the names of clinics should be changed to "psychiatric clinic for children" or some equivalent appellation which will clearly indicate the function of today's services in a medical framework' (ibid.: 158).

The second angle, institutionalisation, takes up the argument that establishing institutional bases proved key to the legitimisation of psychiatry and of child psychiatry. Indeed, the power of psychiatry can be characterised in terms of institutional dissemination. This approach moves away from attributing power to (or imagining that it resides solely with) what seems to be the most obvious influence on the making of the disorderly child: the psychiatrist. This way of thinking follows Foucault, and seeks to avoid attributing power to 'a maker'. As he proposes, 'let us not look for the headquarters that presides over its rationality . . . the rationality of power is characterised by tactics that are often quite explicit at the restricted level where they are inscribed' (Foucault, 1984c: 95). Contemplating power in this way is a means to engage Foucault's fourth point in the analysis of power, 'the forms of institutionalisation'.

Importantly, these institutions do not function separately from the relations of power. They are, through their overlap with the technologies acting on the actions of others, relations of power. This is a challenging concept because of the complexity of the relations of power implicated in the production of conduct disorder. To tackle this complexity it is important to conceptualise the influence of psychiatric and psychological truths not as static institutions, but rather as fluid truths permeating institutions. In the interstices of these relations, the truth of conduct disorder and of the disorderly child invariably interacts with the truths and practices of the institution. From this perspective, this complexity functions simultaneously at levels of truth-making and in the practices of power.

New forms of institutionalisation to detect the dangerous and the mad were necessitated via creating the truth that mental disorder abides beyond the milieu of the asylum. This movement to areas beyond the 'traditional' is noted by Anderson:

> Though in the past the contribution of psychiatry has been largely in the fields of mental disease and mental defect, there is now a rapidly growing interest in the application of its knowledge to other conditions – to the subject of delinquency and dependency as such, to industrial, educational, and other welfare problems.
>
> (Anderson, 1923: 417)

This institutionalisation forms a point of access for the expert as well as a being a site where truthful discourses can be acted upon in the form of dividing practices.

The institutions involved include legal institutions, the penal and juvenile justice system, criminology, the health system, mental hygiene and public health, child guidance, the family, government, and the school. Over the following pages a selective discussion of the mechanisms of institutionalisation is made. Here I focus on three forms: public welfare; the delinquent and the criminal; and, third, the delinquent, the expert and the school.

As well as the individual, the 'expert' on the mind is also interested in the 'welfare of society'. This 'wider' focus is emphasised by Anderson, who states 'Psychiatry devotes itself to the study and treatment of human behavior, particularly that form of human behavior that is now, or may later become, inimical to the welfare of the individual and society' (Anderson, 1923: 417). This 'concern for society' can be conceptualised as connected to the conviction that the disorderly child holds within it a potentially dangerous adult. According to this schema, the child is viewed as a prospective threat, an uncertain variable that poses both present and future danger and so poses a 'public health problem'. Indeed, Ruggles-Brise states that this idea was regarded by Van Waters (1926) as the 'discovery of the century'. This was 'the recognition of the fact that delinquency and disordered conduct in dealing with the young is a Public Health problem; and that America's two outstanding contributions to civilisation in dealing with crime are the Juvenile Court and the Mental Hygiene Movement' (Ruggles-Brise, 1926: ix). Here the child is considered a means to ensure the future wellness of the population, an action that does not merely mean keeping the child well, but involves keeping 'bad' children from those that are well. This connection of the child with future problems provides rationality to act on the actions of the child. The child becomes, through a series of hypotheses, a potential danger and therefore a focal point for the protection of public welfare.

This connection of disorderly children with public health necessitates a range of institutions and technologies to identify, prevent and treat this dangerous child. 'Mental Hygiene' was one of the technologies contrived to deal with this issue. In a presidential address delivered to the History of Education Society in 1982 in New York, Cohen (1983: 124) describes the impact of the mental hygiene movement:

> The mental hygiene movement provided the inspiration and driving force behind one of the most far-reaching yet little understood educational innovations of this century, what I call the 'medicalization' of American education. I mean by this metaphor the infiltration of psychiatric norms, concepts and categories of discourse – the 'mental hygiene point of view' – into virtually all aspects of American education in this century.

According to Ruggles-Brise (1926: ix), in the US 'The first Mental Hygiene Society was founded at Connecticut in 1908. Since then twenty states have organised Mental Hygiene Societies'. In Jahr's estimation the technologies implemented by mental hygiene were anticipated to make great contributions to public health, and the discipline was expected to attain the status of a science. Jahr (1928: 494) declares:

> the mental hygiene movement is with us to stay. It may not have reached the dignity of an exact science, but stay it will, because the principles upon which the practice is based are as sound as any branch of medicine ever can be; it seeks to preserve mental health. It is spreading rapidly.

This value of science is demonstrated in Henderson's claim that mental hygiene provides 'The application of scientific principles to human affairs so as to produce a healthier thinking, healthier acting race' (Henderson, 1939: 7). The racialised motives of mental hygiene are clear in this statement, and so too is the importance of the scientific. This obsession with science suggests how important it was that psychiatry was 'scientific', and how, as a scientist, the psychiatrist is the authorised expert on both public health and the individuals who endanger it.

This quest for public health is not restricted to some 'distant' past. Take for instance this 'call to arms' from the psychiatrist Koplewicz, who advocates action on the actions of toddlers in day care centres:

> Every day care center in America should be on the lookout for obviously aggressive and out-of-control three-year-olds. Nothing is to be gained by watching and waiting to see if these kids will outgrow this behavior by the time they're four or five or 10. By then their behavior will be even more sociopathic; also they'll probably do badly in school and won't have any friends . . . If there is any chance of turning these kids around, it must be done in the early stages of the *disease,* before they've 'progressed' from lying and shoplifting to assault and rape. Left untreated, these kids are at high risk for substance abuse, imprisonment, and death by unnatural causes.
>
> (Koplewicz, 1996: 238, emphasis added)

Possible danger and threatening potential to 'society' provides a rationale for action on children that seeks to identify, intervene and to treat them. Similarly Cadoret *et al.* (1995: 923) raise the question of acting on the threat posed by the deoxyribonucleic acid (DNA) of certain children: 'The interaction results show that antisocial behaviors and aggressivity are increased in the presence of predisposing genetic factors'. Based on this concern, Cadoret *et al.* (1997: 252) recommend a disconcerting course of action: that 'genetic counselling' needs to be instituted for 'patients and their families who are characterized as providing adverse environments'.

Turning to the relationship between the expert, the delinquent and the criminal, it would seem that delinquency in the eyes of the psychiatric expert is frequently perceived as more than the committing of crime. The delinquent can be deciphered as being mentally disordered (the delinquent child has conduct disorder) or having the potential of mental disorder (the delinquent child is at risk of conduct disorder).

This interpretation can be applied in reverse: the child's conduct disorder can be posited as a reason for delinquency, or the presence of conduct disorder can be construed as a risk factor for delinquency. Interestingly, this latter configuration is advocated by Anderson (1923: 425), who suggests that conduct disorders can 'manifest themselves in socially unacceptable and delinquent behavior that later on, if unchecked, develops into what we call a criminal career'. This emphasis on the decipherment of others places the expert as a detective, ever watchful for the presence or possibility of delinquency or mental aberration.

Conceptualisation of the delinquent as defective creates the need for experts and their scientific expertise. Reliance on this expert would, purportedly, act to limit the delinquent, since 'It was through the application of mental science that the reformation of delinquents could be effected' (Henderson, 1939: 6). Following this premise, the actions of mental science would become vital means to alter the trajectory of the delinquent. In this way, psychiatric points of view become implicit to notions of the delinquent. This is apparent in the convergences of psychiatry and juvenile law. The importance of this psychiatric role to the service of psychologic laboratories in the US is noted by Sadler (1947: 146), according to whom 'More and more juvenile courts ... are being served by psychologic laboratories in charge of competent psychiatrists, and some day the courts of our land will treat these young offenders in the light of the findings of these laboratories'. These 'competent psychiatrists' and their 'laboratories' were in the service of the US juvenile courts, an institution that according to Van Waters (1926: 111) 'came into existence to remedy a great evil'. In this statement Van Waters is referring to the 'great evil' of administering adult punishment to children. By creating a 'juvenile court', this 'evil' could be avoided, and the child criminal could be known as a delinquent and connected to psychiatrised actions of 'justice'. Despite this proliferation and dissemination of expertise, delinquency has not been curtailed. Nevertheless, psychiatric knowledge of disorderly children is generally considered to be integral to identifying the juvenile who may perpetrate crime, and in ameliorating the problem.

This relationship between the expert and the delinquent extends to a relationship between the delinquent, the expert and the school: in addition to being linked to mental disorder or its possibility, delinquency is also intertwined with truancy. For example, Eichorn (1965: 308) claims that 'The chief concern with truancy is that it is frequently a forerunner of delinquency'. Once associated with delinquency, truancy by proxy becomes implicated in mental aberration, and can then be said to be more than a descriptor of an absence from school: it is a signifier of difficulty that belongs to the individual, and of potential mental dysfunction or abnormality. This is an association that mandates the school's responsibility for truancy to include the detection of delinquency and, by extension, of individuals with a mental disorder or those harbouring its potential. For example, the school is recognised as having the prime role in the management of truancy, a responsibility that involves the school in the detection of potential delinquency. In this manner, psychiatric expertise extends to the school and the teacher acquires a function in the identification and prevention of delinquency.

Expert knowledge, schools and education

Connections to psychiatric discourses situate the school as an institution where teaching and learning are complemented by specific expertise on the mind. The 'expert' or 'specialist' in education can refer to range of individuals, from school counsellors to behaviour support teachers. What these all are likely to share is a connection to the discourses of disorderly behaviour. My purpose here is to consider how knowing the disorderly child became necessary for teaching and learning. I begin by asking how it is that this expertise of the mind has become necessary for education.

One explanation proposed for the arrival of the expert in education is the increased provision of 'education for the masses'. This line of reasoning is used by Morse (1961: 327) to explain the incursion of mental hygiene into the school: 'When the schools began keeping more children longer, and when they became concerned about their adjustment as well as intellectual learning, new specialists were added'. Another explanation for the incursion of the expert is the increasing numbers of disorderly children in schools, an explanation that is tied to the notion of the 'prevalence' of disorderly children. A third proposed explanation is the recognition of the school as a valuable site for accessing the young. From this perspective the school is a place of experimentation and learning, a laboratory for the expert. This potential was noted in Australia, where it was acknowledged that the special school offers a 'valuable opportunity for psychological research' (Sutton, 1911: 994).

Rather than being lured into a quest for an explanation for the incursion of the psychological expert into the school, I draw on multiple reasonings. This enables me to refer to the three explanations as aspects influencing this phenomenon and, at the same time, not to subscribe to the view that these are the only explanations. These three are drawn on because of their effect on the promulgation of the truth of disorderly children. To simplify this complex network these are considered in terms of two broad means of practising this expertise. One means is the actual incursion of the 'expert' (psychiatrist, clinical psychologist, psychologist and mental health personnel) into the school. The second is the assimilation of expertise by the school personnel, such as the school counsellor or the teacher trained in 'behaviour disorders'.

The incursion of the expert into the school can be witnessed by considering a range of documents. In the early twentieth century in Britain, the medical doctor had a direct role in school management of the 'imbecile' or 'morally defective' or 'mentally deficient child'. As Potts (1983: 188) remarks, 'Not only did doctors direct the placement of children with the state education system and determine the range of provision for children with disabilities, but they also wrote at length about the details of curriculum, time-tabling and teaching.' In NSW, Australia, the school medical service, established early in the twentieth century, was another means used to bring the expert into schools. Medical officers have been employed by the NSW State Children's Relief Board (SCRB) since the 1860s, and since

1903 the NSW Education Department, has had 'an entire School Medical Branch' (Snow, 1990: 30). This School Medical Branch of the NSW Education Department 'carried out a considerable amount of mental testing and psychological examination of mentally backward and defective children' (Machin, 1934: 371). Significantly, the School Medical Branch and the NSW State Children's Relief Board had affiliations that linked them to a particular knowledge about aberration of the mind, crime and segregation. 'Medical Officers from both departments undoubtedly belonged to the Australian Medical Association (AMA), which argued that crime had a physiological basis, that physical unfitness was related to mental unfitness, and that the "mentally unfit" should be segregated from the rest of society' (Snow, 1990: 30). Bringing these experts into the school therefore simultaneously introduced certain beliefs concerning the origin of crime and the 'segregation of the mentally unfit'. Armed with these beliefs, the medical expert provided a means to *know* the defective.

This function of knowing the defective is demonstrated by the line of reasoning posited for having medical doctors in schools. In the case of the Australian state of Victoria, it was declared, 'Not only does education benefit directly and indirectly, but with medical inspection the parent has a guarantee of the real health and progress of the child, and the community a satisfactory surety – the only one that exists – of the welfare of all its children' (Sutton *et al.*, 1915: 86). Such experts are distinguished from their pedagogical colleagues by their ownership of the knowledge of the mental health of the child. Crucially, this 'expertness' translates into the 'non-expertness' of the teacher, who becomes the individual who needs advice and direction from the expert.

For the psychiatrist, the supervisory role is enhanced by combining medical membership with expertise of the mind. Examples of this supervisory position are evident in the literature on child guidance clinics, which were established in Australia early in the twentieth century, For instance, Williams (1949) puts forward the argument in the *Medical Journal of Australia* that the psychiatrist, because of medical affiliations, must direct the child guidance clinic. In making this assertion Williams even admits his own prejudice, stating 'In my opinion, prejudiced as it may be, the lack of this medical direction is decidedly unfortunate' (ibid.: 678). This substantiation of psychiatric leadership is also made by Buckle in the *Australian and New Zealand Journal of Psychiatry*: 'often his biological training will oblige him to coordinate all these therapeutic efforts and he must learn to utilize secondhand observations and reports from different professions' (Buckle, 1971: 170). Similarly, Dawson (1933), a psychiatrist at an Australian child guidance clinic, contends that the psychiatrist must be the 'director' of the guidance clinic. According to this view, not only is the psychiatrist to be the appropriate director of the Australian child guidance clinic, but also 'psychiatric sense' is posited as the revered knowledge. This point is emphasised in Dawson's statement that 'One must, however, admit the capacity for the psychologist to gain through experience a sound psychiatric sense' (ibid.: 544).

Liaison between the school and external specialist services is another means to instill psychiatric expertise into education. In NSW the link to the expert is apparent in the early relationship between the NSW School Medical Service and the teacher. In this relationship 'Teachers are requested to enter on the mental survey schedule and submit for examination any pupils, whether backward or not, showing marked nervous or psychological abnormality' (Machin, 1934: 372). Similarly rigorous surveillance was applied to the teacher in England early last century, with the medical doctor being intimately involved in many facets of educating the mentally defective student (Potts, 1983).

A second means to implant expertise into the school is through making school personnel 'school experts'. To be experts, such personnel would need to be conversant with psychiatric and psychological principles. An example of early involvement of such an expert is the 'visiting teacher', a specialist used in the US who 'began work in the year 1906–1907 in New York City, Boston, and Hartford [Connecticut]' (Nudd, 1926: 277). This visiting teacher assisted and directed classroom teachers with 'problematic' children. What is noteworthy is that the impetus for the creation of this 'expert' did not originate within education, but was prompted by individuals such as the 'director of a psychological laboratory' (ibid.).

More recently, there have been increases in special education 'experts' and 'expertise' for the disorderly child. In countries such as Australia, the UK and the US this expertise is represented by a range of specialist teachers and specialised practices. These include in Australia the support teacher behaviour (STB), and District Behaviour Committee; in the US practices such as IEP (individualised education plan) or FBA (functional behaviour analysis); and in the UK the local education authority 'behaviour support service'. In the US, for example, the FBA is a responsibility, 'mandated by the 1997 amendments to the Individuals with Disabilities Education Act (IDEA)' (Packenham et al., 2004: 9). The FBA is required when there are changes in a child's school placement due to problems with behaviour (for example, removals from school of more than ten days, resulting in changes in placement). As Packenham et al. (ibid.) point out, the FBA is 'a matter of intense concern for special educators'. Such administrative mandates inculcate complex expert tasks into the role of the special educator, connecting the school to a convoluted apparatus that administers the disorderly child.

Although the special education teacher has developed an increasing expertise, it is important to emphasise that a distinction is frequently made between the knowledge of the teacher and that of the expert, particularly the psychiatrist. To illustrate this point I quote this description by a psychiatrist of a mother's encounter with a teacher who was critical of psychiatry:

> Another mother showed up at my office in tears. Her daughter's teacher had told her that medicine – in this case an antidepressant for separation anxiety disorder – is the worst possible thing for a growing child. 'I can't believe you're giving her drugs,' the teacher said to the mother. (This was the same teacher who, only a few months earlier, had told the mother that her six-

year-old daughter Ellen had some real problems, that all she did all day in class was stare down at her desk, cry, and ask to go home to her mommy.) Ellen's mother sputtered a response to the teacher: 'But you told me there was problem. I'm trying to fix it.' The teacher's response: 'I told you to do something, but I didn't mean this.' The fact that with the medication Ellen was able to attend class all day without chronic worries and fears didn't affect the teacher's attitude.

(Koplewicz, 1996: 59)

From this perspective, the expertise of the psychiatrist needs to prevail over that of the teacher and the specialist teacher. In so doing, this expertise has considerable influence – and it is this point that we need to emphasise. It is not that we must convince ourselves that the psychiatrist is 'bad' but, rather, we need to come to terms with the importance of interrogating practices of 'psychiatric power'. We need to recall the relationship between the constitution of the disorderly subject and the designators of the disorderly. As Foucault (1997b: 291) points out, 'the mentally ill person is constituted as a mad subject precisely in relation to and over against the one who declares him mad'. These practices of power require a relatively unique expertise, one at the upper levels of a hierarchy, and one connected to scientific knowledge (if not displayed as analogous to it). In the case of the diagnosing of disorderly children, these practices are not confined to the four walls of the clinician's office. These are practices that circulate more broadly (in newspapers, on the radio and so on) and are able, in myriad ways, to recognise the disorderly child. But it is the preserve of psychiatric practices (and those qualified to be intimate with it, for example the paediatrician, the clinical psychologist) to have the final say.

Chapter 5

Administering disorderly children

Kool Kids Project Turns Naughty into Nice

A groundbreaking program which identifies and manages problem children whose bad behaviour is actually caused by a clinical condition has received a $450,000 shot in the arm from the Bracks Government, the Health Minister, Bronwyn Pike, said today.

(Ryan, 2004)

Successful administration of the disorderly child is, I have argued, tied to a thorough knowledge of the disorderly child, and the expert is integral to both of these. Such expertise makes possible special programmes such as Kool Kids, which identifies and works with conduct-disordered children, turning them from 'naughty to nice'. Referring to Foucault's (1988g: 107) assertion that 'truth is no doubt a form of power', it can be argued that a function of truth is the operation of action on the actions of others. The truth of conduct disorder not only has the function of naming the disorderly child, but can also divide this child from others by certifying actions such as segregation from regular schooling. In this sense the expert can be described in terms of the third point in Foucault's (1983b: 223) analytics of power, as a 'means of bringing power relations into being'. In this sense the administration of disorderly children takes on a more complex dimension: that is, controlling, segregating, disciplining or excluding these children is connected with both complex truths and practices of power. When, for example, a child is segregated from school because they are deemed disorderly, the administrator of this action is not only connected to the truths of the expert, and the truths of diagnosis, they are also 'bringing power relations into being'.

In this chapter I consider the administration of disorderly children through actions on the actions of others. This discussion is organised into two parts, beginning with consideration of these actions as 'dividing practices'. This leads to the second part, in which I discuss 'schooling the disorderly student'. This is focused on disorderly children in public education in the Australian state of New South Wales, with the addition of some discussion of similar practices in the UK and the US. In discussing these technologies I am not attempting a detailed report of service provision in NSW, Australia, or in the UK or the US. Nor am I attempting a 'truthful history' of behavioural disorders and their interlocutors. My purpose is to demonstrate the increasing preoccupation with conduct disorder and behaviour disorders and to argue that this concern has enabled the infiltration of psychiatric knowledges of disorderly conduct into the school.

Dividing practices

Dividing practices are an efficient means to facilitate actions on the actions of others because they function to identify and isolate the individual. These practices, as Foucault points out, have the effect of 'objectifying of the subject': 'I have studied the objectivizing of the subject in what I shall call "dividing practices." The subject is either divided inside himself or divided from others. This process objectivizes him' (Foucault, 1983b: 208). This observation indicates an important point, namely that dividing practices can have *interior* and *exterior* effects. Here dividing practices are considered from the point of view of those mechanisms that divide a subject from others. This leaves the problem of how the dividing practices influence the technologies of the self, a question that is considered in Chapters 6 and 7. This discussion of dividing practices is organised around four practices that have the effect of division and are instrumental in making the disorderly child. These four practices are, first, categories; second, schooling for otherness; third, special education; and, last, making behaviour special.

Categories are integral to dividing practices since they provide a means with which to divide. In this sense categories locate the young person in a specific domain in both a nominal sense and the literal sense of division from others. In NSW, Australia, categories are prerequisite to the provision of additional education support for children with disabilities through practices such as the *Intervention Support Program* (ISP). 'Social/Emotional and Behavioural' is one of the categories of 'disability' listed for support. To qualify under this category requires diagnosis by a 'specialist psychologist, psychiatrist or paediatrician' (New South Wales Department of Education and Training, 2003: 3). Reliance on categories is clearly evident in the explanation of the referral procedure to Swalcliffe Park School, a special school in Oxfordshire, England. On its web page it explains that students will have a Statement of Special Educational Needs (SEN) that 'will contain a diagnosis of EBD (Emotional and/or Behavioural Difficulties) or ASD (Autism Spectrum Disorder)/Asperger Syndrome'. Then, referring to EBD, it is explained that this can 'frequently encompass a number of diagnosed or possibly undiagnosed developmental disorders of special educational needs. These include: ADHD, Dyslexia, Dyspraxia, Dyscalculia, Language Difficulties, Oppositional Defiant Disorder (ODD), Conduct Disorder (CD), Pathological Demand Avoidance (PDA) and Attachment Disorder (AD)' (Swalcliffe Park Special School, 2005). The Judge Rotenberg Center, a 'special needs school' in Canton, Massachusetts, US, also lists a range of categories pertaining to its students. These are 'a wide variety of behavior disorders, including conduct/emotional/psychiatric disorders and autism/developmental disabilities' (Judge Rotenberg Center, 2005).

Repercussions of being categorised can include displacement from the classroom or removal from regular school. In some instances this can lead to placement in specialist services such as adolescent psychiatric facilities. The perceived threat that disorderly children pose to the teacher is one of the rationales for removing these categories of children from the classroom (Saunders, 1987; Walker, 1984). Swinson *et al.* (2003) also cite teacher concern regarding their capacity to cope with these students. Membership of the category 'behaviour disorders' by proxy denotes being unmanageable in the school and a threat to the classroom.

To question the category and illustrate its function as a dividing practice I draw an example of a once acceptable category that would now be considered illogical, the practice of employing genital morphology to categorise the 'female delinquent'. In this example, Talbot (1902: 23–4) reports, 'The genitals in eighty-three cases were normal; in eleven cases were excessively developed and in seven were arrested in development. There was one case of markedly deformed labia'. These claims would now, I hope, be considered outrageous.[3] Dividing practices based on gender have been subject to rigorous critique by several authors, including Blackman (1996). At the time of Talbot, it proved possible to make such connections between female delinquents and their anatomy. It was possible, too, to make connections between bodies and feeblemindedness. Scientific assumptions about morphology were deployed by medical doctors examining children for problems such as 'defective expression'.

> Defective expression is very common. Mobile, changeable features show a want of attention and an unstable temperament, and an apathetic, stolid look may mean that the brain is sluggish, but sometimes appearances are very deceptive. Creasing of the forehead, twitching of the mouth, rolling of the eyes are all common, but it is hard to classify or describe the various characteristics that go to make up a defective expression. It is chiefly want of control of the features. To the practised eye the expression and control of the features and general bearing are a great help in deciding whether the child is feeble-minded, and the habit of rocking to and fro in a mechanical way generally indicates mental vacancy and is found more often in the lower grades of classes.
>
> (Dendy, Appendix, in Lapage, 1911, cited in Potts, 1983: 182)

This quote is taken from a book by Lapage (1911), *Feeblemindedness in Children of School Age*, which, as Potts explains, was accompanied by 'photographs of children's faces'. Potts describes a similar example. '[I]n 1888 Dr Francis Warner published A Method of Examining Children in Schools as to their Development and Brain Condition. This consisted of a slow-motion parade of children in front of the doctor' (Potts, 1983: 182).

This recourse to physical characteristics was done alongside an emphasis on scientific principles that assumed interior problems could be detected via the physiological. Thus, eugenics, as Mitchell and Snyder (2003) contend, was bound up with a fixation on the body's physical marks and signs. This has significant implications. Following Mitchell and Snyder, it is imperative to comprehend eugenics in terms of both disability and 'race', and to attempt to fathom how this may have continuing effects in the present. As they explain, 'if we consider racism to be tethered to biology, as most racism scholars now suggest, then drawing parallels between racism and ableism seems necessary, particularly given that disability is inevitably located within a conception of degraded biology' (Mitchell and Snyder, 2003: 859). This necessitates that the truths produced about disorderly children need to be examined for their ableist and racist assumptions. As Desai warns (2003: 98), 'the simultaneous development of social and scientific constructions of "race" and "mental illness" have resulted in the ideology within psychiatry that madness must be a "natural" state for black people'. This is not an outrageous claim. Conclusions from researchers such as Lau *et al.* (2004) point to 'racial/ethnic bias among teachers' and a tendency to view African Americans as having more 'externalising problems'.

Perhaps one means to think this through is to grasp it more broadly in terms of biopower. Following the outline Foucault provides in the 1976 Lectures at the Collège de France, biopower implicates the state in racism. As Foucault contends (2003: 254), 'the modern State can scarcely function without becoming involved in racism at some point, within certain limits and subject to certain contradictions'. In this formulation, 'racism is the indispensable precondition that allows someone to be killed' (ibid.: 256). This is done in order to preserve one's own 'race', or, as Foucault states, 'the death of the bad race, of the inferior race (or the degenerate, or the abnormal) is something that will make life in general healthier: healthier and purer' (ibid.: 255). In this way racism becomes justification for the state to sanction killing the 'bad race' or the 'degenerate', and permit those in its care to both kill and be killed. Importantly, 'killing' in this sense 'does not simply mean murder as such', but refers to 'every form of indirect murder: the fact of exposing someone to death, increasing the risk of death for some people, or, quite simply, political death, expulsion, rejection, and so on' (ibid.: 256). If we understand 'killing' in this way, then can't the act of demarcating someone as mentally disordered constitute an act of expulsion, rejection – or at the very least, the serious risk of such? Taking this point, we could draw on this perspective of biopower and racism in relation to diagnostic practices – and its associated conceptualisations of the so-called 'abnormal'. Analysing from this perspective is not to make the accusation that diagnostic practices are, fait accompli, racist. Rather, it is to examine these practices for racist implications, and to acknowledge the complexities involved in such an analysis. For example, Stoler points out that 'those with opposing political positions can frequently utter the statement "Blacks are poor because they are black" – and mean totally different things' (Stoler, 2000: 200). Therefore, there is a need to be attentive to the disparate concerns entrenched in discussing racism and the diagnosing of disorderly children.

Current practices of rationalising conduct disorder, those of Lapage (1911) and Talbot (1902) and, more broadly, those of eugenics, share claims to 'scientific reason'. Comparing these, it is more likely that the eugenicists' use of 'scientific' rationality appears strange. However, one only needs to look at practices like the 'measurement of brainwave activity' in young people suspected of ADHD to be struck by similarities (see Laurence and McCallum, 1998b, for an excellent critique of this practice). When considered alongside the more 'dated' practices that checked for delinquency or feeblemindedness, current practices such as measuring brainwaves can be made to appear odd. This strangeness can show up scientific rationality as value-laden and subjective, and raises questions regarding the so-called scientific rationality implicit to notions of the disorderly child.

The variation in categories has prompted proposals for the development of a common category for these disorders. Szaday (1989: ix) takes this one step further, suggesting that this common category needs to be free of psychological and medical implication, one that 'implies no medical or psychological diagnosis of a particular child or adolescent'. The possibility of such a category is doubtful since to be devoid of medical or psychological diagnosis necessitates being free of its dividing practices. This supposed shift would entail removing the expert from the relationship with schooling, which would be a difficult endeavour to say the least. Szaday's (1989) call for a 'common language' is interesting given that eighty years earlier commonality was claimed to have been achieved through the category 'feebleminded':

> There was a time, a few years ago, when one could explain anything by just saying 'feebleminded'. It was a wonderful explanation because it seemed to solve so many difficulties. If a child stole, he was feebleminded; if murder was committed, the murderer was feebleminded; if a child did not want to go to school, he must be feebleminded; and if he did go to school and exhibit unpleasant behavior, surely he was feebleminded. Feeblemindedness was a sufficient explanation for all these things.
>
> (Wile, 1926: x, cited by White, 1996: 185)[4]

The 'wonderful explanation' of 'feeblemindedness' seems to have been made redundant through the scientific endeavours that create categories. Paradoxically, this diversity seems to have caused a dilemma, prompting the need for further scientific exploration to (re)establish commonality.

To securely attach a category to young people it is essential to establish scientific means for its affixation. Psychiatric and psychological expertise forms a basis for substantiating diagnostic categories, making these experts integral to the processes of administering conduct disorder, and to disorderly children. As I have outlined, psychologists and psychiatrists are implicated in the school as sources of referral of specific students, and as interlocutors within the school. Engagement with this external expertise is evident in technologies such as the school psychologist. Significantly, this school-based expert is able to perform their own practices of division, including the administration of tests, a task that is clearly stipulated by the NSW Department of Education and Training (2004: 84), which employs 'school counsellors' (who are required to have psychology qualifications) to 'conduct assessments, support in-school planning and liaise with relevant service providers such as NSW Health'. The school psychologist is thus often a key player in the decision-making that demarcates students into special education services. And these 'psychological' practices can be very much influenced by discourses of the diagnosing of disorderly children. A case in point is the research by Della Toffalo and Pedersen (2005) into the influence of 'psychiatric diagnosis on school psychologists' decision making'. As they report, 'when a psychiatric diagnosis is available as a piece of referral information, the child is more likely to be considered ED [emotional disturbance] and in need of special education services' (ibid.: 58).

In addition to psychological and psychiatric practices, schools have refined various technologies that categorise and separate students. One aspect that perhaps seems less obvious, but arguably contributes to notions of success (and thus failure), is the idea of student progression. This is relevant to notions of conduct disorder since it is frequently reported that conduct-disordered students have low levels of achievement (APA, 1994), a difference that is apparently suggestive of the 'additional diagnosis of Learning or Communication Disorder' (APA, 2000: 96). Linking age with grade became an official practice in school in New South Wales in 1906 (Snow, 1990). Before then students progressed when they were deemed ready to do so. Snow (1990) argues that this age grade content policy produced the 'backward' child, a phenomenon produced when a child did not demonstrate age grade-appropriate knowledge. Subsequent to the implementation of the age grade policy, inspectors conducting a survey on the ages of children in the various grades in primary schools in 1909 reported 'a staggering 50% of students from 3rd to 5th grade were "retarded"' (ibid.: 32). The divisiveness of this association not only produced notions of 'retarded' students, it also made possible notions of 'normality': the student who progressed through each grade in accordance with his or her age. According to Snow, this 'backward' child was interpreted via a eugenics framework, in which the concern with 'backwardness' instigated the

> establishment of a School Clinic in 1919. Staffed by doctors, one of whom was a psychologist, the Clinic was intended to fill a variety of psychology based functions. It was to help establish psychological norms for Australian students, to diagnose and treat students with 'special disabilities in their schoolwork' and to correlate the data on young people in day schools and the Children's Courts which would help to provide insights into the causes of mental deficiency and abnormal behaviour, particularly juvenile delinquency.
>
> (ibid.: 32)

What is significant is that this 'School Clinic' cautioned the teacher to consider an internal deficit as the underlying cause. Snow then argues that the 'school medical service stood poised to utilise the Clinic for *their "long desired attack on the feeble-minded, the most dangerously unfit class in society"*' (ibid., emphasis added). Linking age with grade appears to have created an aberrant individual, and when these aberrations became linked with the knowledge of the mind (the school medical service), it became expertly known in terms of internal deficit.

A number of the dividing practices that pertain to behaviour are located under the banner of 'special education'. Although it now appears familiar, the category 'behaviour disorder' has not always been so easily connected to special education. This raises the question of how conduct disorder (or behaviour disorder) became 'special'. To respond to this question I focus on the experience in NSW, Australia, beginning with a consideration of how special education was required by education and then analysing how behaviour came to be made 'special'. This means considering how the dividing practices of special education were instituted in education and also how 'behaviour' formed a means with which to both categorise the student and administer the effects of division.

The earliest institutional segregation in Australia was specifically for 'deaf and blind' students and was first established 'in mid 1860 ... in Sydney and Melbourne' (Andrews *et al.*, 1979: 14). With the passage of time, segregation increased to include more than vision and hearing. For example, the '1903–04 Royal Commission Reports, NSW led to recommendations for the establishment of special schools for the feeble-minded' (ibid.). The creation of special schools followed these recommendations, with schools such as the Lorna Hodgkinson Home in Sydney in 1923, which provided classes for 'mentally retarded children' (ibid.: 14–15), and the 'Special School at Glenfield', south-west of Sydney, in 1927 (Machin, 1934: 370). An important point to note is that Glenfield Special School differed from the previous schools for the 'deaf and dumb' with its special classes for 'state wards' and 'defective boys' (ibid.). At the time of Machin's article in 1934, Glenfield Special School had 'an enrolment of 108', and other 'special classes' in metropolitan Sydney included a 'special class for State wards at the Brush Farm Home for Girls at Eastwood; and ... a similar class for the defective boys at May Villa, Dundas' and, outside Sydney, a privately funded 'school for defectives at the Newcastle Mental Hospital' (ibid.). The influence of previous special schools for the 'deaf', the 'dumb' and the 'blind', combined with the accentuated import of the medical expert in matters of the defective, ensured that specialness would be conceptualised within a medical framework.

In addition to being subjected to medical categorisation, those individuals placed in the realms of special education may also find themselves associated with another form of otherness, a form presaged with negativity. This connotation is made explicit in a statement by Jackson (1973: 190), who emphasises that 'Special Education has been concerned with those aspects of human functioning which in some ways were thought to deviate in a negative direction from normative standards'. This suggestion may appear an unsubstantiated or biased view of one writer, but similar perspectives are evident in education documents such as the *National Report on Schooling in Australia 1994*:

> A school which requires students to exhibit one or more of the following characteristics before enrolment is allowed: intellectual disability; physical disability; autism; social/emotional disturbance; in custody or on remand. The following are not considered to be special schools: intensive language centres; schools whose distinguishing feature is the lack of formal curriculum; *schools for exceptionally bright or talented students.*
>
> (Ministerial Council on Education, Employment, Training and Youth
> Affairs, 1994: 21, emphasis added)

Locating the 'exceptionally bright' or 'talented' outside of special schools is indicative of the negative connotation of special education. In this statement it appears that policy seeks to ensure that the 'gifted' are not touched by the stigma of 'specialness'.

Although this medicalised view has largely prevailed, there have been efforts to change the medical orientation in special education. For example, the Committee of Review of New South Wales Schools (1989) proposed a definition of special education that sought to move away from medical or disability orientation. The current popularity of the medicalised view of behaviour disturbances and behaviour disorders suggests that efforts such as this to move away from clinical conceptualisation have failed. This failure is patently demonstrated by the increasing use of clinically defined *DSM* conduct disorder as a means to categorise children as disorderly and to divide them from their peers.

The motives for dividing children from their peers are questionable – and, not surprisingly, subject to debate. There are those who contend it is good for the disorderly, while there are others who argue that it is a problem. Then there are the criticisms of a more selfish motive, such as teachers 'mov[ing] children whom they find difficult, disruptive, repulsive, or simply discipline problems out of their classroom and into special education classrooms' (Neal, 1982: 158). A similar observation was made in the 1930s in the *Medical Journal of Australia*, that 'such classes often proved to be a dumping ground for scholastic misfits' ('The problem of mentally defective children in NSW', 1934: 390). By contrast, a recent report by the NSW Department of Education and Training (2004: 84) states that 'the increase in behaviour services means that students with behavioural difficulties get more help, other students get a better learning environment, and teachers and other staff have a better working environment'. These comments cannot be simply dismissed on the basis that they were made twenty or seventy years ago – or on the assumption that the measures are 'just to help'. If, as Swinson *et al.* (2003) note, teachers are reluctant to have EBD students included in their classes, what can be inferred of their attitudes to having them excluded? This point is stressed in relation to ADHD by Jacobs (2004: 16), who argues that if a 'child can be "diagnosed" and drugged, the classroom and the school will run smoothly'. He then points out that 'this dynamic has been so powerful that several US states have had to pass legislation prohibiting non-medical school personnel from diagnosing children and suggesting medication' (ibid.). These remarks prompt scrutiny of the comfortable notion that the behaviourally disordered have a 'special' problem and are therefore in need of special remediation, and this is always offered with benevolent intentions.

The child who is offered 'special' attention is likely to be rapidly drawn into processes that will diagnose him or her as disorderly. This is because invocation of the diagnostic is instinctive to special education. As Thomas and Glenny (2000: 288) point out, 'The child who misbehaves has special needs which are rooted in emotional disturbance, the vocabulary at once invoking psychological, psychoanalytic and psychiatric knowledge. Once need is established, the psychological genie has been released'. Thus, via the architecture of special education that draws on diagnostic practices, the behaviourally worrisome child can be categorised and routinely ostracised (and this could take many forms).

With regard to New South Wales, the category 'behaviour disorders' seems to have emerged as a distinct concern in special education in the early 1980s, although initially specialness seems to have varied. For example, at the beginning of the November 1983 edition of the *Australian Journal of Special Education* there is a short piece titled 'Special Education Requirements in Teacher Training'. In this is a description of children with 'special needs', children who are 'at the extreme . . . are multiply handicapped, the severely intellectually disabled, the emotionally disturbed, the chronically learning disabled, the deaf, the blind who will have special needs for relatively long periods and, in some cases, permanently' ('Special education requirements in teacher training', 1983: 5).[1] Amongst the categories listed in this statement there is no mention of behaviour disorders. In the same journal a year later behaviour disorder is presented as a special education issue. In November 1984 Walker, an American Professor of Special Education and Rehabilitation, states that 'Children who are classified as either emotionally disturbed or behavior disordered appear to stress school systems perhaps more than any other handicapping condition' (Walker, 1984: 25).

Three years prior to Walker's (1984) article, Rees and Irvine make this comment on the published papers of the 1980 Australian Association of Special Education (1981: 114) conference:

> The writings in this book demonstrate that the concept 'persons with special education need' covers children, adolescents and adults with mild or significant learning difficulties, children and adolescents with mild or significant emotional or behavioural disorders, as well as those with severe multiple handicaps.

Concern with behavioural disorders was evident in 1982 when the Working Party on a Plan for Special Education in New South Wales (1982) recommended that among the different consultants made available in regional areas there would be two for 'Behavioural Disorders'. The merging of behaviour disorder with disability and special education is also evident at a federal level, where 'the Commonwealth Schools Commission Working Party in Special Education (1985) . . . identified severely socially/emotionally disturbed children as a target population and included this group in their definition of special education students' (Bain, 1988: 20).

In Britain, the 'EBD' student has been one result of the attention on behaviour and special educational needs. What is intriguing is that, as Thomas and Glenny (2000: 283) explain, EBD

> categories officially ceased to exist following the report of the Warnock Committee (DES, 1978) and the 1981 Education Act. Yet it would be clear to a Martian after five minutes' study of the British education system that for all practical purposes EBD is indeed a category and that it forms in the minds of practitioners, professionals and administrators one of the principal groups of special needs.

They then describe how a search of 'five leading national and international journals' over a ten-year period 'finds not a single paper that discusses the provenance, status, robustness, legitimacy or meaning of the term "emotional and behavioural difficulties" (EBD). This is surely a cause for concern' (ibid.).

Not surprisingly, the interest in behaviour as a special education concern has met with varying responses. For example, there are viewpoints that contend behaviour is definitely a special education concern, a 'special need'. This view appears to be endorsed by Bradshaw (1998: 122), who states in support of segregation, 'it would appear that for many children with behaviour disorders placement in the regular school may not be the most appropriate educational placement'. Conversely, the placement of disorderly children into special education can be viewed as absolving transgression (Murray and Myer, 1998). One perspective even cites the 'pressure' to get disorderly children out of schools: 'there is often a lot of pressure to get kids with severe behaviour disorders "out of my school" and somewhere else. A vast amount of time is wasted by schools dodging their responsibility for such tasks' (Heins, cited from transcripts, Human Rights and Equal Opportunity Commission, 1993: 631–2). Following this line of argument, the placement of students in 'Off-Site Units' could be construed as 'avoiding responsibility'. In spite of such issues, a range of 'segregation' technologies are used as a means to school disorderly children in New South Wales (and in the UK and US).

Schooling disorderly children

The infiltration of psychiatric knowledge into education has meant that specific relations of power have become articulated in schooling. These articulations connect the truth of conduct disorder to the young individual, a connection that facilitates the construction of the disorderly child. Special education is a key site involved in schooling the disorderly child, and one that draws heavily on disorderly discourses. This issue was the topic of an article in the *Times Educational Supplement*, where it was stated 'the SEN [special educational needs] lobby is fast becoming a willing partner in the pathologising of our children. It may be with the best of intentions, but in the long term it could be doing untold damage' (Edwards, 2004). As a dividing practice used in schools, special education has become an increasingly complex and costly enterprise. Taking public education in NSW as a case in point, the attention to special education is evident in the amount of resources it is allocated. In 1989 the NSW Minister for Education and Youth Affairs announced the '$80 Million Special Education Plan' (Metherell, 1989).

In each year of the five-year period of the Special Education Plan, further details on funding were announced, and during this time the emphasis on disorderly children remained a prominent consideration. For example, the *Special Education Plan for 1993–97* incorporated several strategies targeting behaviour disorders (Special Education Directorate, 1993). This pattern of increased funding was repeated for the year 1998–9 with funding for special education technologies quoted as being 'a record $399 million in 1998/99' (New South Wales Department of Education and Training Policy and Planning, 1999: 3). Twenty million dollars of this was allocated to student welfare to specifically target 'welfare and anti-violence programs' that included 'involvement by more than 100 specialist staff in programs targeting violent or disruptive behaviour by students' and 'specialist high schools to support students with behavioural problems'. This emphasis has continued, with the NSW Department of Education and Training (2004) *Annual Report 2003* describing a range of provisions for 'students who exhibit disruptive behaviour'. In terms of money, 'the 2001/2002 State Budget provided an extra 46 million, to be spent between 2001 and 2004 to deal with behavioural problems. The 2003/2004 State Budget provided over 12 million towards the continuation of this program' (ibid.: 83).

The Independent Inquiry into the Provision of Public Education in NSW chaired by Vinson (2002a; 2002b) (commonly referred to as the 'Vinson Report') includes a detailed discussion of such special education provision, and provides information on students with behaviour problems. According to the Vinson Report, the 770 school counsellors in NSW schools 'are the 'primary behavioural specialists in the system' (Vinson, 2002a: 58). It explains there is funding for 'students who have been diagnosed with a mental health problem or who have certain kinds of behaviour disorders (such as Oppositional Defiant Disorder)' (ibid.). Included in the report is a description of the 'continuum of programs' for students with behavioural problems (Figure 5.1).

The seven parts of this continuum closely match Deno's cascade model, a 'pyramidal structure' 'consisting of several tiers' (Flynn *et al.*, 1989: 11). In 1989, Hodges described this model as being used by the NSW Department of Education (as it was then called). In this configuration it had five levels, ranging from children at level 1, who could be 'treated successfully by regular school staff' to children at level 5, who were 'needing placement in a special school' (Hodges,

School level services						District/community services		
TEACHERS AND OTHER SCHOOL - BASED PERSONNEL	FUNDING SUPPORT/ ITINERANT SUPPORT TEACHERS- BEHAVIOUR	GATEWAY PROGRAMS FOR YOUNG PEOPLE 'AT RISK'	TUTORIAL CENTRES – COMBINATION OF DISTRICT AND SCHOOL RESOURCES	BEHAVIOUR SCHOOLS - SEVERE BEHAVIOUR DISORDERS		DET CENTRES FOR STUDENTS WITH EMOTIONAL DISORDERS	SCHOOLS WITHIN DEPARTMENT OF JUVENILE JUSTICE	DET- DEPARTMENT OF HEALTH CENTRES FOR TREATING MENTAL HEALTH DISORDERS

Figure 5.1 Range of programmes for responding to behaviourally disturbed and/or disen-
gaged students and young people. Reproduced with permission from Vinson
(2002a: 57).

1989: 36). Whilst Hodges posits level 5 as the uppermost, Conway (1994a) refers
to an additional 'level 6'. At this level 'The most common educational facilities
at Level 6 are units within psychiatric facilities either in regular hospitals or in
designated psychiatric hospitals' (ibid.: 331). This 'cascade model' can be viewed
as an administrative dividing practice, where at its higher levels individuals can,
as Conway (ibid.) explains, be removed to placements in psychiatric services.
Such a placement would not only *dis*place a young person from their school, but
separate them from 'regular' society.

Linked to these pathologising practices, the school has increasingly become a
space involved in medicating disorderly children. It is almost impossible to ignore
this connection given the increasing rates of prescription of psychostimulants to
school-age children. Berbatis *et al.* (2002) report a 12 per cent average increase per
year for the period 1994–2000 across the countries Australia, Canada, Denmark,
France, the Netherlands, New Zealand, Spain, Sweden, the UK and the US, with
figures highest in the US, Canada and Australia. A recent story on the Australian
Broadcasting Commission's *Radio National* reported on the subject of ADHD
and psychostimulants, and the parliamentary inquiry into the use of the drugs in
Western Australia. The programme commenced with a statement about Western
Australia, describing how it is being described as the 'ADHD capital of Australia
with an estimated 4.5% or 18,000 children on dexamphetamine medication.
Australia has the world's third highest rate of psycho-stimulant consumption in
the world' (Mitchell, 2004). The rates of prescription are a topic of debate and
controversy and, although this debate is often characterised as concerned with
ADHD, the issues with medication have broader implications for 'disorderly
children'. For instance, ADHD is often considered to be 'comorbid' with other
disruptive behaviour disorders such as conduct disorder and oppositional defiant
disorder (Linfoot *et al.*, 1999).

The school must administer medication, supervise compliance by the student,
monitor the effects of the medication and make referrals to outside specialists
– and has been accused of forcing parents into medicating their children. A report

in the UK newspaper the *Observer* says 'parents are being pressured into putting their children on Ritalin . . . or face the children's expulsion from school' (West and McVeigh, 2001). In relation to this concern, Jacobs (2004: 16) argues that parents are 'not consenting' to diagnosis or medication, since they are not 'told of the lack of scientific reliability or validity to the diagnosis' and they are 'often not told about the dangers of psycho stimulants'. The school also has to be vigilant to abuse of these drugs because, as Jacobs (ibid.) points out, the medication is being 'sold and shared by children like candy'.

Whereas special education appears to function as a rubric for action, the teacher could be argued to provide the technology for the dissemination of action. This teacher technology can be conceptualised as a *proxy* for expert knowledge that links the student to the expert, and as a *proxy expert knowledge* that links knowledge of disorder to the student. In the first instance the teacher facilitates the passage of the student to the expert of the mind (school counsellor/psychologist, guidance officer, clinical psychologist, paediatrician, psychiatrist). In the second instance the teacher functions as a type of expert who can attach mental disorder to the student. These functions could both occur on one occasion, for example when the teacher assigns identification on to the young person (e.g. stating that the student has behavioural problems) and refers that individual to the school counsellor.

Since suitably knowledgeable teachers are integral to this technology, it is important that considerable effort be expended to ensure that such teachers are appropriately trained. This has meant administering changes in the content of teacher knowledge, with mounting emphasis on teaching about 'behaviour' (and, therefore, behaviour problems, disorders and so on) in teacher pre-service education. In 1994 the Ministerial Council on Education, Employment, Training and Youth Affairs (1994) declared that public school teachers in NSW are required to have knowledge of special education (which incorporates training on 'behavioural disorders'). Prior to this, teacher training had included subjects on behavioural difficulties and disorders on an *elective* basis, and provision is now often made for undergraduate and postgraduate courses specialising in the 'behaviour disorders'.

Ironically, in tandem with augmenting the numbers of teacher specialists whose task was to keep the behaviourally disordered at school, there have been increases in the provision of 'out of school services'. In the mid-1990s the NSW Special Education Plan created specialist 'off site' units where the disorderly child could be removed from regular schooling, As Bressington and Crawford (1992: 101) explain, in '1989 a student population of severe conduct disordered adolescents had been identified by the Special Education Branch (as it was then known)'. It was based on this 'population' that, according to Bressington and Crawford, 80 million dollars was allocated to special education and that 'Each of the ten regions within the state could write a submission for a pilot unit which would cater for severe conduct disordered students' (ibid.). Segregated conduct disorder services were allocated on a regional basis, with severe conduct disorder units 'established in eight regions to provide for secondary aged students in regular schools who exhibit severe behavioural problems' (New South Wales Department of School Education, 1990).[2] These specific conduct disorder facilities, by region, were 'Metropolitan North Region – North Harbour Unit; Metropolitan East Region – Edgeware SSP; Metropolitan West Region – Blacktown Tutorial Centre, Mt. Druitt Tutorial Centre; Metropolitan South West Region – Campbell House SSP; Hunter Region – Hunter Adolescent Support Unit; North West Region – Tamworth Tutorial Centre; Riverina Region – Kandeer SSP; South Coast Region – Wilderness Enhanced Program' (Conway, 1994b: 13).[3] Six of these are 'units' and three are schools for specific purposes (SSP) (ibid.).[4] SSPs function as 'autonomous and have official staffing establishments including a principal and designated support staff . . . Units, by contrast, are led by a head teacher (or faculty head) and must be attached to a high school (a primary school in one case for location reasons)' (ibid.: 14).

More recently, these services are described as including '28 specialist schools in locations across the State, 34 tutorial centres and alternate behaviour programs in city and country areas, 330 specialist behaviour teachers to assist schools to manage students with behavioural difficulties in normal classrooms' (New South Wales Department of Education and Training, 2004: 83). Additional teacher 'retraining' was offered, with '134 teachers retraining in teaching children with behavioural disorders, learning difficulties or disabilities' (ibid.). The NSW DET also initiated 'District Behaviour Plans' in order to 'ensure that all schools have access to specialist services directed at supporting students with behavioural problems' (ibid.). A list of the services provided for students includes 'school counsellors', 'student welfare consultants and student services and equity co-ordinators based in each district', 'support teachers in behaviour who assist classroom teachers', 'teachers aide funding', 'special schools for students with severe behavioural difficulties' and 'tutorial centres . . . for students with severe behavioural problems' (ibid.: 84). These provisions are promised to be increased: 'Eight new behaviour schools and seven tutorial centres for secondary students will be established by 2007, to add to the 11 new schools and 17 new tutorial centres established during 2001/2002' (ibid.).

Significantly, these services were made physically distinct from the school. For example, to construct the unit called the Metropolitan West Tutorial Centre (also referred to as Blacktown Tutorial Centre) 'a caretaker's cottage outside a local high school was fenced off from the school, refurbished and refurnished' (Lindsay, 1990: 245). This effort to physically separate the disorderly students from the non-disorderly is not an unusual practice. The Vinson Report describes the experience of one of the members of the Inquiry's staff, who encountered just such a fence. This member of staff was 'invited by one student in the unit to join her so that she could introduce two student friends from the general school community with whom she was conversing through the cyclone fence' (Vinson, 2002a: 68). The report goes on to detail the 'explanations that were given', which included the claim that such explicit segregation would motivate the students to improve, and that it assisted in 'preventing' trouble with the regular school's staff and students. It is instructive to pause here to imagine what it would be like to be a disorderly student in one of these services, with cyclone fencing demarcating your difference from the rest of the 'normal' school's population.

It is worth considering these forms of segregation in more detail. To do this I discuss two examples: Campbell House SSP and Hunter Adolescent Support Unit. Campbell House School for Specific Purposes was opened in April 1989, and has a restricted number of places available. Enrolments in 1995 were fifty-five students (New South Wales Department of School Education, 1996: 35), and more recently the NSW DET lists sixty-two students (2005). Campbell House SSP is not sited at a regular school. It is situated in a disused dormitory of Glenfield Park School, a school that was established in 1927 to 'cater for 128 students with a mild intellectual delay aged from 8 to 18 years' (Anning, 1992: 47). With Campbell House SSP in one of its dormitories, Glenfield Park School 'redefined its operation' (ibid.: 48). In 1989 the management of Glenfield was taken over by the Metropolitan South West Region of the Department of School Education with the view to use the 'site as a great opportunity to develop some innovative programs to address the needs of ED/BD students both within and outside the region' (ibid.: 47–8).

In relation to the students at the school, the NSW DET website states that the school 'caters for students with severe behavioural and/or emotional difficulties. Each student has been identified as Conduct Disordered, Emotional Disordered or observed as having other behavioural deficits'(2005). Entry to the school involves 'psychiatric assessment' and this is organised by the 'District Guidance Officer attached to Campbell House' (Henderson et al., 1991: 251). Prior to being diagnosed, prospective candidates need to be first referred to Campbell House SSP. Because candidates for Campbell House SSP are infrequently at school, these referrals come from sources such as 'Home–School Liaison Officers (HSLOs), Juvenile Justice case workers and courts, Department of Community Services (DOCS) case workers and parents' (Conway, 1994b: 17). In Truancy and Exclusion from School the establishment of Campbell House SSP is described as catering 'specifically for conduct disordered students who have experienced multiple school suspensions' (House of Representatives Standing Committee on Employment Education and Training, 1996: 123). This makes an assumption that truancy is contemporaneous with the otherness of the suspended and the conduct disordered. It thus makes the 'truant' much more than an individual who is not at school: with this association with conduct disorder, it gives the category 'truant' leverage to function as a dividing practice in its own right.

Like Campbell House SSP, the Hunter Adolescent Support Unit (HASU) was established in July 1989 (Conway et al., 1992). Unlike Campbell House SSP, it is not situated in a remote location away from regular schools, but 'is located in the grounds of Jesmond High School and provides special education programs for 24 adolescent students with conduct disorder' (Holt, 1995: 67). Conway et al. (1992: 82) state that the HASU was established 'as a Special Education pilot initiative of the New South Wales Department of School Education to address the needs of adolescents of high school age in the Hunter Region who had disturbed behaviours'.

Entrance criteria for HASU place emphasis on a diagnosis of conduct disorder, as it is defined in *DSM-IV* (Conway *et al.*, 1992; Holt, 1995). This is a divisive practice, so that the *DSM* not only facilitates the diagnoses of children as disorderly, but also makes possible their segregation into special schooling. Candidates must also demonstrate that they are 'lucid students who have significant abnormalities in their school behaviour without psychiatric illness, for example (a) students who chronically break rules; and b) students who are chronically aggressive, anti-social, and/or oppositional' (Conway *et al.*, 1992: 83). Altogether there are ten parts to the selection criteria, including being able to 'show some evidence in his/her life of being able to develop a relationship with an adult or peer' and having a 'stable residential address and a responsible parent/guardian' (ibid.). It is striking that these criteria make such a distinction regarding 'home', thereby further differentiating conduct-disordered young people into those who have homes and those who are 'home-less'.

A salient question to pose here is just *who* is being segregated. The research literature indicates that certain children and young people are more likely than others to be considered to have behavioural problems: those from low socio-economic backgrounds are disproportionately represented, as are boys, and there are serious questions to be raised concerning ethnicity. That there is an expectation of who is most likely to have behavioural problems is evident in the *index* for behaviour service allocation used by the NSW Department of Education and Training. This *index* is used 'for the purpose of allocating specialist "behaviour" staff across its 40 school districts according to need. The factors taken into account include population size, socio-economic status, learning difficulties, average daily attendance, and short and long term suspension rates' (Vinson, 2002a: 63). The issue of the representation of socio-economic status (SES) is reported by Reid *et al.* (2002) in relation to prescription of psychostimulants in South Australia. As they note, '[T]he highest SMR's [standardised medication ratio] tended to be located in the northern and southern suburbs [of Adelaide]. These areas are predominantly of lower SES, with high unemployment.' (ibid.: 912). Reid *et al.* (2002) also remark that their findings differ from claims that prescription is usually higher in middle-class parents, arguing that subsidised medical and pharmaceutical care in Australia may contribute to the higher figure reported in their study.

In relation to NSW, the Vinson Report includes reference to the concerns of Aboriginal parents, who 'are concerned about the frequency with which their children are suspended or excluded from school or classified as emotionally or behaviourally disordered' (Vinson, 2002b: 21). As outlined in Chapter 1, there are numerous reports regarding other groups more likely to be diagnosed with behavioural disorders. This includes, for example, boys (Ayers and Prytys, 2002; Sawyer *et al.*, 2000; Scott *et al.*, 2001; US Department of Health and Human Services, 1999) and African American children (Fabrega *et al.*, 1996; Lau *et al.*, 2004; Pigott and Cowen, 2000). Literacy 'problems' seem to be another feature that is overly represented: 'some degree of literacy deficit is present in 90% or more of the individuals in these groups' (Brown, 1997). This raises serious questions regarding what disordered or problem 'behaviour' actually refers to – and to whom the identification and segregation of disorderliness is directed.

What is perplexing is that this mechanism of segregation functions contemporaneously with the notion of integration. This tactic is commented on by Slee, who says with reference to schools in Victoria, Australia, that 'Perhaps the clearest and most ironic expression . . . was the sanctioning of off-site behaviour units as a part of integration policy' (Slee, 1998: 104). This issue of integration of students with behaviour problems is frequently taken up in debate over inclusion. But, as Visser and Stokes (2003) discuss with regard to the UK, the EBD student is certainly disadvantaged in current inclusion discourses. This student is more likely to be segregated, and in 'law' this can be justified. They emphasise that '[T]here is no guarantee that the courts will uphold individual right, as conflicting rights will have to be weighed against one another, i.e. the right of a disruptive pupil to remain in school versus the rights of other pupils to learn unhindered' (ibid.: 72). This situation is made more intractable with the array of diagnostic practices that in essence certify a child or young person as not only *currently* behaviour disordered, but in the *future* a likely candidate for psychopathological and antisocial acts.

These issues are tangible in the way that notions of integration can be voiced amongst the practices that segregate children described as conduct disordered. Consider these two occurrences. In a keynote address to the NSW Council for Intellectual Disability, the NSW Minister for Education, Cavalier, declared, 'it has been obvious to me that there is nothing special about Special Education. All education is special . . . Integration will put "paid" once and for all to some of the most pernicious practices of singling out individual children as "special" first and children second. They are children first and last' (Cavalier, 1986: 2–3, cited in Irvine, 1988). Three years after this public statement, in 1989 the '$80 million dollar Special Education Plan' was launched. In a short period of time the denunciation of 'special' seems to have shifted significantly.

It seems that part of this shift was a corresponding swing in the conceptualisation of special education from a service demarcated by practices of segregation to a service that proved 'special' through its agenda to 'integrate'. Indeed, the integration of students with disabilities or the prevention of the segregation of children with disabilities has become a mandate for special education, with the integration debate being based on the notion of 'equity' (Christensen, 1999). Yet the same notion sustains the rationale for the establishment of segregated services, with the creation of the special school enabling the education system to provide schooling to children that were too difficult for the regular school.

Although the Special Education Plan made specific provision for segregating the conduct disordered, it was recognised that, amongst categories that counted as special, these students were the least likely to be integrated. Take, for example, this acknowledgement by the Committee of Review of New South Wales Schools

(1989: 234): 'It is possible that the full integration of all students with disabilities into regular classes may never be achieved. For students with . . . behavioural disorders, the most that can be achieved may be placement in special units in the regular school'. The right of integration does not appear to apply to students with behavioural disorders or who are described as conduct disordered. These students appear to be outcasts from the integration spectrum. According to data on conduct-disordered students provided by Conway, only 7 per cent are reintegrated into their previous high school and 17 per cent are 'reintegration-unspecified' (Conway, 1994b: 20). This leaves a figure of approximately 80 per cent of students placed into conduct disorder technologies who are not 'reintegrated'. It seems that there is the intention to integrate, but the odds of doing so successfully for those described as behaviourally disordered are minimal. This difficulty in 'reintegration' indicates that the divisiveness of conduct disorder is successful in terms of both the removal of children from regular schools and the prevention of their return to regular schooling.

As I have argued, the practice of segregating children diagnosed as disorderly occurs amidst the rubric of integration. The regular school cannot be expected to manage the 'mentally disordered irregular student' since the school does not possess the relations of power demarcated by psychiatric expertise. The so-called regular school can thus be absolved from the responsibility for the disorderly child. As I have discussed, for some of these young people, it can literally mean having a fence placed between them and regular schooling. Commenting on such practices, Vinson (2002a: 68) stresses 'Schools are not part of the correctional system and the adoption of quasi-custodial practices, even on the most limited scale, should be rejected as being totally inappropriate'. I suggest we take this observation further. With an understanding drawn from Foucault, we need to look further than just fences as the signifiers of custodial practices. We need to understand the complex powers that diagnostic practices really have, grasp the consequences they have on student freedoms and interrogate the panoptic practices that they invoke. In the light of this, we should not be too surprised when the so-called disorderly child tries to resist.

The relations of power implicated in these practices function as a means to connect the truths of disorderliness to the young person. As I have discussed, it is through the effects of certain relations of power that conduct disorder is able to manifest as a scientific truth. From this legitimised manifestation the truth of conduct disorder can, via relations of power, form a relationship with an individual to produce mentally disordered subjectivity. This truth functions in a manner that enables those experts who exercise it to *know* the young person. It is a truth that can function as a dividing practice that assigns categories to students, links them to experts on the mind and connects them to the special practices of schooling. These dividing practices can segregate students into 'off-site' units or 'schools for specific purposes', thereby reinforcing the truth of mental disorder. This can influence young people to understand themselves in terms of mental disorder, yet how can young people come to know themselves in this way? In Foucauldian terms, this is to ask how the relationship between truth and power connects to the young person to produce these disordered subjectivities. To consider this question I move to analyse in the next chapter what Foucault (1988a) terms the 'technologies of the self'.

Chapter 6

Why do children and young people believe they are disorderly?

When a young person has a disordered subjectivity, the question can be posed: 'How is the young person involved in the constitution of that subjectivity?' To respond to this question this chapter turns to the third of Foucault's (1983a) three axes of genealogy, the technologies of the self. In so doing, an analysis is made of the relationship of these technologies of the self to truth and power and the construction of subjectivity. In this chapter the stories from the five young people, Rachel, Kris, Josh, Ben and Jemma, are used to provide examples of the effects of truth, power and the self.

Following Foucault (1997b), I argue that subjectivity is constituted through the mechanisms of truth, power and the self. Foucault (ibid.: 290) explains this conceptualisation in terms of the constitution of the subject, stating:

> What I wanted to try to show was how the subject constituted itself, in one specific form or another, as a mad or a healthy subject, as a delinquent or non-delinquent subject, through certain practices that were also games of truth, practices of power, and so on.

In this analysis Foucault explains that he 'had to reject a priori theories of the subject in order to analyze the relationships that may exist between the constitution of the subject or different forms of the subject and games of truth, practices of power, and so on' (ibid.). Importantly, this subject is not something that occurs solely from being 'acted upon'. The emphasis here is on how this subject can be conceptualised as active or, to put it another way, is involved in its constitution. But this is not some act in isolation – it is done in relation to the games of truth and relations of power.

Truth and relations of power have ongoing and cumulative effects on the means by which young people form the technologies of the self that are implicated in the construction of disorderly subjectivity. This relationship of the self to truth is made explicit by Foucault (1997c: 177–8): 'In every culture, I think, this self technology implies a set of truth obligations: discovering the truth, being enlightened by truth, telling the truth. All these are considered important either for the constitution of, or the transformation of, the self'. In this way the efforts made by a young person to 'tell the truth' can be read as part of the obligation to truth. This suggests that the Foucauldian notion of games of truth can be taken to include not only the processes of making diagnoses such as conduct disorder truthful, but also the multitudinous interactions involved in telling the truth to the young person. By considering the constitution of disorderly subjectivity (and, more specifically, mentally disordered subjectivity) in terms of its relation to truth we can consider how a young person comes to *know* him- or herself as mentally disordered.

As I have outlined, these truth technologies are promulgated and imposed via relations of power. This function of power can be illustrated by asking what actions are being made on the actions of the young person. Foucault (1997b) suggests utilising this function of power as a means to contemplate the way truth influences the self. From this perspective 'knowledge and power . . . is not the fundamental problem but an instrument that makes it possible to analyze the problem of the relationship between subject and truth in what seems to me the most precise way' (ibid.: 290). This implies that relationships of power can be used as a means to analyse the relationships that a young person with a disorderly subjectivity forms with the technologies of truth. In addition to being a means through which to analyse the relationship between subjectivity and the self, the notion of power implies the possibility of contesting subjectivity.

Further means of considering the rupturing of these effects of truth, power and the self can be found in Foucault's observation of the inversion of the need to know the self over the need to care for the self. 'There has been an inversion between the hierarchy of the two principles of antiquity, "Take care of yourself" and "Know thyself." In Greco-Roman culture knowledge of oneself appeared as the consequence of taking care of yourself. In the modern world, knowledge of oneself constitutes the fundamental principle' (Foucault, 1988a: 22). Young people designated with a diagnosis are presented with the inference that, through knowing themselves as disorderly, and through being good subjects, they can take better care of themselves. This interpretation is significant as it situates this need to '*know*' as a practice that needs to be problematised. Of relevance to this point is Marshall's discussion of 'knowing' the self over 'caring' for the self. Here it is pointed out that this 'is a self which is now to be known through the human sciences. To care for one's self in the twentieth century has come to be to fit oneself out, retail, with a set of "truths" which, by being learned, memorised, progressively put into practice, construct a subject with a certain mode of being and a certain visible manner of acting' (Marshall, 1997: 41–2). This remark illustrates the impact of truths and, more specifically, the truths of the 'human sciences', on the notion of 'knowing' the self. From this perspective the games of truth of the 'human science' of mental disorder function as a means to retail the young person with the knowledge that they are disordered. In this chapter I link the argument regarding the persuasiveness of the truth of 'mental disorder' to a conceptualisation of how the technologies of the self respond to truth and power to form disorderly subjectivities.

Truth, power and subjectivity

As was discussed in Chapter 1, the five young people who were interviewed all spoke of being told truths about themselves. These truths included terms assigned to them by their teachers, psychologists, psychiatrists, their families and their peers. In many instances, these truths were influenced by psychiatric discourses. For example, Rachel was also told that she had 'behavioural problems' and 'relating problems' when she was sent to the Adolescent Psychiatric Facility. However, she described how she was dissatisfied with these, and would have preferred a truth that was more definitive:

> At the Adolescent Psychiatric Facility, you know [if] you have [a] problem it was [better to have a] more straightforward one – to have anorexia or bulimia or things like that. Because you know with anorexia or something like that you had a definite label – or something definite or they told you more.
>
> (Rachel, Interviews)

'Behaviour problems' was unsatisfactory because it did not definitively tell her who she was (or what exactly was wrong with her). This prompts questions about the effects of diagnoses such as the nebulous 'EBD' – how do young people respond to being described in this way? Further, what do we do when, in a culture that courts diagnoses, a young person (or parent or a teacher) demands a diagnosis that is as precise as can be on the premise that it will afford them 'straightforward' knowledge of *who they are*?

The influence of psychiatric discourses continued after high school when Rachel encountered Community Mental Health Services. According to Rachel, these services presented her with the knowledge that she had depression and post-traumatic stress disorder (PTSD). Towards the end of her adolescence Rachel was given the precise diagnosis she had yearned for when she was told she had borderline personality disorder (BPD).[1] This disorder is listed in the *DSM-IV-TR*, where the description includes 'The essential feature of borderline personality disorder is a pervasive pattern of instability of interpersonal relationships, self-image, and affects, and marked impulsivity that begins by early adulthood and is present in a variety of contexts' (APA, 2000: 706). As well as criteria such as 'identity disturbance', 'recurrent suicidal behavior' and 'chronic feelings of emptiness', it includes references to 'inappropriate anger' such as 'panic or fury when someone important to them is just a few minutes late or must cancel an appointment (ibid.). With these criteria it could be supposed that BPD denotes disorderly behaviour, but is reserved for adults (especially young adults). When Rachel informed me that she had been recently been given this diagnosis, she explained that, although she was relieved to finally know herself, she was troubled by this confirmation of her mentally disordered identity.

Josh spoke of being diagnosed with ADD, being segregated in a Special Ed class, and being told by his mother that he was 'stupid', would 'fail school', was 'no good', wouldn't 'make it anywhere'. As he explained, 'she never stopped saying it, she always put me down, she affected me' (Josh, Interviews). This precarious relationship with his mother eventually led to Josh's decision to leave school: 'I left cos I didn't have any stable accommodation when I got kicked out of home . . . I was passing school with flying colours, I just had to leave cos of my accommodation situation' (ibid.). Josh's ADD diagnosis would have been taken from *DSM-III-R* (APA, 1987), which differentiated between 'Attention-Deficit Hyperactivity Disorder' and 'Undifferentiated Attention-Deficit Disorder (without Hyperactivity)'. This interpretation changed in *DSM-IV* (and subsequently *DSM-IV-TR*), where these two mental disorders were 'integrated' 'into one overarching category' (APA, 1994: 775). As Josh was given his ADD knowledge prior to the creation of *DSM-IV*, he had a very real but outdated diagnosis.

The truths told to Jemma by adults included that she belonged in the 'slowest class' and was put in the ESL class (English as a second language). Jemma never understood why this occurred as, although she spoke both French and English, she considered English her first language. Jemma was told by some adults that she was dumb and stupid, her friend's mum said she had dyslexia, her doctor told her she had 'depression', and she described how her parents called her a 'slut', 'no good at anything and useless'. She explained that her parents called her a 'slut' because 'they actually thought it was my fault' (Jemma, Interviews). Jemma's peers told her truths including that she was 'dumb', 'stupid', a 'fat heifer', a 'black mamma', a 'slut', and teased her because she was 'no good at school'. This truth-telling by her peers included references to 'the colour of my skin' (Jemma, Interviews). Being told she was 'stupid' led Jemma to form the belief that *she was stupid*, a truth that has 'just stuck with me ever since' (Jemma, Interviews). This meant Jemma experienced this truth-telling as an ongoing subjectivity, the truth of being told she *was* stupid became the subjectivity of *being* stupid. Jemma felt she had been so influenced by these truths that her only option was to completely change who she was, to change her identity completely. This change of identity from 'Kathy' to 'Jemma' is discussed in the next chapter.

Ben and Kris also experienced the discourses of diagnosis. Ben was diagnosed with conduct disorder and Kris was diagnosed with borderline personality disorder. Kris also described being diagnosed with anorexia and anxiety problems. Each of the young people was affected by the discourses of diagnosis even though there is difficulty defining 'mental disorder'. As declared by Frances (1994: vii, emphasis in original), 'it is by no means clear just what *is* a mental disorder'. Despite the ambivalence of experts, these young people knew themselves as being mentally disordered. The relations of power involved in the making and administration of conduct disorder are vital to its legitimacy and authority as a knower of young people, so much so that, despite there being questions regarding its definition, young people can be definitively diagnosed.

Power is a fundamental consideration in analysing the construction of mentally disordered subjectivity. In the previous two chapters I outlined the potential for using power as a means to grasp its effects in the diagnosing of disorderly children. I employ power here to consider the relationship between the reflexivity of the subject and the telling of truths. In a quote cited previously, Foucault (1998b: 451) makes this reference to reflexivity: 'I wish to know how the reflexivity of the subject and the discourse of truth are linked'. Power can be used to analyse the relationship between truth and the reflexivity of the subject. By employing power in this manner it can be utilised as a tool in the analysis of the construction of disorderly subjectivities.

In relation to education, segregation both in and out of school influenced the young people and their understandings of themselves as disorderly. Both Rachel and Ben were segregated from their 'regular' peers when they were placed in adolescent psychiatric facilities, and Kris experienced segregation through his forced admission to hospital and then to an adolescent psychiatric hospital. These forms of segregation had the forceful effect of emphasising to the young people that they were *different* from students who attended 'regular' school. However, segregation does not necessarily have to involve removal from school. As Jemma and Josh described, another effective method is to be segregated from peers whilst remaining within the school. For Jemma and Josh this meant being placed into a 'slow' or 'special' class.

Although Jemma and Josh both experienced being segregated *within* their schools, they spoke about their experiences quite differently. Josh explained that he 'liked the Special Ed class' and was of the opinion that placement in this class enabled him to 'get a better education'. The reason for this was because the Special Ed class 'was better than the mainstream classroom, the teacher had more time to spend with you, not like in the mainstream classroom where there's so many kids, there's only about six or seven in the Special Ed class' (Josh, Interviews). Josh commented that one of the advantages of the special class was its similarity to primary school: 'It was just like primary school again, the same class, we didn't move out into the high school . . . in a way you felt that someone wanted you, being such a big school' (ibid.). In particular, Josh was of the opinion that the organisation of primary school was superior to that of high school: 'If you stayed at primary school through to year twelve I reckon you would be better off than if you go to high school. I think the primary school way is better because you've got smaller classes and one teacher and then maybe one teacher comes in and helps now and again' (ibid.). Josh also attributed the length of time he managed to remain at school to his placement into this class, where, he states, he 'learnt more'. Whilst he points to these benefits, Josh also experienced the very real effects of power in his removal from 'normal classes' and placement into the 'special class'. He indicated that this segregation meant he was different from the 'normal students' and that he had a disability. Segregation reinforced the truth of his ADD and the belief in his need for psychostimulant medication.

The connection of ADHD (or, in Josh's case, ADD) disorderliness to pharmacological intervention is arguably a commonplace assumption in schools, in teacher education, in the media, and often for parents/caregivers. This was evident in the comments from the young people in the focus groups on prescription and over-the-counter medication. Two comments by high-school-aged students indicate that quite clear associations are made between ADHD and psychostimulants. One young person said, 'I know people who are junkies who are on that, we call them prescription junkies. We don't really associate with [those] people. Yeh no-one really talks to people who take Ritalin and all that' (sixteen-year-old male, Focus Group 1, 2004). A participant in another focus group similarly commented, 'apparently according to one of my friends, all the people that he doesn't like are on Ritalin. It's stuffing with their minds. That's what they are saying anyway' (seventeen-year-old male, Focus Group 3, 2005). Other descriptions used in this focus group included 'they are crazy' and 'they are unwell' (Focus Group 3, 2005).

The parents that I interviewed also raised the issue of the social consequences of taking psychostimulants. In relation to her son's refusal to take psychostimulants at school, one mother observed 'you just go to the office and they'll give you a tablet and of course any child going to the office . . . stand[s] out' (Parent Interview 1, 2003). Reflecting on this issue, she commented on both this visible practice and her son Brad's response:

> There's a queue of children lining up at the office every lunch time for their medication because there's asthma sufferers, there's diabetics, there's the children with behaviour problems. So really a lot of children will do it and they're able to cope with their label or their illness or whatever. But flat refusal – he just would not do it.
>
> (Parent Interview 1, 2003)

Another parent similarly remarked on what she sees as the issue of medicating at school, stating that it is an issue for the 'little kiddies as well and especially as they get older, I've been in schools and you see the kids going to the front office to get their medication and I think that must have all sorts of social feelings for them too' (Parent Interview 2, 2003). To manage this issue, this parent chose to put her son Andrew on 'slow-release Ritalin', which she explained meant that he didn't require a tablet at school. In spite of her doing this, her son continued to experience 'segregation'. This parent described how other parents would not let their children play with her young son, Andrew, because he was 'on speed'. One parent stopped her child's long-standing friendship with Andrew (including regular house visits) when she discovered that he was taking Ritalin. Segregation for young people diagnosed with ADD or ADHD can therefore comprise much more than a Special Ed class or 'special' measures situated within the 'regular' classroom. It includes public medication routines, and social effects such as being viewed by other young people as a 'prescription junkie'.

While Josh described enjoying the Special Ed class, Jemma 'hated' that she had been put in the 'slow' class, stating that she felt that she 'could not learn' *because* she was in this class. She argued that this segregation taught her she could not learn, told her she was 'slow', a 'failure' and 'was a nobody' and that it happened at a time in her life when she was experiencing traumatic personal events.[2] Jemma explained that the class 'meant my ideas and thoughts that I was stupid just got worse and worse . . . I was just going through so much and my life was just so fucked and school was just not one of the good things'. She then concluded, 'actually, school ended up making me feel worse about myself – and that just kept getting worse' (Jemma, Interviews). Jemma was saddened by her experience of school, recounting that before the slow class she 'enjoyed everything about school like sports days and all that stuff, but after I was in the slow class everything just changed and I didn't want to be at school' (ibid.).

The segregation of Jemma and Josh is an example of a practice of educational power that has significant effects on the subjectivity of the young person: it teaches them that they are different and that there is something *wrong* with them. Jemma's placement in a 'slow class' and Josh's removal to the Special Ed class are both examples of what I term the administration of dividing practices. These dividing practices separated them from their peers and posited them as individuals who were 'other', a designation premised on the assumption of 'internal deficit'. For Jemma, this designation occurred because particular individuals within the school had the expertise to designate certain individuals as 'slow'. Josh was initially designated 'other' through the ADD diagnosis he was given by the 'expert on the mind', which was later reinforced by the proxy expertise within the school when he was placed in the Special Ed class. Although Josh didn't discuss the details of his medication whilst at school, it seems that the very act of being prescribed the medication authenticated his understanding of himself as having ADD, and the placement in the special class reinforced that he had a disability. These two experiences illustrate how the teacher can both function as a proxy for the experts on the mind (those who are officially able to diagnose mental disorder) and also have his or her own expertise through the practices of segregation and designation of otherness.

Each of the five young people experienced being told the truth that they were mentally disordered. Although they had been diagnosed as having a mental disorder, not all of them chose to enter into a discussion of this experience. Both Jemma and Josh referred to this experience only briefly. By contrast, Rachel, Kris and Ben discussed at length their experiences of the process of being diagnosed as disorderly. Rachel began her relationships with experts on the mind when she was in kindergarten, where she recalled, 'I first started seeing the school counsellor' (Rachel, Interviews), and was told how she had 'problems'. Being physically sent to this specialist in the school served as reinforcement of the truth that she was a 'problem'. Not surprisingly Rachel disliked her future relationships with the school counsellors, stating, 'I hated the whole thing about school counsellors' (ibid.). In addition to being differentiated at school, Rachel was further posited as different through her placement in an adolescent psychiatric facility, which she described as 'a place for people that have problems – it can be from anorexia to school problems, um, anything that people have problems with basically' (ibid.). Rachel was required to live at this facility during the week and went home at weekends. Even though she had complied with these instructions, she resented being made to go, and described it as 'scary'. Being placed in this facility emphasised to Rachel the dominating effects of psychiatric power and acutely accentuated the truth of her 'difference' and status as a 'problem'.

The adolescent psychiatry facility was also the site where Rachel underwent the first of her many experiences of psychiatric power's chief instrument, the diagnosis. Here the diagnostic process obliged Rachel to perform a gamut of tests and procedures so that she could be assessed, and she was required to undergo this testing without being given access to the results. Initially Rachel was told it was suspected that she had attention deficit disorder, a suspicion that was later retracted. Rachel stated that when this possibility was first suggested she knew that it was wrong, but that she still had no choice but to complete the tests. As she described, 'well to start off with they first looked at ADD . . . but that was shown up as a no no, I could tell that before they did the testing but anyway' (ibid.). This experience taught Rachel where she was situated in the relationship of power with psychiatric and psychological testing. It was not until six or seven years later, when her counsellor requested these results on Rachel's behalf, that she was able to personally examine the results of these tests.

As described previously, Rachel was told that she had behaviour problems, a truth that implied she was 'disruptive'. She had initially been told this by her teachers: '*I was still labelled disruptive and anything went wrong it was always "Where's Rachel?"*' (ibid., emphasis added). Later this truth was made 'official' when it was reiterated to her by psychiatric power. The effects of this 'reiteration' were increased by the ongoing repetition of the problems: 'when it's said over and over and over again you remember it for sure' (ibid.). These tactics of diagnosis and repetition emphasised to Rachel that she was, indeed, a problem. Rachel was to undergo similar experiences after she left the adolescent psychiatric facility. When she went to university she was forced into a relationship with the local community mental health team and was sent to see more psychiatrists for further diagnosis.

Like Rachel, Kris came to believe he was mentally disordered through the procedure of diagnosis. Prior to experiencing any specific psychiatric subjectivisation Kris experienced being diagnosed with asthma and was put on a steroidal drug 'permanently', which had side effects, causing him to gain a considerable amount of weight. At that time in his life Kris described himself as 'big and fat'. In an effort to control the weight gain he went to Weight Watchers, a popular weight loss programme. He described this strategy as 'successful', and explained that he decided to continue dieting even after he had reached his 'ideal weight'. This continued to the point at which Kris found himself admitted to hospital and was 'tube fed'. He then spent a considerable amount of time in hospital, spending his 'seventeenth and eighteenth birthday in hospital . . . and I had very little time in between where I was out of hospital so basically I was in hospital for about a year all up' (Kris, Interviews). Initially Kris had been placed in an adolescent ward at the hospital, but he was later moved to an adolescent psychiatric hospital.

Being situated in this hospital proved to be an action with powerful connotations for his belief in his 'mental disorderedness' and his sense of being a 'problem' and 'abnormal'. This was because the action of being admitted to hospital precipitated the first of Kris's interactions with psychiatrists and diagnosis. Kris recalled this first conversation with the psychiatrist quite clearly, stating that it began with, 'Hello I'm the psychiatrist and I'd like to have an interview, I'd like to talk to you for a while so' (ibid.). Kris described this further:

> I'd talk to her and tell her how I feel and then she said 'Well I think that you are depressed and clinically depressed and that you have certain anxieties that need to be addressed and I want to put you on an anti-depressant'. See at that stage we were pretty cautious about what drugs to take because of the asthma drug, we were really worried about what the side effects might be. So mum and dad and I had an interview with Dr X and she told us that there were little side effects with the anti-depressant.
>
> (ibid.)

Although this was the first time Kris met with psychiatric diagnosis, it was not the first time he had met a medical specialist. With the recollection of this experience, when he was given the anorexia diagnosis, his reaction was 'I felt as though, here we go again, here's another thing I've collected to my collection of diagnoses' (ibid.). Kris described this initial experience of meeting psychiatric power and its action of diagnosis as entering the 'psychiatric mousetrap': 'that's when I first got into the sort of the psychiatric mousetrap' (ibid.). The metaphor of this relation of power places Kris in a position of little power, since he is the 'mouse' that has been caught in the 'trap'. Kris emphasised this sense of being 'trapped' and powerless when he explained this metaphor: 'they don't let you go as soon as they get you' (ibid.). These powerful effects of diagnosis not only limited Kris in regard to his relationship with himself and with his psychiatrists, they also appeared to give others the right to exert actions on him. For example, Kris told how his grandmother had recently interrogated him in regard to his eating. In doing this, it seems his grandmother considered she had the right to exert actions on Kris *because he had been diagnosed with anorexia*. For Kris this translated to continuing his occupancy in the 'psychiatric mousetrap'.

Two weeks prior to our interview Kris had again experienced the 'psychiatric mousetrap' when he was diagnosed with borderline personality disorder. He explained, 'One of them had said a few months ago that I had borderline personality traits but they never told me that I actually had the disorder until two weeks ago' (ibid.). When he was told he had this diagnosis he was also informed that he could go into psychotherapy for treatment. Even though Kris had researched this new self-knowledge, he stated he couldn't 'really understand it'; the only clue he had was that it might be 'brain chemistry' or 'delayed development' (ibid.). It seems then that, via the powerful action of psychiatric diagnosis, borderline personality disorder presented an ultimate explanation for who Kris was, a knowledge he could not understand, yet was obliged to accept. These actions had a cumulative effect on Kris, as he explained: 'when I see it's all linked in together it all points to where I am now' (ibid.). At the time of our interviews Kris was worried by his 'abnormality' and the fear that he could never be 'normal'. Kris had come to know himself as someone who is 'different', who has many problems and who needs psychiatric treatment. Indeed, for Kris to know himself he had to subscribe to certain psychiatric knowledge about himself, and armed with this he could then take care of his mentally disordered self. Kris had effectively been instructed that he must *know* himself and be a good psychiatric subject, in order to care for himself.

Unlike Kris, Josh spoke very little about the effects of psychiatric power on his understanding of himself. He did describe how 'It was a psychiatrist who diagnosed me with ADD' (Josh, Interviews). When this diagnosis occurred Josh was quite young: 'well, when I was eight years old I was diagnosed ADD and I was on Ritalin for two years and then after that they changed me to dexamphetamine. For seven years I have been taking that drug, I'm still taking it' (ibid.). At seven years of age this was the youngest age of psychiatric diagnosis of all the five young people. However, this is not uncommon. Children are often diagnosed at early ages; Rapoport and Ismond (1996) even suggest that children as young as three may exhibit oppositional defiant disorder. Two of the mothers I interviewed for the parent study described how their children had been diagnosed with behavioural disorders (such as ADHD) at the age of five – and how at the same consultation as this first diagnosis both mothers were offered prescriptions, one for dexamphetamine, the other for Ritalin.

With hindsight Josh described this diagnostic process as something he experienced as 'being done to him', something he had to partake in that he did not fully understand. As he recounts, 'I remember going to the hospital and the next minute taking these drugs' and 'the drugs were meant to make me better' (Josh, Interviews). He took the drugs even though 'at the time I felt they weren't doing anything for me' (ibid.). Later Josh changed his mind and came to the opinion the drugs were 'doing something'. This 'compliance' with his medication makes Josh a good psychiatric subject, and demonstrates the influence of psychiatric power on the way Josh construed himself as a disabled young man with ADD. Josh could be understood as drawing on technologies of the self that subscribe to the psychiatric notions of treatment in order to carry out what he has been taught is 'caring for himself', that is, taking his dexamphetamine as prescribed.

Ben's initial experience of psychiatric power was similar to Rachel's in that he too was forced to attend an adolescent psychiatric facility (they attended different facilities). Rachel was made to attend an adolescent psychiatric facility by her parents and the school, whereas Ben was compelled to go as a result of a court order. Ben's parents had reported his theft of his mother's car and this led to Ben having to go to court. The magistrate did not convict but instead ordered him to have counselling and attend the adolescent psychiatric facility. 'Cos when I stole my mother's car . . . I had to see counsellors and all that and so the decision of the court was I had to attend school for twelve months, that was part of my thing. I had to go to the adolescent psychiatric facility and they were trying to get me back into school . . . and um that didn't work out' (Ben, Interviews). Ben emphasised that he did not get a criminal record for stealing his mother's car. Even though he managed to avoid the juvenile justice system, he did find himself legally compelled to attend an adolescent psychiatric facility. In addition, whilst Ben was subjected to the segregation of the adolescent facility as a means to 'try to get him back to school', he was not reintegrated into regular schooling. This seems, as I argued in Chapter 5, an apposite example of segregation premised on the rhetoric of 'integration'.

This practice of relocating the 'delinquent' into a psychiatric paradigm is possible when the young person in question is changed from the status of delinquent to that of mentally disordered. In Ben's case, this meant being diagnosed with conduct disorder. This shift is acceptable *because*, as a mental disorder, conduct disorder is aligned with the medical model. In this way the action of stealing a car can be responded to within the framework of health and medicine or, specifically, the action of psychiatric diagnosis and hospitalisation. One wonders whether the outcome for Ben would have been different had Ben been subjected to 'discipline and punishment' as opposed to 'discipline and psychiatric medicine'. It could be asked how Ben might have experienced things differently had his actions been viewed as naughty and a 'discipline and punishment' solution administered – as opposed to being diagnosed as conduct disordered and having psychiatric care imposed.

Once Ben was situated in the adolescent psychiatric facility he found himself experiencing the powerful effects of psychiatry and its ability to 'know him', learning tasks such as keeping appointments with the psychiatrist and his counsellor. Fortunately, Ben liked his counsellor and formed a relationship with him that was unlike the other relationships he had with the adults in his life. Ben said that he 'liked him a lot . . . he was really good' (ibid.). One of the key features that made this relationship work for him was that this counsellor 'hung in there'. This proved to be crucial to their relationship, Ben explained: 'I had a tendency then to push people to the limits to see how much they cared about me, so no one could ever care about me enough. That's one of my biggest problems in that sense – but I've gotten over that yeah' (ibid.). When Ben's counsellor 'hung in there' he surprised Ben and passed the 'test'. Ben was of the opinion that 'kids' do this because 'they want to see how much you care about them' (ibid.). From a Foucauldian perspective this action of 'pushing people to their limits' is an exercise of power that a young person can exert on adults around him or her.

Diagnosing disorderly children runs the risk of indicating that the adult thinks they know the young person better than they know themself. The young person then has choices, such as resisting these actions, or acquiescing to psychiatric knowledge and 'retailing' themself with the self-knowledge that they are mentally disordered. By acquiescing, the young person is folded into the rhetoric that agreement with the expert of the mind is a practice of caring for the self. Alternatively, resistance to this knowledge could be construed as an action that *cares for the self* through its attempt to resist the psychiatric dictum of *knowing thyself*. As can be seen in the instances of Rachel, Kris and Ben, diagnosis entailed significant encounters with psychiatric expertise and with proxy psychiatric experts such as the teachers whose task it is to teach the special student who is 'mentally disordered'. Furthermore, the experience of being placed in psychiatric facilities was especially influential in the way in which Rachel, Kris and Ben considered themselves to be 'other' and mentally disordered. These forms of segregation provide a means for relations of power to manifest that can substantiate the legitimacy of mental disorder as a knower of their selves and, consequently, influence the construction of their disorderly subjectivity.

Technologies of the self

Here I move to consider how the young people constructed their disorderly subjectivities. To do this, I have structured the discussion around the question, 'How is it that young people perform work on themselves to construct a mentally disordered or problem subjectivity?' More precisely, it could be asked how the technologies of the self are influenced by the truths of disorder and the actions of power that are involved in the diagnosing of the disorderly child. These questions imply considering the self not only in relation to truth and power, but also in terms of the relation of the self to itself.

Technologies of the self are those practices performed by individuals upon themselves and which, through their interactions with truth and power, create subjectivities. I am suggesting here that these technologies of the self form a pivotal function in the production of subjectivity. This raises questions regarding how the relationship with truth and power influences the way in which individuals perform work on themselves. This is not to only ask how these technologies function in relation to truth and power, but also to ask how they act on and modify other technologies of the self. Foucault states that the technologies of the self

> permit individuals to effect by their own means or with the help of others a certain number of operations on their own bodies and souls, thoughts, conduct, and way of being, so as to transform themselves in order to attain a certain state of happiness, purity, wisdom, perfection or immortality.
>
> (1988a: 18)

Technologies of the self can be understood as a means that permit the individual to perform 'certain operations' on him- or herself. Thus, when considering subjectivity, the self needs to be considered in relation to the effects of truth and power. This representation of subjectivity illustrates how the self can be conceived as holding a strategic position in the production of subjectivity. This position is necessarily crucial since, to construct a disorderly subjectivity, truth and power must necessarily meet with the self (or what could more accurately be termed the technologies of the self).

Drawing from Foucault, it can be argued that to grasp the mechanisms of the technologies of the self one *must* simultaneously be cognisant of the effects of truth and power. Indeed, Foucault's (1988a) description of technologies of the self is confined to the performance of these technologies in relation to truth, to knowledge, to the relationships of power and to the formation of subjectivity. What is not clear from Foucault, or what is left to our imagination, is how these technologies work amongst themselves to form subjectivities. For example, the question could be posed, 'How may some technologies of the self prevent alternate technologies of the self from creating "non-disordered" subjectivities?' To respond to this I refer to Foucault's (1988h: 148) use of the term 'rationality': 'we are thinking beings, and we do these things not only on the ground of universal rules of behaviour but also on the specific ground of a historical rationality'. My intention is to borrow from Foucault's notion of 'rationality' and apply it to what could be tentatively termed the 'historical rationality of the technologies of the self of a young person'. This rationality could then be viewed as a historical rationality of the technologies of the self, acting as a 'lens' of interpretation in the construction of other subjectivities. For example, being mentally disordered can evince further constructions of difference and otherness.

This discussion must necessarily occur contemporaneously with an acknowledgement of the possibilities of the influences, namely of other subjectivities, technologies of the self, games of truth and relations of power. Indeed, there are interdependent relationships between different subjectivities and technologies of the self. These relationships contribute in various ways and at varying times, and respond to the telling of truths and the mechanisms of power to perform the construction of subjectivities. Linked to this, subjection to subjectivities influences acquiescence to the dictum that one must listen to the 'expert' and 'know thyself'. As suggested earlier in this chapter, the urge to know oneself forms a technology of the self that interacts with the effects of truth and power to produce disorderly subjectivities. To consider how the technologies of the self are involved in such constructions involves analysing the formation of the five young people's disorderly subjectivities in terms of the work the self has performed on the self.

The technologies of the self that influenced Rachel's construction of her disorderly subjectivities include those that caused her to believe she was unable to socialise, unwanted, unable to learn and a nuisance, and had mental disorders. Placement in the adolescent psychiatric facility forcibly differentiated Rachel from her school peers. The extent to which Rachel felt 'different' was conveyed in her description of her move to the adolescent psychiatric facility:

> That was a big thing, it was like when I was leaving school. I wanted to say goodbye to some people that I was kind of friendly with because I knew in a way, yeah, I'd be back next year but I knew in a way that I wouldn't be back at all like . . . I said 'No I'm just going to another school'. You know I didn't actually tell anybody. No I didn't tell anybody what actually the adolescent psychiatric facility was. I just said I was going to another school because in a way I was quite ashamed that I had to leave the school.

(Rachel, Interviews)

Not only was Rachel again feeling 'unwanted' and 'different', she was also overwhelmed by a sense of shame at having to go to the adolescent psychiatric facility. This sense of difference enforced by the distinct physical segregation also occurred when, at the adolescent psychiatric facility, she was required to attend her regular school for one or more days each week. These attendance regimes were observed and commented on by the 'normal' students at her high school: 'I got all these questions, "Why do you only come one day a week or two days a week?" Or you know "three days a week?" Yeah it was like they kind of come up with something and it stuck' (ibid.). This is a poignant comment given that the practice of sending students from segregated settings to schools for 'day visits' is employed as a procedure to 'reintegrate' disorderly children.

Rachel seemed to deploy similar technologies of the self when she attempted a course at TAFE college, explaining that as a result of her experiences at high school she started this course with the conviction that 'I'm not going to know anything' (ibid.). This meant that when Rachel met with tasks that required her to learn she applied her technology of the self to them, her own truthful subjectivity that she *is a person that cannot learn*. For example, Rachel explained:

> Like sometimes it can take ages and ages to get around to actually sitting down and trying to do it because your mind says you can't do it and you believe it. Just the impact of years of people saying 'you can't learn' or 'you misbehave too much to learn' or on the other hand teachers just don't know what to do with you so they would just send you out. So you didn't learn either. I think it's the fact of it's just so many years of your bloody life, it's forever being drilled into you. You can't but listen to it because it's always there.

(ibid.)

This description provides an example of how Rachel applied technologies of the self to produce an ongoing knowledge of herself as someone who *can't learn*. We also need to take note of her germane comment regarding the assumptions made about misbehaviour and an inability to learn. It is likely that this is another truth that young people experience, and from which, ironically, they learn.

Added to this were new truths introduced to Rachel via the truth of psychiatric diagnosis. At the start of her first year at university Rachel was told she had depression and 'some idiot said post-traumatic stress disorder' (ibid.). She explained that this was later added to:

> I'd gone back to education and these mental health workers have thrown in some new labels . . . And now it's like [with] my psychiatrist something different has been said. They told me I had personality disorder and it's just like my head's – just like my head's just like – ohhh what am I meant to think, you know? With all these different diagnoses that have been thrown at me through education and it's just like 'ohhh hold on, what have I got?' kind of thing.

> (Rachel, Interviews)

These intrusions by psychiatric power did not only build on Rachel's educationally deficit subjectivities and technologies of the self; they also gleaned effectiveness from Rachel's previous psychiatric encounters at the adolescent psychiatric facility.

Like Rachel, Kris experienced the cumulative effects of being disordered. In terms of the concept of a historical rationality, his interactions with truth, power and the technologies of the self have conjured a rationality that knows Kris as disordered. The rationality that seems to frame his technologies of the self is one that construes *who he is* as abnormal and as disordered. This means that each of Kris's technologies of the self is swayed by this rationality – they are affected by the rationality of abnormality and disorderedness. The rationality of Kris's technologies of the self has been influenced largely by his interactions with psychiatry and to a lesser extent by education. These different domains (the psychiatric and the school) interacted with one another, so that at school Kris experienced being other because of his psychiatric otherness.

Kris divided the effects of schooling into two aspects, 'the academic aspect and then the social one' (Kris, Interviews). In terms of the 'academic aspect', Kris stated that although he 'went ok' overall it was not good because he hadn't completed his HSC (Higher School Certificate). Yet Kris had missed a substantial amount of this final year because he was in the adolescent psychiatric hospital. In relation to the social aspect, Kris explained that he couldn't 'interact'. This was reinforced by psychiatric opinion when he was diagnosed with 'social anxiety' (in *DSM-IV-TR* the preferred term for social anxiety disorder is 'social phobia'). Kris learnt of his social anxiety when he saw his 'treating doctor's report' for the Department of Social Security. This action corroborated Kris's rationality of his technologies of the self, mounting its persuasion. This influenced the way in which Kris interpreted himself as being unable to do many things *because* of his social anxiety. For example, in relation to his parents' plans to go to a festival he said, 'There will be a lot of people there, and I think to myself "how am I going to cope?" I want to go but how am I going to cope with all these people there because *I've got this anxiety disorder*' (ibid., emphasis added).

This psychiatric truth has dramatically affected Kris: 'I realise that maybe I'll never get over it'; and it made him feel 'bad inside' (ibid.). He also explained that this aversion to social situations meant that his 'personality had changed'. For Kris, having his personality change was something that was a fait accompli; once changed it could not change back. This conceptualisation is quite different from considering self-knowledge in terms of subjectivity, for, whereas the changed personality is irreversible, the constructed subjectivity can be deconstructed through the technologies of the self. This point adds to the critique of diagnosing disorderly children, for what are the implications of diagnosis when it carries such intractability – and such foreboding?

As previously discussed, for Kris, an outcome of his dietary vigilance was hospitalisation, the diagnosis of anorexia and placement in an adolescent psychiatric hospital. Being diagnosed with anorexia meant more than being given a mental disorder, it was meant what Kris called a 'girls' disease' (ibid.). Having a 'girls' disease' made Kris feel even more alienated: 'I never met any other boys with what I had, at the hospital there was another anorexic there and she said she knew a guy with it' (ibid.). What this meant for Kris was that not only was he told the truth that he had anorexia and was forced to experience the powerful effects of being in hospital and tube fed, he simultaneously experienced the effects of feeling different because his disease did not belong to *his* gender. This influence of gender was clearly significant for Kris, and these truths, and the powerful means by which they were persuaded, colluded with and encouraged the technologies of the self that Kris had which created his subjectivities of being anxious and afraid of social interaction. With this 'girls' disease' subjectivity Kris felt the distance to the cricket nets or the soccer field was ever increasing.

The experience of hospital, the experience of feeling alienated at school and the experience of being diagnosed convinced Kris that he is 'a problem' or, as Kris puts it, '*I'm the problem*'. What seems to have occurred is that the rationalities dominating Kris's technologies of the self have changed from specific defects (such as being unsociable or fat) to an overall sense of being 'a problem'. This effect and influence of truths (or, as Kris calls them, labels) was further explained:

> These labels made it more difficult for you to do your work because you seem as though you are different to everybody else. You have got something wrong with you literally, and you are almost like a disabled person. You can't do it . . . and sometimes you get into that the victim mentality when you think 'well how should I be able to do this' or 'I've got that'. And you get angry with it, and you and get angry with school, you get angry with parents and you get angry with everything else. So it did affect the way I was at school and because I was in hospital so much.
>
> (Kris, Interviews)

These diagnoses then were not just things he was told, but were taken on by Kris and used as a technology of the self, a technology which meant he had a productive role in the formation of his mentally disordered subjectivities.

Unlike Kris and Rachel, Josh's sense of 'being different' was not reinforced by placement in an adolescent psychiatric facility; it was made palpable by his segregation into a Special Ed class. This action confirmed both the truths of his mental disorder and his mother's 'put-downs'. The combined effect of these truths and actions was not only persuasive enough to produce technologies of the self that subscribed to the disability subjectivity, it also made disability a persuasive rationality. This rationality served to confirm Josh's knowledge of himself as disabled, with him believing that his disability and the things he has been told about himself were responsible for his inability to get work, his homelessness and his use of marijuana as a means to deal with his problems. Josh was so convinced of this knowledge that he had a low expectation of fitting into employment and believed that the best thing for him was to go on disability pension: 'I should be on a disability allowance not the dole as I have a disability' (Josh, Interviews).

This pervasive belief in his disability did not only depend on a rationality of disability, it also required the truth of the internal defect. It is important to emphasise that segregation made this 'truth' convincing. This is because, as I discussed in Chapter 5, practices such as segregation are frequently premised on the notion that students have internal defects or deficiencies. In essence, the very action of segregating Josh signified that there *must* be something wrong with him. This belief was so influential that Josh did not accept that good things and his disability could co-exist:

> It's hard to come to terms with whether I've got a disability or not. It's like is it there or isn't it there? I think it is there when I think I'm dumb in myself, when I think that I'm not going to get anywhere. I think it's not there when something good's finally gone right and my disability hasn't stuffed it up for me.
>
> (ibid.)

To participate in the dialogue of disability Josh has had to come to know himself as an individual *with* an internal defect. This means that, when Josh experiences something outside of the realm of disability (such as 'when something good's finally gone right'), he must interpret it in terms of an inexplicable absence of his disability. This internal defect *must* be present when Josh feels like giving up, but mysteriously disappears when something 'good' happens.

One of the reasons for Ben's forced attendance at the adolescent psychiatric facility was to ensure he returned to regular school. Despite this intervention, as I described earlier, Ben did not return to high school on a regular basis. This experience of not being able to 'successfully' return to regular schooling had the effect of further enforcing a sense of difference from the majority of his peers. This compounded Ben's beliefs that he was different and a potential problem. Whilst Ben was nonchalant about his conduct disorder diagnosis, he stated that his worst fear was that he would become a psychopath. This belief had been imposed through his attendance at the adolescent psychiatric facility, where he was forced to recognise not only that he was different, but that his diagnosis of conduct disorder implied the possibility of psychopathy. Ben's reference to 'psychopathy' is to an 'out-of-date' term. In 'correct' diagnostic vernacular the term used is antisocial personality disorder. Ben's potential psychopathic subjectivity was not only premised on the truth of his mental disorder, it also existed in relation to how he conceptualised the way he was perceived by other people. Ben feared that people who knew him might think his 'morality' was wrong and infer he was psychopathic. Ben had come to believe that by virtue of the conduct disorder diagnosis he had the inherent potential to manifest a psychopathic subjectivity. This belief could be re-described in terms of rationality, where the overwhelming persuasiveness of a rationality (such as psychopathic potential) can convince a young person of the truth of his or her inherent disorder, and sanction the belief that psychopathic potential is an inherent attribute.

The truths, relations of power and technologies of the self that impacted on Jemma seemed to revolve principally around her segregation in the slow class, the personal trauma she experienced at age eight or nine and the repercussions of these events. The ramifications of these experiences were especially far-reaching, causing Jemma to conceptualise herself as a complete problem, or, more exactly, that her previous identity, 'Kathy', is a complete problem. These technologies of the self created an impasse, a position in which Jemma believed she had to completely change *who she was* (change from Kathy) in order to create alternative subjectivities. Grasping how Jemma's previous identity became an irrevocable problem involves considering truth, power and the technologies of the self. In the research interviews Jemma tended to refer specifically to Kathy only in relation to her change of identity. At other times when she described past experiences (at school for example) she didn't use the name Kathy. I have followed this convention and, in this and the following chapter, refer to Jemma's previous identity, 'Kathy', either when Jemma used this name in the interviews or when I am discussing this change of identity.

Jemma explained that being placed in the slow class at primary school significantly affected her in several ways. One of these effects was that she became convinced that she was 'unwanted', a belief instigated by her interpretation of the slow class placement as a means for her teachers to 'get rid of her'. She reasoned that her teachers must have thought, 'Oh, there's one kid less that I'll have to worry about so I won't even bother' (Jemma, Interviews). This gives pause to those arguments that critique segregation on the premise that it is a tactic for teachers to remove 'troublesome' students. At the very least, it shows how practices of segregation may be interpreted by the segregated. Believing she couldn't understand her teachers was another consequence of her insertion into the slow class, where she found she couldn't understand the 'special' way that she was taught in the slow class. At the time of this placement in the slow class Jemma was experiencing what she described as a 'personal trauma', something she described as 'definitely terrible' (ibid.). This personal trauma began when she was eight or nine and made it impossible for her to concentrate and study. Jemma said that, although she was distressed by the personal traumas, 'all the teachers or any of the adults that were around me never picked up on them' (ibid.). In hindsight Jemma believes that the teachers misinterpreted her reactions to this personal trauma and mistakenly used her reactions to it as a rationale for segregation into the slow class. These events resulted in Jemma concluding 'I was the problem', explaining that 'then I was just being treated like a worthless piece of shit . . . you're a nobody, you can't do this, that and the other so therefore you can't do anything' (ibid.). She emphasised that she has fond memories of her life before the slow class: 'to me everything was fine before I was in those classes' (ibid.). The action of segregation exacerbated Jemma's personal situation, amplifying the trauma she was experiencing and her sense of alienation. Segregation consequently had a profound impact on both her sense of helplessness and feelings of 'fault' in relation to her personal trauma.

To be told such truths and have these enforced (and reinforced) by actions such as segregation clearly influenced Jemma's technologies of the self. The interplay of these three, the self, truth and power, produced subjectivities that included 'slow', 'problem' and 'nobody'. But these subjectivities did not 'go away' when she left primary school. She continued to describe herself as 'slow' at high school, a description that had deleterious effects on her schooling and future attempts to re-engage with education. For example, Jemma explained that when she attempts study 'I give up in the end and just think oh I'm such a fuckin' failure that I just don't bother about other things any more' (ibid.). One of the results of this rationality of the technologies of the self is that when confronted with study, 'I just turn off the idea' and have the thought that 'I can't do it', and this happens 'all the time. I have that idea all the time' (ibid.). Consequently, these technologies of the self influenced how she worked on herself in relation to learning. Jemma described this experience: 'Often when I try to learn something the word failure definitely comes back. It gets in the way of trying to learn something – it totally puts a hold on it and then after that it just totally irritates me' (Jemma, recording through writing, Interviews). It was difficult for Jemma to explain what happened when she met with something she felt she could not learn. She did state, 'I'd just go insane thinking about it, so I'd put it off and just keep putting it off' (Jemma, Interviews). Here the insertion of disorderly discourse (especially her sense of the risk of going insane) appears to have influenced her, and so, when confronted by her own technologies of the self that instruct 'You can't learn and can't study', Jemma chooses the safest option: she gives up.

When Jemma engages in education she is alert to anything that signifies that she cannot learn, suggesting that this 'can't-do learning rationality' actively listens for 'can't-do truths'. The work Jemma's self performs on itself thus has a significant relationship to the effects of truth and power *and* to the effects of the technologies of the self. Here we could envisage that the technologies of the self modify one another through their effects on the self. This implies that being a *complete problem* involved a complex cacophony of influences derived from the effects of truth, power *and* the influences of the technologies of the self *on* the technologies of the self. It was not the issue of a few rationalities dominating Kathy's technologies of the self; it was the case of there somehow being a *complete* identification of the self with subjectivities of *inadequacy*. These powerful discourses of failure were intertwined with uncompromising discourses of disorderliness. Remarkably, as I discuss in the next chapter, Jemma was able to find fissures that enabled her to challenge this subjectivity.

Each of the young people was described in varying ways as disorderly. This included psychiatric classification and demarcation as problems by their schools, by parents/caregivers/grandparents, and by their peers. Whereas some of these ascriptions fitted with the categories 'behaviour disorder', 'behaviour problems', 'conduct disorder' and 'attention deficit disorder', others such as borderline personality disorder, or depression or social phobia appear quite distinct. My point is to argue that, although differing, the effects demarcated the young people as disorderly in one way or another. For example, there was a disorderliness about Kris that, although he was not designated as 'behaviour disordered', could have had him designated as an 'E' (emotional) in the configuration 'EBD'. His 'problem', like those of the other young people, was that he didn't fit with the practices of the school and, like the other young people, he was markedly affected by his experiences of diagnosis. Furthermore, Kris and Rachel's borderline personality disorder diagnosis was tantamount to recognising them as disorderly.

Technologies of the self connected each of the young people to truth and power and were integral in the formation of disorderly subjectivities. For example, the truth of mental disorder convinced one of the participants that she is 'not just Rachel': she is not normal. As argued in the earlier chapters, diagnoses such as conduct disorder function as truthful knowledges that designate otherness via the assumption of aberration within the individual. For these young people, the effects of mental disorder were persuasive enough to influence their technologies of the self and the interplay between truth and power, producing disorderly subjectivities where they came to *know* themselves as disorderedly. Here I emphasise it is instructive to contemplate subjectivity not just in terms of how certain forces construct the subject (the diagnosis, segregation), but in terms of how the young person is involved. From this perspective, the work individuals perform on themselves is pivotal in creating these persuasive knowledges of the self – and, crucially, in resisting certain knowledge of the self. In the following chapter I move from analysing how technologies of the self are involved in producing disorderly subjectivities to considering how the self can be involved in questioning them.

Chapter 7

Questioning the diagnosing of disorderly children

> . . . what different forms of rationality offer as their necessary being, can perfectly well be shown to have a history . . . [these] reside on a base of human practice and human history; and that since these things have been made, they can be unmade, as long as we know how it was that they were made.
>
> (Foucault, 1988c: 37)

Taking up the challenge in the above quotation does not imply that, by knowing how disorderly children are made, we can simply 'unmake them'. Rather, it can be drawn on to cross-examine the rationality that diagnoses disorderly children, those practices that segregate, refer to, label or describe them as disorderly. In making the above statement Foucault is alluding to how history can be used 'to show how that-which-is may no longer be "that-which-is" ',

> by following lines of fragility in the present – in managing to grasp why and how that-which-is might no longer be that-which-is. In this sense, any description must always be made in accordance with these kinds of virtual fracture which open up the space of freedom understood as a space of concrete freedom, i.e., of possible transformation.
>
> (ibid.: 36)

This connects to Foucault's genealogical work and, in particular, his attention to contingencies. The crux of this argument is to employ practices of description that work with these 'lines of fragility in the present' and, in so doing, describe the kinds of virtual fracture possible.

To critique the diagnosing of disorderly children we can engage with the fragility of its discourses, and show that the that-which-is of these discourses might no longer be that-which-is. Appreciating the mechanisms of truth, relations of power and technologies of the self, and the complexity of their interactions, therefore provides a means to describe virtual fractures. In so doing, it permits us to grasp both how children can be diagnosed as disorderly and how other possibilities may be possible. Such an understanding can draw attention to how subjectivities are 'made' and, in so doing, provide clues to how to interrogate or subvert the rationalities implicated in their production. This introduces the decisive point that, via rupturing the truths and the relations of power that administer such truths, an individual can challenge subjectivities. Subjectivities can be challenged (and transfigured) by strategically rupturing the very mechanisms that lie at the root of their creation, namely the technologies of the self, games of truth and relations of power. In this chapter I interrogate truth, power and the self by considering how the five young people sought to rupture the persuasions of truth, power and the technologies of the self, and how this rupturing challenged their disordered or problem subjectivities.

Interrogating truth

The young people made attempts to rupture the 'truth-telling' that identified them as disorderly. I discuss attempts by Rachel and Jemma to rupture the subjectivities of 'educational failure', Ben's attempts to rupture the persuasive truth that he is delinquent and the attempts by Rachel, Ben, Kris and Josh to rupture the truth of mental disorder. Education is important to consider because, for the young people, it was often a context for being made disorderly. Both Rachel and Jemma spoke extensively about being an educational failure and their attempts to rupture this truthful persuasion. Rachel tried to challenge her failure subjectivity by re-engaging with education, firstly attending a TAFE College, and then attempting university. Although she left in the first year of university and did not complete her studies, the experience of *going to university* contributed towards her efforts to rupture the 'failure' subjectivity. It had this effect because it signalled she had achieved something educationally. In particular, it rendered problematic her school teachers' predictions that 'you're going to be doing absolutely jack-shit with your life' and 'you're going to be doing nothing with your life' (Rachel, Interviews). She said, 'if only I could see a teacher now and say you know "Now I've got a really really good job." I'm like, you know if I could turn the pages around [and say] "look what I'm doing now" it'd just be just like "woooo hoooo"' [laughs] (Rachel, Interviews). This strategy helped Rachel to create educational experiences that had the effect of rupturing the persuasive truths that she was *totally* an educational failure. Unsettling the truth of subjectivity is an integral step in the process of challenging the rationality of her disordered subjectivities. Nevertheless, she still came to the conclusion that 'I don't think that it's still been challenged for me' (ibid.). Although at times Rachel had disrupted aspects of the truth of failure, she had not completely ruptured the persuasions of truth, power and the technologies of the self, and therefore had not sufficiently challenged this subjectivity.

Like Rachel, Jemma experimented with education as a means to rupture 'failure', and this included a variety of courses and training at TAFE colleges, private training academies and government-funded courses. In her repeated attempts Jemma was continually confronted by her failure subjectivity, which resulted in her wanting to give up: 'I've felt I just want to give up and I do give up for a while and then I just go back and try again and again' (Jemma, Interviews). Given she was so beleaguered by this concept of failure, it is extraordinary that she had the determined belief that educational achievement was the secret to rupturing failure. As she stated, 'it is a major struggle, but I just try and prove to myself that I can actually do something good for once in my life' (ibid.). She explained that when she had not given up and 'done ok', that 'these times when it works are important as I don't feel like a failure as much, I just know that I am doing something good in my life, something worthwhile' (ibid.). Getting 'good grades' and finding that she 'can learn some things' was an experience that helped Jemma to rupture the failure subjectivity. This had enabled her to cast a critical eye over her experience of the slow class. For example, she wrote:

> Now that I look back on it, I know that I wasn't so dumb mainly because I've done quite a few things in my life. For example, a lot of courses and getting into this literacy enhancement course where I was working on a one to one basis with students who had a great deal of difficulty with their literacy.
>
> (Jemma, recording through writing, Interviews)

As a result of this 'keep trying education' strategy and her new skill in teaching literacy, Jemma was able to rupture the persuasion of her failure subjectivity and challenge the truths that she was 'dumb' and 'a failure'. This critique also extends to an understanding of how the 'personal trauma' she experienced affected her schooling and her awareness that it may have been 'happening to other students as well'.

Jemma's attempts to rupture (or partially rupture) the failure reached fruition when she was enrolled in a childcare assistant course at TAFE college. Even though she didn't finish the course, she commented 'if I had stuck at it all I would have had a certificate for it so I would have passed' (Jemma, Interviews). She had asked for time off from the course because she felt 'sick most of the time . . . depression and feeling down in the dumps', explaining that the main reason she was feeling so depressed was because a friend had committed suicide. She commented that 'if I didn't have depression I would've actually finished the course' (Jemma, Interviews). Being 'depressed' seems to have validated Jemma's non-completion in a way that didn't construe her as a failure. This is an interpretation of diagnosis that could possibly be read as 'positive'. But one wonders at what cost, given that it resulted in her believing there is something 'wrong with her'. This depicts the complexity of these discourses; these diagnoses at times seem useful but, arguably, they are of limited use because of the effects they can have on the young people knowing themselves *as a problem*.

Whilst education was influential in the formation of the failure subjectivity for both Jemma and Rachel, it proved instrumental in challenging this subjectivity. This apparent incongruity indicates that education does not only act on a young person in the formulation of failure subjectivities, but can also be used to form different relationships that can contribute to 'successful subjectivities'. Their attempts indicate that, to some degree, they had begun to question the *totality* of their subjectivisation as failures by honing a style of questioning that *destabilised* the persuasion of the games of truth that contributed to their problematic subjectivities. This possibility of rupturing through engagement in education suggests that the school is not only a site where, as I argued in Chapter 5, the truth of being 'a problem' or 'disorderly' is administered. Rachel and Jemma's experiences indicate that the school can also be a place where a young person can administer his or her success. More ominously, it must be acknowledged that this site could contribute to the creation of further 'problematic subjectivities'. These ramifications indicate the extent of the power of education or, more precisely, the potentially dominating effects of relations of power with education. Furthermore, this relation of power is evident in the paradox that, whereas education seems to be open to critique when its messages are deficit, it is an accepted teller of truths when its messages are good.

Of the five young people Ben was the only one who had been told that he was a delinquent, a truth that prompted Ben to believe that he *was a delinquent*, which he defined as a person who was 'destructive' and who chose to express himself 'in a more violent and criminal way than yeah just talking to someone about it' (Ben, Interviews). Delinquency as Ben understood it was something very much associated with psychiatric truth and legal enforcement. Ben was *made* a delinquent by the juvenile court and *ordered* into psychiatric care because he was a delinquent. Ben's knowledge of himself as a delinquent was influenced by his view of himself as 'antisocial': a conviction that was linked to the truths of psychiatric power because a diagnosis of conduct disorder signifies being 'antisocial' and, moreover, is considered predictive of the likelihood of adult mental disorders such as antisocial personality disorder. Because Ben's delinquency was connected to conduct disorder, to rupture delinquency he must also question this 'antisocial' subjectivity. This meant that to *effectively* rupture the persuasive truth of delinquency Ben would have to challenge several subjectivities connected to extremely persuasive truths that had diagnosed him as disorderly. For Ben, the connection of the delinquent with the psychopathological increased the difficulty of rupturing the delinquent persuasion. What is perplexing, however, is that there is *debate* over whether crime can indeed be connected to pathology of the mind. Yet in spite of such theoretical disagreement, via his acts of crime Ben was connected to psychopathology. This does not suggest that crime and psychopathology are connected within the interiority of the individual but, rather, that certain exterior relations of power can act on actions of crime and connect them to psychopathology. Thus, although there is debate regarding this connection, the relations of power with the juvenile court forced Ben to attend the psychiatric facility and, in so doing, connected him to psychopathology.

Although Ben had been told he had conduct disorder and been subjected to the effects of psychiatric power, he had been able to rupture the truth of this mental disorder, stating 'I believe conduct disorder as a disorder doesn't exist' (ibid.). This was then further ruptured via his argument that the psychiatrists who diagnose conduct disorder are 'just wrong':

> Well you can't really diagnose conduct disorder in a person because what they are trying to look for is a person who is more immature for their age basically. You can't really look for it. And you can play with the psychiatrist, it's easy, there's no set rule to conduct disorder. It's more a name that they give to people when they can't give them other proper mental illnesses.
>
> (ibid.)

Because conduct disorder is not a 'proper mental illness', according to Ben, it is diagnosed in order 'to fill in the gap to make them feel – just to give a name to someone that they can't diagnose' (ibid.). For example, he argued that conduct disorder is used to 'fill a gap' for the juvenile court:

> You see well most people who have been to a juvenile justice court and all this sort of thing, they will be said to have conduct disorder, cos it is just the way they do it if they can't give them a proper name like manic depressive. That was the other one I was hoping for and they couldn't give me that. My dad wanted a name so they gave me conduct disorder.
>
> (ibid.)

Based on these critiques, Ben had concluded that conduct disorder did not exist and that, 'I think well you should just say that person is a little bit immature' (ibid.). Through denying the pathology of conduct disorder and construing himself as immature, Ben was able to rupture the persuasion of this truth and challenge the conduct-disordered subjectivity. In terms of power, Ben employed this query of the truth of conduct disorder to question, first, the authority of the expert who defines conduct disorder and, second, the authority of the expert who administers it. This suggests that grasping how conduct disorder is constructed can assist in mounting a critique of the way it influences a young person. It is relevant to note that, although Ben was critical of the existence of conduct disorder, he had difficulty criticising the prediction that because of his conduct disorder he could become psychopathic.

To rupture the delinquent and 'antisocial' subjectivity Ben chose to differentiate between what he called his delinquent stage and his knowledge of himself as a delinquent. Ben considered his delinquent stage to be a period during his early teenage years when he stole and was destructive, the time in his life when he was sent to court and ordered to attend the adolescent psychiatric facility. In this 'delinquent stage' he described how he did not care about life and, so, didn't care about being a delinquent. This 'not caring about life' was quite literal; he questioned the purpose of living: 'Well, yeah, I didn't know if I wanted to live first of all, well there's still pain and suffering in someone's great life so is it really worth living with all that pain and suffering?' (ibid.). His ambivalence towards life during his delinquent stage was hindered by what Ben described as being 'too scared to commit suicide': 'Yeah cos everyone has bad times now and again. You just feel hopeless and you were too scared to commit suicide so you just wanted to destroy yourself slowly – or hope that someone else would kill you or people'd feel sorry for you that sort of thing' (ibid.). Somehow Ben stopped not caring about life and decided he wanted to live. This seemed to happen at the same time as he re-engaged with education:

> I had more to live for. I think I slowly started to feel yeah that I could have a life. I think that was when I started going to TAFE. I was thinking more about my future life and I was thinking the next thing I'm going to do, um, my HSC and then I'll go to Uni and that . . . so yeah, it was about that time it was sort like yeah, instant I decided yeah, I have hope.
>
> (ibid.)

The realisation of hope meant that Ben now had 'something to lose' if he remained in his 'delinquent stage'. He explained, 'I just realised that for me I had more of a life, so I needed to change in that sense and focus on education. Focus on just having a good life in that sense. Like if you're delinquent you end up in jail and those sort of things cos yeah crime doesn't pay' (ibid.). From this perspective, Ben's interpretation of the delinquent stage was synonymous with not caring and so to change one of the pair necessarily included changing the other. It is significant that it was through his reconnection with education that Ben found his sense of hope. Again, education seems to have the potential to enable young people to reconfigure their 'lack of hope' but, more perilously, it also figures prominently in young people losing hope.

Ben's decision to re-engage in education was based on his opinion that education could improve his life: 'I think yeah, if you want to have a proper life you need to be educated yeah so I've just got to somehow get the education' (ibid.). He reasoned that if he successfully re-engaged with education he could get his Higher School Certificate (HSC), go to university, and could have a life; or, as Ben put it, 'yeah that there is a chance for me' (ibid.). Ben described feeling positive about education, commenting 'Yeah now that I feel that I can, I'll take more of an interest. Before I just thought that I couldn't do it so I never bothered. I'd given up hope before they even began to educate me' (ibid.). It is remarkable that Ben made the decision to return to education given his past experience of being 'bored by education' and his self-described 'lack of discipline'.

Through his decision to reconnect with education Ben gained two important insights on his delinquency. He realised that to move from the delinquent stage he had to formulate 'philosophies and theories' about his problems and how to deal with them and reasoned that 'everyone has a bad life – it's how you deal with the problem that matters' (ibid.). Then he described becoming aware of how his view of gender had influenced his knowledge of himself, explaining 'like when I was that age I couldn't express myself verbally cos you had to be a man and all this sort of stuff' (ibid.). Ben used this second insight to develop an understanding of the way he had responded to problems during his delinquent stage. Ben explained 'you had to be a man . . . you weren't allowed to let your problems get you down so you just did it like violent, and that's why you express yourself I hate life everything yeah without saying it' (ibid.). In reconsidering this view of 'having to be a man' he began to think 'more philosophically about the world and that sort of thing', reconsidering how it is possible to respond non-violently to problems. Coming to this insight was a turning point since it became a successful strategy to rupture his belief that to be a man he must necessarily be both violent and aggressive. These are interesting comments given the way that conduct disorder is allegedly more prevalent among males. Young men, it seems, are more likely to be subjected to diagnostic practices that demark them as disorderly. This suggests that there is the need for an analysis of diagnosing disorderly children that draws on the critical literature on gender and masculinities. Indeed, these practices need to be subjected to closer critique in terms of several concerns, including the pressing issues of 'race', ethnicity and diagnosis, and the assumptions about 'low income'.

Unlike Ben, Josh had not been able to rupture the truth of his mental disorder. Josh had been told he had attention deficit disorder when he was seven years old and since that time he had come to think of this truth as 'my ADD'. Josh described how he finds this truth perplexing: 'I haven't worked this one out, I am still trying to. I find it very confusing to understand and why they call it that and why they call it a disability or should they call it a waste of time that the government doesn't want to deal with you' (Josh, Interviews). Because he had been segregated into the Special Ed class and told that he had attention deficit disorder, he had concluded that there was a problem with him and that problem *must* be a disability. However, when Josh used this self-knowledge to apply for disability support (instead of unemployment payments) he discovered his view was not shared by Australian government departments such as the Department of Social Security (now called Centrelink). This view directly conflicted with Josh's self-knowledge and prompted him to ask, not 'do I have a problem?', but rather '*what is my problem?*' Josh had not been able to rupture his ADD truth, nor had he been able to rupture his belief that he 'had a problem'. What he had started to do was to consider the question, 'just what is my problem?' Unlike Ben, Josh had chosen to accept the legitimacy of his mental disorder and did not question the authority of the experts who had assigned his diagnosis or prescribed his medication over the past six years. As part of this acceptance it appears that Josh was beginning to investigate the intricacies of his diagnosis.

Like Josh, Rachel was unable to rupture the truth of her most recently diagnosed mental disorder, borderline personality disorder. She had received this diagnosis a few days prior to our last interview. It may be that the immediacy of this truth contributed to Rachel's inability to develop a strategy to rupture its persuasiveness. This might suggest that time is a critical factor for some young people in the formulation of strategies to rupture persuasive truths. In addition to the closeness of the diagnosis, the experience of the adolescent psychiatric facility was a persuasive influence in the acceptance of the mental disorder. Being forced into this facility emphasised that she was disordered and that there was something wrong with her. This point indicates the potentially persuasive effects of the segregation of a young person into a psychiatric facility, or to off-site units or schools for specific purposes, or pupil referral units. Such physical differentiation can function as an indicator for the supposed mental aberration within the interiority of the individual. From this perspective, such dividing practices both designate and reinforce the otherness of the young person and, significantly, make it difficult to rupture the persuasion being diagnosed as disorderly.

Kris described the borderline personality disorder diagnosis as adding to his 'collection' of mental disorders ('major depression', 'anorexia', 'anxiety disorder', 'social anxiety'). He did not know the purpose of this diagnosis, stating 'what it has done for me is just given me something else to worry about' (Kris, Interviews). This is ironic given that another of the truths Kris has been told is that he has 'anxiety problems', an irony that was not lost on Kris. As a consequence of being told he had borderline personality disorder Kris concluded that he definitely was 'not normal', interpreting this diagnosis as an absolute knower of himself, a signifier of his status as someone with an internal deficit. Part of the reason Kris found it difficult to critique these truths was because his disordered subjectivities had distanced him from what he called 'the mainstream' and meant he was not normal, he was 'abnormal'. As he described, 'I've always just gone along with the label – that's the group that I belong to' (ibid.). To challenge his disorderly subjectivities Kris had to simultaneously confront his position outside the mainstream. As he explained, 'it's a vicious cycle because once you think that you're abnormal you think that it is not going to get better and that you're not as good as anybody else, I mean it just goes downhill from there' (ibid.).

Although Kris felt restricted to a specific positioning by his mental disorders, he had cultivated reasons to explain the use of these persuasive truths. 'By designating others we can then designate ourselves . . . that's what I think' (ibid.). This reasoning not only provided Kris with an explanation of why these persuasive truths are used, it also informed a strategy he used to question his own positioning as disordered and abnormal. Kris's strategy was to view other people as having a problem or mental disorder, and shift what he saw as the fine line between normal and abnormal, a procedure that, for him, increased the boundaries of normality. For example he said, 'You could say to yourself that I am not the only one who has this disorder. So then I'm not unique. Which means there are other people with the same thing, which means, I suppose, that it was normal if there were more' (ibid.). Kris gave the example that the more he recognised other people were anxious, the more normal being anxious seemed. This prompted Kris to conclude, 'so that's how I think you can challenge those thoughts by thinking that sort of thing' (ibid.). This method helped because he could argue, 'everybody has probably got something wrong with them . . . mentally' (ibid.).

As this discussion indicates, it is possible for a young person to engage with truth and question the authority of such truth. For some of the young people interviewed, one means to achieve this was to re-engage with education to challenge games of truth such as failure. However, it seems that re-engagement with the games of truth of mental disorder was a more problematic enterprise, for it appears that to engage with the institution conveying psychiatric truths risks the nomination of disorderedness. Unlike education, whhich holds out the possibility of engagement as the non-other (e.g. the successful student) or the other (e.g. the 'Special Ed kid' or the 'slow kid'), engagement with psychiatric expertise is invariably premised on the 'other'. Connecting this point to the argument that psychiatry exists via the 'psychopathological objects it speaks into existence', it seems that re-engagement with the expert of the mind can only occur simultaneously with the risk of becoming one of its objects. Drawing from this, it would therefore seem that rupturing psychiatric truths has a substantial degree of difficulty.

Interrogating power

> It seems to me that power *is* 'always already there'. That one is never 'outside' it . . . But this does not entail the necessity of accepting an inescapable form of domination or an absolute privilege . . . To say that one can never be 'outside' power does not mean that one is trapped and condemned to defeat no matter what.
>
> (Foucault, 1980c: 141–2, emphasis in original)

This conceptualisation of power does not mean we cannot take up the idea of 'virtual fracture' and describe how 'that-which-is might no longer be that-which-is' (Foucault, 1988c: 36). Questioning these discourses and describing the possibilities of 'that-which-no-longer-is' does not require one to be outside the power of discourses of diagnosis. This carries the implication that to critique these discourses, to work against them, or in terms of one's own disorderly subjectivity, one doesn't have to accept power as an 'inescapable form of domination or an absolute privilege' (Foucault, 1980c: 141–2). At times, then, when the young people ruptured or considered rupturing the relations of power that persuaded them that they were disorderly, they were not outside that power.

In relation to teachers, Rachel described a moment where she 'got even' with the teachers when she received a school merit award. Unlike Rachel, Jemma's experiences of the effects of the teacher came directly through her location in the 'slowest class', where she thought her teachers presumed she was 'acting dumb'. In post-secondary education she described meeting teachers whom she understood, who, if she had problems, 'weren't really hesitant . . . they would teach me another way of doing it' (Jemma, Interviews). She explained she 'didn't know that you had like you had a few different ways at that stage of teaching the students' (ibid.). In primary and high school she had interpreted her lack of understanding as a signal that she was 'dumb' and a 'failure', and 'couldn't learn', but with hindsight she decided that the teachers at primary and high school weren't 'teaching me properly'. The experience of this 'different teaching' enabled Jemma to cast a critical eye over her experiences of learning at school, and rupture the effects of the persuasive actions of the teachers that she could not understand. Kris also used encounters with 'exceptional teachers' as a strategy to rupture teacher persuasion. Kris discussed two secondary teachers who encouraged him to feel different about himself, one who had a high opinion of Kris, and another in year 9 who said 'I was awesome' (Kris, Interviews). Unfortunately, these experiences were cut short by 'getting negatives from year 9 onwards'. Although this distressed Kris, the memory of these two teachers permitted him to maintain the belief that there was a time when he was good at school, when he was valued by his teachers. This memory was vital to Kris's holding on to the hope that there was the possibility that he could again be successful at education.

Ben did not describe any experiences with exceptional teachers but, like Rachel and Jemma, he employed a critique of teaching methods as a strategy to rupture the power that told him he was a problem at school. What differentiated Ben from Rachel and Jemma was that he was aware of the problems of the teachers' methods *whilst* he was at school. He explained, 'the problem was, like, if you gave me a test I wouldn't have passed the question in that sense. When they taught me, they didn't teach me in a way that I felt I was learning. It just went straight past me, like I wasn't there. So they couldn't teach me, yeah' (Ben, Interviews). By contrast, he spoke of how he knew he could learn, giving the example of when he watched a video at school and how he could 'memorise everything . . . But the way teachers were telling me to read a book or something you know it just went straight out the window' (ibid.). Despite this criticism of how he was taught, Ben's issue with learning appeared to be a barrier to his connection to education until he later commenced post-secondary studies.

In relation to segregation, Josh accepted his 'special' designation and did not consider it necessary to rupture its persuasion. What Josh did feel he needed to rupture was being 'called plenty of names' by his peers; as he emphasised, this was essential because it ridiculed his Special Ed identity. In this next quote Josh recounts the strategy he employed for managing these persuasive actions: 'I learnt to live with it because I was doing better than them. It was hard getting called those names. But I knew I was doing better than them, I knew I was going to pass my schooling' (Josh, Interviews). Although this differs from the strategies devised by the other young people, it seems 'learning to live with it' reduced the effects of these persuasions, and permitted him to remain in school. Whereas Josh approved of the technology of the Special Ed class (particularly the small class numbers), he objected to suffering the degradation caused by 'being special'. In this sense 'learning to live with it' was a strategy to rupture the persuasiveness of name-calling.

Quite distinctly, Jemma opposed her segregation into the slow class; it was the issue she spoke most about and the one she knew least how to rupture. Perhaps this difficulty in strategising rupture was proportional to the extent to which she had been affected by the slow class. This difference between Jemma's and Josh's views of segregation could be tied to the degree of influence of the expertise that made these segregations. In both instances these placements had appreciative effects; however, Jemma's placement was not associated with psychiatric incursion whereas Josh's placement was. Josh was diagnosed with ADD and his placement in the Special Ed class was linked to this diagnosis. It would seem that rupturing the persuasion of the Special Ed class is also tied to rupturing the persuasion of his ADD diagnosis. Thus, for Josh, questioning his Special Ed subjectivity implied a twofold process of questioning the expertise of the psychiatrist and the school. By contrast, Jemma needed to rupture the expertise of the teachers who told her she was 'slow', and not the authority of the expert on the mind.

The young people also had differing strategies to rupture the power of psychiatric persuasions. Rachel concentrated on the points where she had 'proved' psychiatric persuasion wrong, Ben formulated a critique of psychiatric diagnosis, Kris focused on criticising the way psychiatric power is used, and not trying to rupture his diagnosis, and Josh questioned why he had been diagnosed with attention deficit disorder. Jemma did not concentrate on rupturing her subjectivities by developing strategies to question psychiatric power; instead she concentrated on rupturing the persuasions of her technologies of the self.

Rachel found it difficult to rupture the persuasive truths she had been told through her interactions with psychiatric power. This difficulty stands in contrast to her more successful efforts at rupturing the educational persuasions. This difference indicates the persuasiveness of psychiatric power and the influence of psychiatric expertise in the legitimation of the truth of mental disorder and being diagnosed as disorderly. It seems that the numerous interactions Rachel had with psychiatric power had emphasised the authority of this form of persuasion. However, in spite of the struggle psychiatric power presented there were some occasions when, although Rachel did not rupture this authority, she did manage to defy its persuasion. For example, in the interviews Rachel discussed several moments when she questioned the action of psychiatric truths. An example she discussed was when she defied a prediction made by a member of a mental health team (who have the responsibility for working with people in crisis with their 'mental health'). She described how 'they virtually told me, "you're going to end up, you're just going to kill yourself" ' (Rachel, Interviews). After relating this to me Rachel commented, 'But I'm still here.' This meant because she was 'still here' she had proved the predictions wrong and had questioned the psychiatric truths.

Rachel also considered how to rupture the psychiatric persuasion that told her she has a behaviour problem. Throughout most of her childhood and adolescence she had been persuaded that she had a behavioural problem, which was especially effective when delivered by psychiatric power. Rachel attempted to counter this by contending that her behavioural actions were a logical response to the events in her life. This prompted Rachel to view herself not as an individual with a behaviour problem, but as someone who was responding to harassment, someone whose responses to those difficulties were 'made worse by what happened at school' (ibid.). This strategy normalised the reactions she had to her experiences at school: 'like you just don't go through a horrible school life and expect, you know, to be happy at the other end' (ibid.). With this perspective Rachel was able to critique the psychiatric persuasion and question why this persuasive power expected her to be happy after all that she had experienced at school. In this sense the practice of blaming needs to be read more carefully: the blaming of someone else could be viewed as a technique that supports a young person in a strategy to rupture the persuasions of power.

Changing the view Rachel had of herself as a victim was also important to Rachel's attempts to rupture psychiatric persuasions. This was because this victim subjectivity prevented Rachel from believing that in the face of persuasions she could 'fight back'.

Rachel explained that the decision to fight back came as she got older and because she was 'fed up with it'. As she stated, 'I think just years of putting up with it and realising you know nothing was being done doesn't get you anywhere either. I got fed up with it and just turned around and said, "You're not getting away with it any more"' (ibid.). The urge to fight back and the decision that 'you're not going to get away with it' were particularly aimed at the persuasions of her teachers, her peers and the psychiatric persuasion that told her she was a behaviour problem. However, Rachel did not find a way to fight back against the diagnosis of borderline personality disorder. This diagnosis catapulted Rachel back to feeling that she was a victim. She explained it was a relief to at last know what was wrong with her, and that she wanted to accept having borderline personality disorder. However, she found acceptance difficult and was overwhelmed that she had been diagnosed with this mental disorder.

The strategy Ben used to rupture the persuasion of psychiatric power differed significantly from Rachel's. Whereas Rachel attempted to create specific strategies against some of the psychiatric persuasions she had been assigned, Ben chose to formulate an overall critique of the persuasive power of diagnosis. As he maintained,

> The labels and the psychiatry profession makes people, just makes people worse generally speaking. They do little to help people because very rarely do people get diagnosed under the right disorder. I think, yeah, there's a few different depressions and they're usually the easiest to diagnose. But, like borderline [borderline personality disorder], and then there's heaps of other ones, they are harder. They're much more harder to diagnose because they are very close – there's lots that are very close to each other.
>
> (Ben, Interviews)

Ben argued that, although there are some mental disorders that are valid, most of them (including conduct disorder) are not 'real'. Ben carried this proposition further by contending that these disorders are created because of demand: 'I think most of them – simply that people want to be sick, yeah, they want to know why life's so bad to them and so we're creating these disorders for people' (ibid.).

Ironically, the time Ben spent at the adolescent psychiatric facility proved to be the major contributor to his critical understanding of psychiatric diagnosis. As Ben described, 'I learnt like all my names and that down there, I learnt all about the depressions – the range of depressions you can get and what they are and I learnt all about the mental side of it, mmm' (ibid.). Ben stated that attending the adolescent psychiatric facility was like 'I went to university and studied psychology' (ibid.). So thorough was this knowledge that Ben said he could trick a psychiatrist: 'I feel like I could sit with any psychiatrist and trick them into thinking I've got a disorder or that I don't have a disorder, yeah, it's pretty easy (laughs)' (ibid.). Ben went on to elaborate on his reasons for this:

> That is a flaw with psychiatry. Like once someone knows, like I don't think you could ever diagnose a psychiatrist with something cos they know what you are looking for in that sense. So once I'd learnt the disorders I could make a psychiatrist think I had anything in the world I wanted him to think. So, yeah, it's only good when the person you are interviewing doesn't know anything about it.
>
> (ibid.)

Ben had recognised that psychiatric knowledge was the key to the attempts by psychiatric power to persuade him of *who he was*. As he explained, 'That's the reason adolescent psychiatric facility first got me, like they were they were messing with me and they were starting to get inside of me. But once I'd learnt about it, yeah, you get used to it and you know how to trick them' (ibid.). Ben found when he did not have this knowledge the adolescent psychiatric facility could 'mess with him', but with this knowledge he could shift the way in which this relationship of power manifested. This meant that Ben could know himself through his own actions on himself, as opposed to submitting his knowledge of himself to the persuasion of the adolescent psychiatric facility. Related to this, Ben also formulated a critique of diagnosis:

> The biggest problem is trying to work out exactly what someone has got. I don't think there's enough set rules or enough understanding of how to diagnose the disorders. The disorders exist but they're done in university tests and it's how they come up with the disorders in that sense. Then you put them out in the open world with the statistics – the setting's all changed, people are not the same. So you have different things and, yeah, I just don't think they can come to the disorder properly.
>
> (ibid.)

While stating that disorders 'exist', Ben was critical of the difference between the science of the laboratory and the unpredictability of the real world. Building on this distrust, he was sceptical of diagnosis and argued that we are 'shaping society to have these disorders' (ibid.). Ben suggested mental disorders are being applied unnecessarily and that in the past, 'you know, if you had a problem you had, um, a breakdown for a couple of weeks and then you were back to work and you acted normal and I think that was, yeah' (ibid.). Ben held the view that, 'I think we're allowed to collapse now, society is trying to let people feel more and, oh yeah, people aren't getting emotionally educated enough so yeah we're sort of creating it with the pressures from society and that' (ibid.). What Ben concluded about the diagnostic procedure was that 'we're making names for things that probably don't exist' (ibid.). Not only did Ben question the existence of many mental disorders, he also questioned the way in which these names are applied to people. Specifically he made the argument that diagnosis is not applied in a manner that suits the individual, but rather it is awarded in compliance with statistical mandates, that first they 'say there's blah blah blah people have this in Australia', and 'then once they've worked out the problem they can just go to their textbooks and then they look up the medications and those sorts of things and they solve it that way' (ibid.). This view interprets diagnosis as basically a management strategy that is premised on out of touch practices.

For all the 'learning' it afforded, Ben intensely disliked the adolescent psychiatric facility, stating he 'hated it' and though 'it made me learn more at the mind side of things but yeah, I wish I hadn't been to the adolescent psychiatric facility, that's my gut feeling' (ibid.). This 'learning' and his critique of diagnostic techniques did not permit Ben to critique the existence of psychopathy; he still lived in fear of his psychopathy possibility. Whilst he had not challenged psychopathy, this critique had alerted Ben to how 'easy it is to influence others', a point that he reflected on in relation to his newly born child. As he described it, 'you can change people easily . . . you've just got to give them the right environment and you can make their thoughts change' (ibid.). As he stated, 'well that's the whole thing; it is complex to work out how to bring up a child . . . cos there's so many different views on it, so many different opinions' (ibid.). It would be instructive to know how, as his child gets older, Ben responds to the discourses of disorderly children, and whether he has to endure assumptions about his parenting (and his child) because of his own 'history' of diagnosis.

Like Ben, when Kris contemplated the persuasiveness of psychiatric power he also criticised what he saw as the limited use of diagnostic practices. In Kris's opinion 'it seems that's all that psychiatrists can do, they can only just put labels on you' (Kris, Interviews). This comment was made in reference to Kris's recent diagnosis of borderline personality disorder, a mental disorder he had been told 'is hard to treat; you'll have psychotherapy for five years' (ibid.). Whilst he was influenced by the persuasion of this diagnosis, he pondered the dilemma of psychiatric labels, explaining this by comparing asthma with mental disorder:

> But there would be a difference, wouldn't there, if a label of asthmatic is put onto you compared to a mental disorder. It's diagnosable. But if, say,

somebody's diagnosed as conduct disorder . . . it's nothing tangible, it's a psychiatric evaluation. Whereas you can put your finger – if somebody's got angina or diabetes or something like that it's a label put on them but it's something that's real. Whereas things in psychiatry are different. It's how the person feels.

(ibid.)

Yet he remained affected by this diagnosis and was extremely sceptical of the grounds for the diagnosis, stating there was no purpose in 'telling me that's what I have' (ibid.). This point was brought home when Kris said, 'I mean ignorance is bliss, isn't it? If I didn't know that I had it, then I wouldn't be' (ibid.).

In contrast to Rachel, Ben and Kris, Josh had only briefly discussed his issues with psychiatric persuasions. The relationships Josh had with psychiatric power were mainly confined to his being diagnosed with attention deficit disorder and the ongoing interactions with the doctors who prescribed his psychiatric medication (Josh had taken Ritalin for two years and dexamphetamine for five years). Because he believed in its existence, Josh did not seek to rupture the persuasion of ADD; he was of the opinion that people 'really did have ADD . . . Yeah, I think people really have ADD because I've been there' (Josh, Interviews). It is not clear what Josh means by this comment. Perhaps it could be interpreted as an example of the effects of the very real experience of being diagnosed as disorderly. Since Josh had decided to accept the truth of his ADD he saw no reason to question the persuasiveness of the psychiatric power that gave him this diagnosis. Indeed, 'my ADD' was a subjectivity with which Josh closely identified; he did not try to rupture it, because, like his specialness, it was knowledge he had chosen to accept.

Although Josh accepted this diagnosis, he spoke of some choice in 'having it': 'ADD doesn't bother me, not at all, just doesn't bother me any more – in some ways I still I have it, in some ways I don't, and I can't explain how because I still haven't worked it out' (ibid.). This seems to contradict his previous statement that people 'really have ADD'. This curiosity prompted Josh to consider some of the ways he has come to know himself as having ADD:

> I do also think that the mother and the father have something to do with it too, because you just don't have it on your own. There's got to be something there to continue it on with. Like, in my case, my mum always telling me I was no good and putting me down all the time. That was my stop point you know, I couldn't go any further because she was always saying that.

(ibid.)

Josh further expanded on his view by associating his mental disorder with disability and then explaining that he believed it all comes down to 'lifestyles':

> With disability it all comes down to lifestyles. If you lead a lifestyle where

your mum always puts you down, always tells you that you're not going to make it, then you're more likely to have a disability than everybody else because you're always getting put down all the time. But other kids' lifestyles – they get everywhere, they do everything because their mum doesn't put them down, says 'good job' you know.

(ibid.)

In addition to his mother telling him he was no good, Josh stated that he did not get taught correctly at school. He considered this to be part of the cause of his 'disability'. At one point in our conversation Josh stated, 'Saying you've got a disability is really saying you've got an excuse in a way' (ibid.). Despite this comment, Josh was not searching for a means to rupture the persuasion of his disorderly status; he was trying to find a way to validate the authenticity of his disability.

Although located 'within' power, the young people variously attempted to rupture the persuasion of power by locating inconsistencies in the scientific truth of their mental disorder. For example, Ben's critique drew attention to the arbitrary and subjective manner in which mental disorder is constructed. In a different way, Kris questioned the dividing practices of mental disorder by suggesting that many people are like him so, therefore, he is more 'normal' than abnormal. These criticisms position mental disorder as problematic via a process of questioning its notions of legitimacy, authority and practices of division.

Interrogating the technologies of the self

Because subjectivities are produced through interactions between the self and truth and power, the technologies of the self have a pivotal role in the formation of subjectivities. In considering subjectivity as being produced via a relationship between the self, truth and power, the self can be conceptualised as a point where both truth and power must negotiate in order to construct the disorderly subjectivity. It follows then that, to rupture subjectivity, the young people not only had to rupture the persuasions of truth and power, they also needed to tackle their own technologies of the self. This is a task located within relations of power, and a task for which one needs to have some conviction that the 'that-which-is' does not necessarily need to be so.

It is important to emphasise that the technologies of the self are themselves sites of contestation in the effort to challenge subjectivities. This implies that rupturing the persuasion of technologies of the self can be attempted from two approaches. First, the young person could concentrate on rupturing the way the technologies of the self respond to truth and power. Practically, this means asking questions such as how the technologies of the self are influenced by truth and power. Second, the young person could focus on the actions of technologies of the self on other technologies of the self (the self on the self). This would include attempting to rupture dominating rationalities of the technologies of the self. To contemplate how these two modes of rupture can be attempted I consider how two of the young people sought to rupture their technologies of the self. I begin by discussing Ben's efforts to develop a strategy to rupture the technologies of the self that persuaded him to believe he had the potential to become a psychopath. I then turn to Jemma's efforts to rupture her identity as Kathy and create a 'new me', an individual she called Jemma.

Ben ruptured the persuasive truth of conduct disorder and questioned the persuasion of diagnosis but reached a hiatus in his struggle to rupture the technologies of the self that persuaded him of his potential psychopathic subjectivity. Initially Ben had not wanted to rupture this potentially psychopathic subjectivity.

> The only thing I was happy about was when this person told that me when you have conduct disorder, when you turn like twenty-five or something you can move up a level and go to psychopathic . . . Yeah, but you had to be like twenty-one or twenty-five before you can be legally psychopathic, so that was the only thing I was proud about . . . Oh, I just thought it would be cool to be psychopathic, yeah.
>
> (Ben, Interviews)

It was cool to have this psychopathic potential because it elevated Ben's status amongst his peers in the adolescent psychiatric facility. A second reason why Ben did not dispute his psychopathic potential was because at that time in his life he didn't care about himself. As Ben explained, 'Oh no it never feared me in that sense, I was really at a stage where I didn't care about myself, didn't care and so, yeah, it's just like I thought it would be cool' (ibid.). Ben explained that this view began during his delinquent stage and continued until recently when, as the father of a newly born child, he began to worry about the consequences of becoming psychopathic. When Ben decided to care for himself he changed his opinion about his psychopathic potential, stating 'I'm fearful that the psychopathic thing is going to hurt me so, yeah, and that connects more to it, mmm' (ibid.). This fear drove Ben to search for a way to rupture the technologies of the self that had persuaded him that he could become psychopathic.

One of the difficulties Ben had with rupturing his own persuasive technologies of the self was that he believed in the existence of psychopathy. Ben knew that to be psychopathic 'You have to be reasonably intelligent, they're usually like IQs of 150 and above and between twenty and thirty I think, yeah, they're young males and they usually have social problems – those sort of things, so they're rare to come across' (ibid.). Because he believed so firmly in the existence of psychopathy and was so influenced by this persuasion, he managed to overlook the infrequency of its occurrence, and remain persuaded he had the potential to become psychopathic. As a consequence he hoped he would not become psychopathic but lived in fear that he might.

As discussed previously, Ben was able to rupture the persuasive truth of conduct disorder on the premise that 'it did not exist' and challenged his conduct-disordered subjectivity. But, because he believed psychopathy *did exist*, he could not utilise this strategy. This seems illogical: if he could rupture conduct disorder, then why not potential psychopathy? Perhaps this absence of 'logic' is suggestive of the extent of the power of this persuasion. Since Ben had subscribed to the truth of psychopathy, it seemed that one of the few recourses he had to rupture his technologies of the self was to try to prove to himself that he wasn't psychopathic, and this meant being vigilant to the signs of psychopathy.

> I guess the way I would challenge it is [by] saying, well, the social bits of the psychopathic – like that they feel isolated and these sort of things – they don't exist with me. I don't feel isolated, yeah, and I can be close to people. Psychopathics, they feel, yeah, isolated, they feel locked in – but that doesn't happen to me . . . So I'd challenge it in that way.
>
> (ibid.)

Another criterion of psychopathy that Ben challenged was his intelligence. Ben emphasised that he thought he was smart but not crazy, stating, 'like you see that the most intelligent people are a bit, um, yeah crazy, a bit weird' (ibid.).

Whilst he scrutinised himself for signs of psychopathy, Ben attempted another strategy by trying to question the way he performed work on himself. In particular, he had noticed that he 'feared' the opinions of other people, *especially* those affiliated with the psychiatric and psychological professions. Adding to Ben's fear of psychiatric opinion was his suspicion that his psychopathic potential had been recorded somewhere, explaining, 'Like, I don't think I am, but there's still a fear that maybe people will think I am, I guess because well I think it's probably written down, I don't know – I don't know' (ibid.). The possibility that somewhere someone has written that he could become psychopathic was a powerful persuasion for Ben's already persuasive technology of the self. Because Ben had been told he could 'become a psychopath', he reasoned it was likely to have been written down somewhere. Certainly, regardless of whether it is recorded in Ben's personal files, it is written down extensively in the research literature, and invoked often in media stories about bad/mad children.

Ben tried to reinterpret the psychopathic suggestion by viewing it as a beneficial action of his counsellor. To do this Ben posed the question, 'Like, if they hadn't told me, maybe I would have become psychopathic earlier cos now I'm more fearful of it' (ibid.). Ben wondered whether, if he had not been told of his 'potential', he might have definitely become psychopathic. He hypothesised that this might have occurred because he would not have been aware of the things that could lead him to psychopathy. However, it seemed Ben remained unconvinced of the merits of this particular strategy.

Despite these efforts it seemed that Ben could not rupture the psychopathic suggestion. This led him to draw the conclusion, 'only time will tell'. In the interviews I asked Ben if he could imagine what it would have been like had he not been told he could become psychopathic. One thing Ben thought would be different was that he would not have been questioning his thoughts. This would have made some difference to Ben since at the time of the interviews Ben described how he constantly questioned his thoughts and searched for signs of psychopathy, worrying whether his thoughts, such as his criticism of society and of pollution, were signs of impending psychopathy. He also explained, 'when I think about it, yeah, like laterally or, I don't know, literally, I don't think it is twisted. I think I'm just being open-minded but the sort of fear that maybe it is' (ibid.). This caused Ben to be fearful of his ability to be both open-minded and critical of the world he occupied. The consequence of the psychopathic suggestion was an ongoing technology of the self that persuaded him to constantly monitor his thoughts and be vigilant for any psychopathic ideas. The degree of influence of this technology of the self indicates the effectiveness of the truths and relations of power involved in the construction of this potential psychopath subjectivity. The convergence of these to produce such an effect indicates the consequences of the scientificity of conduct disorder and, in particular, the associated discourses of 'prediction'.

The strategy that had the greatest potential to rupture Jemma's problematic persuasions was to *change herself completely*. In our interviews Jemma spoke at length about this change and her philosophical attitude towards the change. It could be interpreted that, unlike the four other young people, Jemma was able to engage in rupturing her technologies of the self because they were not totally tied to a disorderly subjectivity. Whilst Ben's potential psychopath subjectivity was very much linked to the truth of mental disorder and the authority of the expert, Jemma's association with these relations of power was limited to the diagnosis of depression. This was a diagnosis that she interpreted as reflecting the effects of her experiences of being in the slow class and being told she was a 'failure'. She seemed to conceptualise herself as a failure first, and being mentally disordered formed part of the rubric that ascribed her with failure. Perhaps it was because she considered herself a 'failure' in having a mental disorder that she was able to engineer a strategy to rupture the technologies of the self.

For Jemma, changing herself meant changing her identity, 'the whole package' (Jemma, Interviews). Jemma had decided to erase Kathy because Kathy was someone she didn't need – she wanted to 'try and put the rest behind me . . . my whole history and life whatever you want to call it' (ibid.). With a new identity she would be able to dispense with the subjectivities she disliked and the technologies of the self she had not been able to rupture. Although Jemma stated that she wanted to change everything, she did state that in this process of changing herself 'there's a few things that I do want to remember' (ibid.), but that she was not sure what these things were. She explained her reasoning for stepping into this unknown was because 'I've got nothing else to lose, the sooner I do this or the faster I do this the better' (ibid.). This 'failure' subjectivity was an integral part Jemma wanted to erase. This was because she didn't want to be

So much of a failure any more because I hate being a failure. Even though I try so hard I still get called a failure and everything and I'm just really sick of it . . . I know I'm a quitter . . . I've just gotten sick of all my life and becoming a failure and all the rest.

(ibid.)

Jemma was determined to attempt this change of identity strategy even though she was unsure if it would 'challenge what I think of myself or what, but I don't know I just want to try it and give it a go – see how I feel then' (ibid.). In the face of her own uncertainty this decision demanded 'a lot of courage and a lot of time and patience . . . [with] people, myself . . . relatives, friends' (ibid.). It was vital to have this courage because Jemma knew her family and friends would ridicule her intentions. The courage to attempt this 'experiment on myself' was buttressed by curiosity and motivated by the knowledge she had of people who had changed, who 'have been failures and then changed their lifestyle . . . and now they're not failures and now they do what they do because they love doing what they do' (ibid.).

To get rid of 'Kathy' Jemma decided to perform certain work on herself. She would move locations, change her name, and change 'everything about herself'. Whilst Jemma spoke about the racist taunts she received at school, she did not mention this when discussing the change from Kathy.[1] It is not clear how to comprehend her silences. There is, perhaps, a point to be made regarding racism and disability. In their article, Mitchell and Snyder (2003: 851) emphasise that their 'overriding effort is to demonstrate the ways in which disability came to be construed as a socially dehumanising construct in tandem with theories of racial degeneracy'. Is it possible to say that Jemma's 'slow class subjectivity' could be bound up in racialised notions of inadequacy? But, because of the silences, it is not possible for me to discuss what challenging this 'slowness' may have meant in terms of racialised practices.

Moving locations was a tactic Jemma considered crucial to reinventing herself, so that she could 'start afresh' and 'Just see how things go, like, see if I can get a job or do another course or something like that. Just stay somewhere else, somewhere away from this city' (Jemma, Interviews). Jemma said that by moving to a completely new location she could escape from the expectations and knowledges people had of her as Kathy (and avoid those people who ridiculed her plan to change identity). It seems Jemma considered that being free of people's expectations was crucial to evading the truths and actions of power that persuaded her technologies of the self to construe her as a failure.

Reinventing herself also meant she had to change physically and 'just doing other stuff I don't usually do' (ibid.). This physical change was integral to the creation of the new person because Jemma was 'sick of the way I look and feel now, I'd just be a lot better off not so much being a stick but you know sort of dressing differently, dressing nicer' (ibid.). Jemma believed that if she lost weight then she wouldn't be a 'failure', and, while she did not necessarily believe that 'fat people are failures', it seems she did consider that her 'fatness' contributed to her failure subjectivity. Perhaps this was because Jemma's knowledge of herself as the 'fat heifer' was intricately bound up with being Kathy. It was therefore paramount to discard this subjectivity in order to change from Kathy. Jemma was adamant that through these different changes (her name, her location, her appearance and her actions) she would be able to alter not only what other people thought of her, but also *who she thinks she is*. This reinvention and its accompanying 'happier self' would be free of what Jemma called her 'old memories', memories that would 'go at the back of the book . . . apart from a few things here and there' (ibid.). Being free of these old memories perhaps could be interpreted as being free of the technologies of the self that made her Kathy.

At the time of the interviews Jemma was not always able to 'free' herself from Kathy but, on the occasions when she did shift the dominance of Kathy, she experienced things very differently; she emphasised that as 'Jemma' she is adventurous; when she is 'Jemma' she has more power. When Jemma is not 'Kathy' she feels people treat her differently, including her mother. Jemma did not know how to describe the feeling that she had changed, but she did describe how 'a lot of more people are actually noticing and calling me, or starting to call me Jemma until they forget' (ibid.). What she was able to describe was that 'Jemma' was a stronger person: 'I don't know, I don't know if it is just me or what. I feel that Jemma is more of a stronger person than Kathy ever was' (ibid.). Likewise, in terms of truth-telling when she is 'Jemma', she is not a failure, nor is she dumb and stupid. It seems there is a substantial divergence between the technologies of the self used by 'Kathy' and those used by 'Jemma'. She gave this example:

> Like people I meet now I just instantly say 'I'm Jemma'. I don't know why, it just happens and then like I just feel a lot better about myself when I say that instead of Kathy. Like sometimes when I go to a pub or to a club somewhere or just when I meet people and I say 'my name's Jemma', I'll just like keep a conversation going. Whereas if I'm Kathy, if I say I'm Kathy, I just block them out sort of thing and go into a daydream or just won't speak to them that much and be depressed.
>
> (Jemma, recording through writing, Interviews)

Being 'Kathy' was restrictive – or, as Jemma graphically describes it, 'Kathy has a collar over it' (Jemma, Interviews). By contrast, the identity 'Jemma' is something unrestricted, something that is 'exploding' because as Jemma 'there is nothing she can't do' (ibid.). Jemma's rupture of 'Kathy' drew on two approaches for rupturing the persuasion of the technologies of the self: rupturing how the technologies of the self respond to truth and power, and rupturing the technologies of the self (the self working on the self). The key strategy for rupturing 'Kathy' was the work that the self performed on itself, and this was supplemented by questioning the relation the self (as 'Kathy') had to certain truths.

Jemma ruptured truths such as failure by questioning their pervasiveness: 'I don't know, looking back on it now, I know I wasn't always those things, but people didn't really pursue to look on the other side of me, they just looked at the one side and just kept it at that' (ibid.). Even though she deployed this criticism of these truths as *complete knowers of herself as Kathy*, they still impinged on the way she knew herself as Jemma. She had recently encountered one of these truths when she was told she was a 'slut', a truth familiar to the 'Kathy' identity. Although she was 'affected badly', Jemma did not take this to be a knower of herself; she interpreted it as an action of someone 'giving her a name'. She explained that she didn't see the *name as herself* 'because I don't see myself as a slut . . . I'm not a slut, I just don't see myself as being classed as one, so therefore I don't think that they have the right to say whether I am or I'm not' (ibid.). This alternative interpretation suggests that the technologies of the self that met with this truth were not the same as those that met with similar truths when she was Kathy. When Jemma believed she was 'a slut' she *knew herself as Kathy*. Because she *knew herself as Kathy* she was able to assimilate this truth as further knowledge of herself. By contrast, when she identified as Jemma, the truth of 'slut' was not assimilated as a knower of herself, and was just 'something someone said'. Jemma also focused on the relationship between the self, truth and power when she attempted to rupture the technologies of the self that construed her as a 'nobody'. Previously Jemma had interpreted being told she was a 'nobody' as a knower of herself, but when she recast this knowledge and made it a label it became less powerful. In these two examples, the truths of 'slut' and of 'nobody', Jemma had ruptured persuasions by questioning *who she was* in combination with questioning how she processed truth. These tactics also contributed to Jemma's being able to challenge the people who called her names *by challenging her own reactions* to these names. In this manner Jemma formulated how she could rupture the technologies of the self that threatened to succumb to these damaging truths. Whilst Jemma was able to rupture 'slut' and 'nobody', she did not know how to rupture the persuasion of her 'stupid' subjectivity. In this sense it is apparent just how important it was for Jemma to reinvent herself. Nevertheless, being Jemma instigated different management of the truths of failure, the actions of power communicating the truths and the technologies of the self that formulated the 'Kathy' subjectivity.

In spite of the differences reinventing herself made to her technologies of the self, Jemma acknowledged that there were some occasions when she was influenced by 'Kathy'. For example, Jemma stated that receiving criticism about the way she learns might still affect her, and that she might think 'I was dumb or useless' (ibid.). She also added, 'I still think that to this day that I'm a nobody' (ibid.). Significantly, this 'feeling like a nobody' or 'thinking I'm dumb and useless' was conditional on 'feeling like Kathy'. It is crucial to emphasise that lurking amongst 'dumb' and 'useless' and 'nobody' is the nagging voice of Jemma that asks '*Am I dumb and useless?*' The presence of this voice suggests that Jemma had questioned a certain way of knowing herself. Drawing on the discussion in Chapter 6, this type of questioning can be analysed in terms of Foucault's (1988a) discussion of the 'inversion' between the two technologies of 'knowing the self' and 'taking care of the self'. It seems that in some way Jemma had managed to unsettle the dictum that she must *know* herself first, and *care* for herself second. In doing this Jemma had to formulate a means for her self to relate to itself and, in this position, she was able to care for herself by inciting the self to work on the self. Via her actions Jemma reconfigured the way her self related to itself and thereby reformulated how her self related to the outside world.

Jemma's story is an example of how we could interpret one young person replying to the question, 'How can I rupture the domination of the dictum that mandates I must necessarily know myself in order to care for myself?' The strategy used by Jemma was very different from the ways in which the other young people attempted to rupture the persuasion of their self technologies and challenge their subjectivities. Jemma's work on her technologies of the self was different because she grappled with the self technology that demanded her to know herself according to the truth of Kathy. Jemma had examined her experiences and resolutely decided that the only thing to do was to put her self to work on her self. She had decided to take care of herself by renouncing the knowledge of herself as 'Kathy'.

Compared with Jemma, Rachel, Kris, Ben and Josh were not always successful in their attempts to rupture the persuasion of diagnosis or to challenge their disorderly subjectivities. In contemplating this difference, the effects of a psychiatrically legitimised diagnosis need to be taken into account. It is likely that such a clinical diagnosis (in some instances, several diagnoses) implicated the young people in the diagnostic apparatus such that they had tremendous difficulties rupturing the persuasions of diagnosis. However, their efforts can be interpreted as beneficial because in some instances they were able to engage with the *possibility* of rupturing persuasion.

Disorderly subjectivities can be questioned through the action of rupturing key points that support a particular subjectivity. For some of the young people, the action of rupturing self or truth or power was sufficient to weaken and question the subjectivity. In other instances, attention needed to be directed on all three components or a combination of the three. Also, acting on specific points can lead to destabilising other points in the relationship. For example, querying the truth of mental disorder may not directly challenge that disordered subjectivity, but it may expose another point for rupturing. Or in other instances, rupturing some truths might destabilise one subjectivity, but not another. For Ben, critiquing delinquency and conduct disorder ruptured the persuasion, but not his potential psychopathy. This does not suggest that rupturing persuasions or challenging subjectivities are actions that are either wholly successes or completely failures. Rather, it is to propose that we must conceptualise these as *ongoing* processes.

Virtual fractures

In *The Birth of the Clinic* Foucault makes the following point in relation to medical disease: 'The sign no longer speaks the natural language of disease; it assumes shape and value only within the questions posed by medical investigation. There is nothing, therefore, to prevent it being solicited and almost fabricated by medical investigation' (Foucault, 1994: 162). Can we suppose that the signs of disorderly children 'assume the shape and language' of much more than merely the medical, the psychiatric, the psychological, the educational clinic? Although in this book I have focused on conduct disorder, the *DSM*, and the expertise of psychiatry, I have argued that the relations of diagnostic power are not confined to the psychiatric clinic. What we have is a clinic that circulates far more broadly: across conversations by young children in schoolyards, between parents and care-givers as they puzzle over hyperactivity, in the song lyrics on the MP3 players of young people, displayed in fine detail on 'behaviour disorder' websites, and across an ever-growing spectrum of new media. Accompanying this is the clini-cal touchstone: the sacred site where the psychiatrist dispenses diagnoses, and where various other experts of the disorderly child can knowingly nod as they put children through tests, record laborious notes, write research papers and prepare reports. In short, we have a larger-than-life clinic, one where certain qualified expertise can bestow diagnosis (the psychiatrist *et al.*), and where more general knowledges can, citing science, distinguish the disorderly child. Furthermore, this elaborate clinic must be interrogated from a multifaceted perspective; its way of designating 'gender' or 'low income' or 'race' or 'ethnicity' or 'social factors' or 'geography' must be treated as suspect, and recognised for its prejudices.

What seems to unite these, if we dare to speak in this fashion, is that, despite protestations to the contrary, they invariably draw on assumptions of a 'within-child' hypothesis. Although there may be attempts in education in countries such as the UK to move away from the 'straight up' diagnostic models such as the *DSM*, they fail to achieve a goal of 'non-labelling'. Take, for example, Swinson *et al.* (2003), who, in their discussion of emotional and behavioural disorders, are critical of the way educational practices assume a 'within-child' factor. Or consider the point by Thomas and Glenny (2000: 284) that 'The term "EBD" induces a clinical mindset from which it is difficult to escape' and 'The language of the clinic, though, invariably steers the response of professionals towards a child-based action plan'. Furthermore, with the increasing use of terms such as ADHD and spiralling numbers of prescriptions for psychostimulants such as Ritalin, can it be said that one can operate outside the power of diagnosis or, more exactly, away from the influences of diagnostic discourses informed by the *DSM*?

We clearly need to scrutinize the discourses that diagnose disorderly children – and this does not mean interrogating only those that have a recognised location in psychiatric parlance. The proliferation of psychopathological discourses means that saying a child has 'behaviour problems' or 'behaviour difficulties' is likely to connote the spectre of the diagnosis of disorderliness. It is therefore crucial to comprehend the workings of rationalities such as those that deem diagnosis apposite and to describe these in terms of their virtual fracture. We can take up the idea of virtual fracture and set about the task of thinking through how the 'that-which-is' disorderly child was 'made', and, in so doing, listen for the lines of fragility. This is a task I have attempted in this analysis of how games of truth, relations of power and technologies of the self are implicated and interrelated in the diagnosing of the disorderly child.

Games of truth produce disorderly truths such as the purportedly 'scientifically valid' conduct disorder, and relations of power are involved in the construction and administration of disorderly truths. To grasp how it is that young people can consider themselves as mentally disordered it is crucial to contemplate the complexities and inter-relationships between truth, power and the self. Technologies of the self operate in a way that works with these effects of truth of power. In this view the self interacts with truth and power in an *active fashion* that provides for the possibility to accept, reject or change these influences (Foucault, 1997b). Although this is a key point in conceptualising the technologies of the self, it is not a simple matter of the individual just 'deciding' whether they will accept, reject or change the diagnosis. It is far more complex, and the effects of truth and power must be taken into account. When a child or young person is diagnosed as disorderly, the expectation is that he or she will submit to the diagnostic gaze and, in so doing, know his or her self as disorderly. Foucault's (1988a) reference to the hierarchical inversion of 'know thyself' and 'take care of thyself' provides a conceptual tool to describe the process by which disorderly young people are expected to come to *know who they are* in order to care for themselves. This carries the implication that through knowing themselves they can take better care of themselves and, paradoxically, become a good disorderly subject. In the diagnostic configurations this means accepting the diagnosis, complying with treatments such as counselling and medication, and obeying the conventions of segregation.

The reference to 'know thyself' and 'take care of thyself' can also be drawn on to better comprehend the challenges to those scientific knowledges that allege to *know who you are*. This can posit actions of challenging such knowledges as actions that *care for the self*. This style of thinking can be used to differently comprehend acts of struggle against a tyranny of imposed diagnoses. Because the self interacts with truth and power in an *active fashion*, it has a pivotal role in the possibility of disrupting the dictum to 'know thyself'. Based on this, challenging disorderly subjectivities is tied to contesting games of truth, disrupting relations of power and disturbing the way the self relates to itself – and to truth and power. We can deploy this idea to think differently about the imposition of diagnostic knowledge. In so doing, this may afford different perspectives on how acts of resistance may be bound up in acts that seek to defy the imposition of diagnostic knowledge. We must ask ourselves, 'Doesn't a young person have a right to refuse this imposition?' Likewise, don't we need more than ever to ensure that children who are in jeopardy of being subjected to diagnosis, those from low-income families, with 'criminal' parents, 'boys', racial minorities, those with 'single-parent mothers', are able to resist?

Questioning this priority of *knowing* may enable an alternative perspective that disputes the import attached to the psychiatric truths that retail a young person with disorderly knowledge of him- or herself. This provides, I contend, the opportunity of creating a technology of the self that calls into question the knowledge of the expert. This brings me to the matter of how a Foucauldian perspective can be used as a practice. Without taking up this idea of 'know thyself – care for thyself', Laws and Davies (2000) draw attention to the ways in which a poststructuralist perspective can be deployed in educational work with 'disorderly' children. They argue that 'a take-up of poststructuralist discourse enables a radical disruption of the taken-for-granted readings of educational practices, so opening up moments in which the participants can go beyond the conditions of their subjection' (ibid.: 220). This brings to the fore the related question, 'What about how others consider the issue of disorderly children?' What happens when the that-which-is of disorderly children is accepted? What are the implications for teachers who just 'see it that way'? This is a predicament to be grappled with across the many institutions and professions that work with children and young people. Some pointers can be taken from Biering's contention that 'Mental health nurses working with children and adolescents also need to define their stance on the medicalization of their clients' behaviour problems and emotional suffering' (Biering, 2002: 67). Biering then adds, 'We are, after all, whether we like it or not, a part of the psychiatric establishment and share its disciplinary power' (ibid.). It makes cogent sense then to ask, 'How are teachers implicated? What are the consequences if preservice teachers are taught with textbooks and curriculum that instruct disorderly children as "that-which-is"? What are the consequences of not including in teacher education discussion of lines of fragility, such as the debates over definition and diagnosis?'

There are, then, two inter-related areas that a critique of diagnosing disorderly children needs to address: the discourses of disorderly children (the way they appear as truth, the relations of power); and the way that these discourses are implicated in the production of disorderly subjectivities. In this critique we must not lose sight of the importance of the possibility that the 'that-which-is' might no longer be so. It is also important to consider the possibilities that are afforded by conceptualising technologies of the self as active, including the potential to disrupt the diagnosis. But this rupture needs to be carefully understood. This is not to say that, once disrupted, the game is 'over', that one is no longer affected by the dictum of 'science' to know thyself. What it suggests is that, in an ongoing way, it is possible to resist, subvert or challenge those things presented to us as that-which-is. To return to Foucault, using contingency and drawing out lines of fragility, the 'virtual fracture . . . open[s] up the space of freedom understood as a space of concrete freedom, i.e., of possible transformation' (Foucault, 1988c: 36). This freedom, or what Philips refers to as 'concrete freedom', 'exists in the fractures within existing relations of power, at the points of contingency within which no clear path can be prescribed' and, further, 'the emergence of a contradiction within discourse concomitantly involves the opening of a space for freedom' (Phillips, 2002: 336). Such breaks or fractures are transient, quick. If we imagined it happening now we would not be outside discourse or power;

we would remain immersed in it. But perhaps in an interleave a differing view is possible. To cite O'Leary, perhaps we can think of it as a 'condition of our striving':

> Freedom, for Foucault, is not a universal historical constant . . . Freedom, therefore, is not a state for which we strive, it is a condition of our striving; and as such it can also function as a yardstick for that striving. Freedom is not a substance. It is as relational as power, as historically pliable as subjectivity . . . Rather, like power . . . freedom exists only in the concrete capacity of individuals to refuse, to say 'No'. To say 'No', for example, to being governed in a certain way, or to governing oneself in a certain way.
>
> (O'Leary, 2002: 159)

We need to think about truth and power and the technologies of the self and the interplay between them – and consider how thinking about these may help us to look differently at young people and the struggles they are likely to have in responding to these disorderly discourses. Importantly, we need to find ways to talk about, and to write about, the lines of fragility. We must describe the kinds of virtual fracture, so that, amongst the ever-increasing diagnostic imperatives, freedom can be a condition of striving, and young people have the possibility to say 'No'.

My analysis of diagnosing disorderly children runs the risk of being criticised for not offering 'alternatives'. This is a difficult problem, and one discussed eloquently by Baker (2002: 689). As she asks, 'how could any alternative avoid recirculating the salvific and redemptive efforts being problematized'? She later makes the point that 'the challenge as I see it then is not how to tinker with the school, the university, examinations, or substituted portfolios but whether it is even possible to imagine the world otherwise' (ibid.: 696). Perhaps engaging in the kinds of virtual fracture is a way to work through this, to explicitly write descriptions of things where the 'that-which-is' is no longer that-which-is, and perhaps, in so doing, imagine the world otherwise.

Notes

1 Introduction

1 Throughout this text I use lowercase when referring to mental disorders such as conduct disorder. Capitals are used for abbreviations, such as CD, ODD. Quoted material is presented as in the original.
2 Quotations and references to the interview material with the five young people are all cited in this manner.

2 Disorderly children

1 Transcript of this segment made by Harwood.
2 I acknowledge the issues related to the apparent 'androcentrism' in Foucault's texts. For discussion see Ramazanoglu and Holland (1993) and Sawicki (1991).
3 I make a convention of using the plural terms 'themself' and 'their'.

3 Disorderly conduct and the truth of the disorderly child

1 This task force was responsible for overseeing the creation of *DSM-IV.*
2 The author of this article is not specified.
3 Noble (1929) does not provide a date for the formation of the NSW Council for Mental Hygiene, but indicates it formed 'recently', thus a date can be approximated as being close to the publication of Noble's article in 1929.
4 Travis (1908) is citing New York Juvenile Asylum. *Annual Report of the New York Juvenile Asylum* (51st Report). Travis does not provide a date for this citation.
5 'Alienist': a 'specialist in mental disorders; modern usage prefers psychiatrist' (Drever, 1981: 12).
6 The quote from Strecker (1928: 139) states 'turning in fire alarms', which appears to mean 'turning on fire alarms'.
7 This paper was later published in *Archives of Neurology and Psychiatry*, December 1920.
8 The gender composition was '74.4% boys . . . 24.6% girls' (Anderson, 1923: 424).
9 Breggin and Breggin (1994) are citing Kendler (1992) Twin studies. *Psychiatric Times,* December.
10 Lorei and Vestre (1969) citing Buss, A. (1966). *Psychopathology*. New York: Wiley.
11 The 'x' in these categories is used to denote 'disorders of psychogenic origin or without clearly defined tangible cause or structural change' (APA, 1952: 7).

4 Interrogating the power to diagnose disorderly children

1   Opsonic index is 'the ratio of the number of bacteria destroyed by phagocytes in the blood of a test patient to the number destroyed in the blood of a normal individual' (Hanks, 1981: 1032).
2   Kevles (1985: 315) indicates the source of this citation to be from the American Eugenics Society (1922). *The Fitter Families Eugenic Competition at Fairs and Expositions.*
3   Dividing practices based on gender have been subject to critique by authors such as Blackman (1996).
4   From Wile (1926). The relation of intelligence to behavior. *Mental Hygiene.* Volume details of journal are not provided by White (1996).

5 Administering disorderly children

1   No author details provided for this insert in the *Australian Journal of Special Education* (1983).
2   Pages in this document are not numbered.
3   According to Conway 'two regions, North Coast and Western, did not operate a specific regional facility. Instead, these regions provide funding for specific initiatives in high schools or clusters of high schools' (Conway, 1994b: 13).
4   The 'Wilderness Enhanced Program', unlike the other programmes, was not a site-specific service.

6 Why do children and young people believe they are disorderly?

1   Rachel did not specify what type of 'depression'. *DSM-IV-TR* describes categories of 'Depressive Disorders'; these 'Depressive Disorders' are subdivided into three types: 'Major Depressive Disorder', 'Dysthymic Disorders' and 'Depressive Disorder not Otherwise Specified'. The term 'personality disorder' is used to refer to a 'family' of disorders to which borderline personality disorder 'belongs' (APA: 2000).
2   Jemma asked that this be described as 'personal trauma', 'major yucky thing' or 'yucky experiences'.

7 Questioning the diagnosing of disorderly children

1   In Rasmussen and Harwood (2003) we use the Butlerian notion of performativity to discuss the injurious speech acts Jemma endured, and, drawing attention to the intersections of racism and sexism, we examine the implications of these speech acts on her identity.

References

Achenbach, T. M. (1998). Diagnosis, assessment, taxonomy, and case formulations. In H. Ollendick and M. Herson (eds), *Handbook of Child Psychopathy* (3rd edn). New York: Plenum Press, pp. 63–87.

Alexander, F. G. and Selesnick, S. T. (1967). *The History of Psychiatry: An Evaluation of Psychiatric Thought and Practice from Prehistoric Times to the Present*. London: George Allen and Unwin.

American Academy of Child and Adolescent Psychiatry (1997). *Summary of the Practice Parameters for the Assessment and Treatment of Children and Adolescents with Conduct Disorders*. Retrieved 6 March 2005, from http://www.aacap.org/clinical/parameters/summaries/CONDCT~1.HTM

American Psychiatric Association (1980). *Diagnostic and Statistical Manual of Mental Disorders (DSM-III)*. Washington, DC: APA.

—— (1987). *Diagnostic and Statistical Manual of Mental Disorders, Third Edition, Revised (DSM-III-R)*. Washington, DC: APA.

—— (1994). *Diagnostic and Statistical Manual of Mental Disorders, Fourth Edition (DSM-IV)*. Washington, DC: APA.

—— (2000). *Diagnostic and Statistical Manual of Mental Disorders, Fourth Edition, Text Revision (DSM-IV-TR)*. Washington, DC: APA.

American Psychiatric Association Committee on Nomenclature and Statistics (1952). *Diagnostic and Statistical Manual of Mental Disorders (DSM-I)*. Washington, DC: APA – Committee on Nomenclature and Statistics.

—— (1968). *Diagnostic and Statistical Manual of Mental Disorders (DSM-II)*. Washington, DC: APA – Committee on Nomenclature and Statistics.

Anderson, V. V. (1923). The psychiatric clinic in the treatment of conduct disorders of children and the prevention of juvenile delinquency. *Journal of Criminal Law and Criminology*, 14, 414–56.

Andrews, R. J., Elkins, J., Berry, P. B. and Burge, J. A. (1979). *A Survey of Special Education in Australia: Provisions, Needs and Priorities in the Education of Children with Handicaps and Learning Difficulties*. Canberra: Schools Commission.

Anhalt, K. and Morris, T. L. (1998). Developmental and adjustment issues of gay, lesbian, and bisexual adolescents: A review of the empirical literature. *Clinical Child and Family Psychology Review*, 1(4), 215–30.

Anning, G. (1992). Glenfield Park family program. In B. Willis and J. Izard (eds), *Student Behaviour Problems: Directions, Perspectives and Expectations*. Hawthorn, Victoria: ACER, pp. 47–56.

Atkins, R. (1884). Half-yearly reports – report on nervous and mental disease. *Dublin Journal of the Medical Sciences* (March), 245–6.

Ayers, H. and Prytys, C. (2002). *The A to Z Practical Guide to Emotional and Behavioural Difficulties*. London: David Fulton Publishers.

Bain, A. (1988). Issues in the suspension and exclusion of disruptive students. *Australasian Journal of Special Education*, 12(2), 19–24.

Baker, B. (2002). The hunt for disability: The new eugenics and the normalization of school children. *Teachers College Record*, 104(4), 663–704.

Barkley, R. A. (1987). The assessment of attention deficit-hyperactivity disorder. *Behavioral assessment*, 9, 207–333.

Barone, T. (1992a). On the demise of subjectivity in educational inquiry. *Curriculum Inquiry*, 22(1), 25–38.

—— (1992b). Beyond theory and method: A case of critical storytelling. *Theory into Practice*, 31(2), 142–6.

—— (1995). Persuasive writings, vigilant readings and reconstructed characters: The paradox of trust in educational storysharing. *International Journal of Qualitative Studies in Education*, 8(1), 63–74.

Bennett, J. (2004). *(Dis)ordering Motherhood: Mothering a Child with Attention Deficit Hyperactivity Disorder (ADHD)*. Unpublished PhD, University of London, London.

Berbatis, C. G., Sunderland, B. V. and Bulsara, M. (2002). Licit psychostimulant consumption in Australia, 1984–2000: International and jurisdictional comparison. *Medical Journal of Australia*, 177(10), 539–43.

Biering, P. (2002). Caring for the involuntarily hospitalized adolescent: The issue of power in the nurse–patient relationship. *Journal of Child and Adolescent Psychiatric Nursing*, 15(2), 65–74.

Blackman, L. M. (1996). The dangerous classes: Retelling the psychiatric story. *Feminism and Psychology*, 6(3), 361–79.

Blau, B. I. (1996). Oppositional defiant disorder. In G. Blau and T. P. Gullotta (eds), *Adolescent Dysfunctional Behavior: Causes, Interventions and Prevention*. Thousand Oaks: Sage, pp. 61–82.

Bogardus, J. A. (1997). *Ordering Conduct, Conducting Order: Conduct Disorder and the Production of Knowledge*. Unpublished doctoral dissertation, Simon Fraser University, Burnaby, BC.

Bogenschneider, K. and Gross, E. (2004). From ivory tower to state house: How youth theory can inform youth policy making. *Family Relations*, 53(1), 19–25.

Bradshaw, K. A. (1998). The integration of children with behaviour disorders: A longitudinal study. *Australasian Journal of Special Education*, 21(2), 115–23.

Braithwaite, K., Duff, J. and Westworth, I. (1999). *Conduct Disorder in Children and Adolescents*. Retrieved 20 January 1999, from http://www.adhd.com.au/conduct.html

Breggin, P. R. (1994). *Toxic Psychiatry: Why Therapy, Empathy and Love Must Replace the Drugs, Electroshock and Biochemical Theories of the 'New Psychiatry'*. New York: St. Martin's Press.

Breggin, P. R. and Breggin, G. R. (1994). *The War against Children: How the Drugs, Programs and Theories of the Psychiatric Establishment are Threatening America's Children with a Medical 'Cure' for Violence*. New York: St. Martin's Press.

Bressington, R. and Crawford, G. (1992). Edgeware school – a centre of excellence for work experience for severe conduct disordered adolescents. In B. Willis and J. Izard (eds), *Student Behaviour Problems: Directions, perspectives and expectations*. Hawthorn, Victoria: ACER, pp. 101–22.

Brindle, D. (1999). Young poor 'have more disorders'. *Guardian*, 26 November 1999. Retrieved 7 March 2004, from http://www.guardian.co.uk/uk_news/story/0,3604,253105,00.html

Brown, P. (1997). Co-existence of behavioural problems and literacy problems in young male schoolchildren: Some issues for consideration. *The Weaver: A Forum for New Ideas in Education*, http://www.latrobe.edu.au/www/graded/PBed1.html, 1.

Buckle, D. F. (1971). The changing tasks of child psychiatry. *Australian and New Zealand Journal of Psychiatry*, 5, 167–72.

Bunting, M. (2004). *Today's Youth: Anxious, Depressed, Anti-social*. Retrieved 8 October 2004, from http://www.guardian.co.uk/print/0,3858,5014337–103690,00.html

Burdick, C. (1928). The importance of knowing the personality makeup of the criminal. *Psychiatric Quarterly*, 3, 456–9.

Buss, A. (1966) *Psychopathology*. New York: Wiley.

Butler, J. (1999). Revisiting bodies and pleasures. *Theory, Culture and Society*, 16(2), 11–20.

Cadoret, R. J., Yates, W. R., Troughton, E., Woodworth, G. and Stewart, M. A. (1995). Genetic–environmental interaction in the genesis of aggressivity and conduct disorders. *Archives of General Psychiatry*, 52(11), 916–24.

Cadoret, R. J., Yates, W. R., Troughton, E., Woodworth G. and Stewart, M. A. (1997). Genetic–environmental interaction in the genesis of aggressivity and conduct disorders. *Year Book of Psychiatry and Applied Mental Health*, 7, 251–2.

Cameron, K. (1955). Diagnostic categories in child psychiatry. *British Journal of Medicine and Psychology*, 28(part 1), 67–71.

Campbell, S. B. (1998). Developmental perspectives. In T. H. Ollendick and M. Herson (eds), *Handbook of Child Psychopathology* (3rd edn). New York: Plenum Press, pp. 3–35.

Canavan, M. M. and Clark, R. (1923). The mental health of 581 offspring of non-psychotic parents. *Mental Hygiene*, 7, 770–8.

Caplan, P. (1995). *They Say You're Crazy: How the World's Most Powerful Psychiatrists Decide Who's Normal*. New York: Addison-Wesley.

Carvel, J. (2002). NHS may fund parenting lessons. *Guardian*, 24 August 2002. Retrieved 5 August 2005, from http://www.guardian.co.uk/uk_news/story/0,,779948,00.html

Cavalier, R. M. (1986). Keynote address to the Annual General Meeting of the NSW Council for Intellectual Disabilities, Sydney.

Census Office (1988). *Report on the Defective, Dependent and Delinquent Classes of the Population of the United States as Returned at the Tenth Census* (June 1, 1880). Washington, DC: Government Printing Office.

Christensen, C. (1999). *Social Justice, Equity and Disability in Schools: Educational Views*. Retrieved 24 February 1999, from http://www.uq.au/education.ced-sjust.html

Clarizio, H. F. and McCoy, G. F. (1970). *Behaviour Disorders in School-Aged Children*. Scranton: Chandler Publishing.

Cohen, P., Provert, A. G. and Jones, M. (1996). Prevalence of emotional and behavioral disorders among childhood and adolescence. In B. L. Lewis and J. Petrila (eds), *Mental Health Services: A Public Health Perspective*. New York: Oxford University Press, pp. 193–209.

Cohen, S. (1983). The mental hygiene movement, the development of personality and the school: The medicalization of American education. *History of Education Quarterly*, 123–49.

Collishaw, S., Maughan, B., Goodman, R. and Pickles, A. (2004). Time trends in adolescent mental health. *Journal of Child Psychology and Psychiatry,* 45(8), 1350.

Comings, D. E. (1997). Genetic aspects of childhood behavioral disorders. *Child Psychiatry and Human Development,* 27(3), 139–50.

Committee of Review of New South Wales Schools (1989). *Report of the Committee of Review of New South Wales Schools.* Sydney: NSW Government.

Conway, R. N. F. (1994a). Behaviour disorders. In A. Ashman and J. Elkins (eds), *Educating Children with Special Needs* (2nd edn). Sydney: Prentice Hall, pp. 148–86.

—— (1994b). Meeting the needs of adolescents with conduct disorders. In M. Tainish and J. Izard (eds), *Widening Horizons: New Challenges, Directions and Achievements.* Hawthorne, Victoria: ACER, pp. 12–27.

Conway, R. N. F., Holt, G. and Davies, K. (1992). Hunter adolescent support unit (HASU): A regional program for adolescents with conduct disorders. In B. Willis and J. Izard (eds), *Student Behaviour Problems: Directions, perspectives and expectations.* Hawthorn, Victoria: ACER, pp. 82–9.

Cooksey, E. and Brown, P. (1998). Spinning on its axes: DSM and the social construction of psychiatric illness. *International Journal of Health Services,* 28(3), 525–54.

Cooper, C. (2002). Researching secondary school exclusion and projects of docility. *Research Policy and Planning,* 20(3), 31–41.

Costello, E. J., Compton, S., N., Keeler, G. and Angold, A. (2003). Relationships between poverty and psychopathology – a natural experiment. *Journal of the American Medical Association,* 290(15), 2023–9.

Cunningham, K. S., McIntyre, G. A. and Radford, W. C. (1939). *Review of Education in Australia* 1938. Melbourne: Melbourne University Press and Oxford University Press.

Danforth, S. and Navarro, V. (2001). Hyper talk: Sampling the social construction of ADHD in everyday language. *Anthropology and Education Quarterly,* 32(2), 167–90.

Davidson, N. (1996). *Abnormal Psychology* (6th edn). New York: John Wiley & Sons.

Dawson, W. (1933). The psychopathic child. *The Medical Journal of Australia,* 2(October), 538–45.

Della Toffalo, D. A. and Pedersen, J. A. (2005). The effect of psychiatric diagnosis on school psychologists' special education eligibility decisions regarding emotional disturbance. *Journal of Emotional and Behavioral Disorders,* 13(1), 53–60.

Department for Education and Skills (2004). *Special Educational Needs in England, January 2004* (No. SFR 44/2004). London: Department for Education and Skills.

Department of Health and Department for Education and Skills (2005). *Wired for Health.* Retrieved 4 August 2005, from http://www.wiredforhealth.gov.uk/doc.php?docid=7261

Department of Human Services – Community Care Early Childhood Services (2004). *Conduct Disorder and Associated Challenging Behaviours in Children – Fact Sheets for Health Professionals.* Retrieved 10 February 2005, from http://hnb.dhs.vic.gov.au/commcare/ccdnav.nsf/childdocs/

Desai, S. (2003). From pathology to postmodernism: A debate on 'race' and mental health. *Journal of Social Work Practice,* 17(1), 95–102.

Donzelot, J. (1979). *The Policing of Families.* New York: Pantheon.

Drapes, T. (1906). A note on psychiatric terminology and classification. *Journal of Mental Science,* 52(216), 75–84.

Drever, J. (1981). *The Penguin Dictionary of Psychology.* Harmondsworth: Penguin.

Edwards, M. (2004). Too many tablets to swallow. *Times Educational Supplement,* 13 August 2004. Retrieved 13 January 2005, from http://www.timesonline.co.uk

Eichorn, J. R. (1965). Delinquency and the educational system. In H. C. Quay (ed.), *Juvenile Delinquency*. Princeton, NJ: D. Van Nostrand.

Elze, D. (2002). Risk factors for internalizing and externalizing problems among gay, lesbian, and bisexual adolescents. *Social Work Research,* 26(2), 89–99.

Evans, R. (2004). Ethnic differences in ADHD and the mad/bad debate. *American Journal of Psychiatry,* 161(5), 932.

Fabrega, H., Ulrich, R. and Loeber, R. (1996). Adolescent psychopathology as a function of informant and risk status. *Journal of Nervous and Mental Disease,* 184, 27–34.

Farrar, C. B. (1905). On the methods of later psychiatry. *American Journal of Insanity,* 61(3), 437–66.

Fergusson, D. M., Horwood, L. J. and Beautrais, A. L. (1999). Is sexual orientation related to mental health problems and suicidality in young people? *Archives of General Psychiatry,* 56(10), 876–80.

Fernald, W. E. (1904). Care of the feeble-minded. In *National Bulletin of Charities and Corrections*, Vol. 72, pp. 427–37.

Flynn, K., Ford, K. and Saunders, J. (1989). Half and half: A service model for behaviour-disordered children in adjustment classes. *Special Education Journal,* 1, 11–14.

Ford, T., Goodman, R. and Meltzer, H. (2003). The British child and adolescent mental health survey 1999: The prevalence of DSM-IV disorders. *Journal of the American Academy of Child and Adolescent Psychiatry,* 42(10), 1203–11.

Foucault, M. (1972). *The Archaeology of Knowledge*. New York: Pantheon.

—— (1977). Nietzsche, genealogy, history. In D. F. Bouchard (ed.), *Language, Counter-Memory, Practice: Selected essays and interviews*. Ithaca, NY: Cornell University Press, pp. 139–64.

—— (1978). The history of sexuality: interview. *The Oxford Literary Review,* 4(1), 3–14.

—— (1980a). Confessions of the flesh. In C. Gordon (ed.), *Power/Knowledge: Selected interviews and Other Writings* 1972–1977. New York: Pantheon, pp. 194–228.

—— (1980b). Two lectures. In C. Gordon (ed.), *Power/Knowledge: Selected Interviews and Other Writings* 1972–1977. Sussex: Harvester Press, pp. 78–108.

—— (1980c). Power and strategies. In C. Gordon (ed.), *Power/Knowledge: Selected Interviews and Other Writings* 1972–1977. Sussex: Harvester Press, pp. 134–45.

—— (1983a). On the genealogy of ethics: An overview of work in progress. In H. L. Dreyfus and P. Rabinow (eds), *Michel Foucault: Beyond Structuralism and Hermeneutics* (2nd edn). Chicago: University of Chicago Press, pp. 229–52.

—— (1983b). The subject and power. In H. L. Dreyfus and P. Rabinow (eds), *Michel Foucault: Beyond Structuralism and Hermeneutics* (2nd edn). Chicago: University of Chicago Press, pp. 208–26.

—— (1984a). Polemics, politics, and problematizations. In P. Rabinow (ed.), *The Foucault Reader*. London: Penguin, pp. 381–90.

—— (1984b). What is enlightenment? In P. Rabinow (ed.), *The Foucault Reader*. London: Penguin, pp. 32–50.

—— (1984c). *The History of Sexuality: An Introduction* (Vol. 1). Harmondsworth: Peregrine, Penguin.

—— (1986). *The History of Sexuality: The Care of the Self* (Vol. 3). New York: Pantheon.

—— (1988a). Technologies of the self. In L. Martin, H. Gutman and P. Hutton (eds), *Technologies of the Self: A Seminar with Michel Foucault*. Amherst, MA: University of Massachusetts Press, pp. 16–49.

—— (1988b). The concern for truth. In L. D. Kritzman (ed.), *Politics, Philosophy, Culture: Interviews and Other Writings* 1977–1984. New York: Routledge, Chapman & Hall, pp. 255–67.

—— (1988c). Critical theory/intellectual history. In L. D. Kritzman (ed.), *Politics, Philosophy, Culture: Interviews and Other Writings* 1977–1984. New York: Routledge, Chapman & Hall, pp. 17–46.

—— (1988d). Truth, power, self: an interview. In L. Martin, H. Gutman and P. Hutton (eds), *Technologies of the Self: A Seminar with Michel Foucault*. Amherst, MA: University of Massachusetts Press, pp. 9–15.

—— (1988e). Politics and reason. In L. D. Kritzman (ed.), *Politics, Philosophy, Culture: Interviews and Other Writings* 1977–1984. New York: Routledge, Chapman & Hall, pp. 57–85.

—— (1988f). The dangerous individual. In L. D. Kritzman (ed.), *Politics, Philosophy, Culture: Interviews and Other Writings* 1977–1984. New York: Routledge, Chapman & Hall, pp. 125–51.

—— (1988g). On power. In L. D. Kritzman (ed.), *Politics, Philosophy, Culture: Interviews and Other Writings* 1977–1984. New York: Routledge, Chapman & Hall, pp. 96–109.

—— (1988h). The political technology of individuals. In L. Martin, H. Gutman and P. Hutton (eds), *Technologies of the Self: A Seminar with Michel Foucault*. Amherst, MA: University of Massachusetts Press, pp. 145–62.

—— (1990). *The History of Sexuality: The Use of Pleasure* (Vol. 2). New York: Vintage.

—— (1994). *The Birth of the Clinic: An Archaeology of Medical Perception*. New York: Vintage.

—— (1996a). The return of morality. In S. Lotringer (ed.), *Foucault Live, Interviews, 1961–84*. New York: Semiotext(e).

—— (1996b). An aesthetics of existence. In S. Lotringer (ed.), *Foucault Live, Interviews, 1961–84*. New York: Semiotext(e).

—— (1997a). For an ethics of discomfort. In S. Lotringer and L. Hochroth (eds), *The Politics of Truth: Michel Foucault*. New York: Semiotext(e), pp. 135–46.

—— (1997b). The ethics of the concern for self as a practice of freedom. In P. Rabinow (ed.), *Michel Foucault, Ethics, Subjectivity and Truth. The Essential Works of Foucault* (Vol. 1). New York: The New Press, pp. 281–302.

—— (1997c). Sexuality and solitude. In P. Rabinow (ed.), *Michel Foucault, Ethics, Subjectivity and Truth. The Essential Works of Foucault* (Vol. 1). New York: The New Press, pp. 175–84.

—— (1998a). Return to history. In J. D. Faubion (ed.), *Aesthetics, Method, and Epistemology. The Essential Works of Michel Foucault* (Vol. 2). New York: The New Press, pp. 419–32.

—— (1998b). Structuralism and post-structuralism. In J. D. Faubion (ed.), *Aesthetics, Method, and Epistemology. The Essential Works of Michel Foucault* (Vol. 2). New York: The New Press, pp. 433–58.

—— (2000). Truth and power. In J. D. Faubion (ed.), *Power, The Essential Works of Michel Foucault* (Vol. 3). New York: The New Press, pp. 111–33.

—— (2003). *Society Must Be Defended: Lectures at the Collège De France 1975–76*. New York: Picador.

Foxe, A. N. (1947). Classification and the criminotic individual. In R. M. Lindner and R. V. Seliger (eds), *Handbook of Correctional Psychology*. New York: Philosophical Library, pp. 24–34.

Frances, A. J. (1994). Foreword. In J. Z. Sadler, O. P. Wiggins and M. A. Schwartz (eds), *Philosophical Perspectives on Psychiatric Classification*. Baltimore: The Johns Hopkins University Press, pp. vii–x.

Frick, P. J. (1998). Conduct disorders. In T. Ollendick and M. Herson (eds), *Handbook of Child Psychopathology* (3rd edn). New York: Plenum Press, pp. 213–37.

Galli, V., McElroy, S. L., Soutullo, C. A., Kizer, D., Raute, N., Keck, P. E. J. and McConville, B. J. (1999). The psychiatric diagnoses of twenty-two adolescents who have sexually molested other children. *Comprehensive Psychiatry*, 40(2), 85–8.

Gelder, M., Gath, D. and Mayou, R. (1989). *Oxford Textbook of Psychiatry* (2nd edn). Oxford: Oxford University Press.

Gimpel, G., A. and Holland, M., L. (2003). *Emotional and Behavioral Problems of Young Children*. New York: Guilford.

Goodman, R., F. and Gurian, A. (2001). *About Conduct Disorder (CD), NYU Child Study Center*. Retrieved 17 September 2004, from http://www.aboutourkids.org/aboutour/articles/about_conduct.html

Gordon, R. G. (1938). The neuro-psychological basis of conduct disorder. *Edinburgh Medical Journal*, 45(Jan.), 43–59.

'Graveyard mugger jailed for five years', *This is Lancashire*, 22 February 2003. Retrieved 8 February 2005, from http://www.thisislancashire.co.uk/lancashire/archive/2003/02/22/NEWS2ZM.html

Group for the Advancement of Psychiatry – Committee on Child Psychiatry (ed.) (1974). *Psychopathological Disorders in Childhood: Theoretical Considerations and a Proposed Classification* (2nd edn). New York: Jason Aronson.

Hamill, R. C. (1929). Enuresis. *Journal of the American Medical Association*, 93(3 July), 254–7.

Hanks, P. (ed.) (1981). *Collins Dictionary of the English Language*. Sydney: Collins.

Harms, E. (1960). At the cradle of child psychiatry: Hermann Emminghaus' Psychische Stoerungen des Kindesalters (1887). *American Journal of Orthopsychiatry*, 30(Jan.), 186–90.

Harper, D. J. (1996). Deconstructing 'paranoia': Towards a discursive understanding of apparently unwarranted suspicion. *Theory & Psychology*, 6(3), 423–48.

Harris, J., and Simmonds, L. (2002). *Youth Horizons Trust Programme for Young People with Severe Conduct Disorder*. Paper presented at the Association of Children's Welfare Agencies: What Works!?

Harwood, V. (2001). Foucault, narrative and the subjugated subject: Doing research with a grid of sensibility. *Australian Educational Researcher*, 28(3), 141–66.

—— (2004). Subject to scrutiny: Taking Foucauldian genealogies to narratives of youth oppression. In M. L. Rasmussen, E. Rofes and S. Talburt (eds), *Youth and Sexualities: Pleasure, Subversion and Insurbordination In and Out of Schools*. New York: Palgrave, pp. 85–107.

Harwood, V. and Rasmussen, M. L. (2004). Studying schools with an ethic of discomfort. In B. Baker and K. Heyning (eds), *Dangerous Coagulations? The Uses of Foucault in the Study of Education*. New York: Peter Lang, pp. 305–21.

Healy, W. (1920). Nervous signs and symptoms as related to certain causations of conduct disorder. *Archives of Neurology and Psychiatry*, 4(6 Dec.), 680–90.

Healy, W. and Bronner, A. F. (1926). *Delinquents and Criminals: Their Making and Unmaking*. New York: Macmillan.

Hempel, C. G. (1965). *Aspects of Scientific Explanation and Other Essays in the Philosophy of Science*. New York: The Free Press.

Henderson, D. K. (1939). The nineteenth Maudsley lecture: A revaluation of psychiatry. *Journal of Mental Science,* 85(354), 1–21.

Henderson, S., Frew, J. and O'Brien, D. (eds) (1991). *Student Behaviour Problems: Context, Initiatives, Programs*. Hawthorn, Victoria: ACER.

Henn, F. A., Bardwell, R. and Jenkins, R. L. (1980). Juvenile delinquents revisited: Adult criminal activity. *Archives of General Psychiatry,* 37(10), 1160–3.

Henriques, J., Holloway, W., Urwin, C., Venn, C. and Walkerdine, V. (1984). *Changing the Subject: Psychology, Social Regulation and Subjectivity*. London: Methuen & Co.

Henry, J. and Day, M. (2004). He's not naughty he's an ODD child. *Sunday Telegraph,* 4 November 2004. Retrieved 8 October 2004, from http://www.telegraph.co.uk

Hewitt, L. E. and Jenkins, R. L. (1946). *Fundamental Patterns of Maladjustment. The Dynamics of their Origin: a Statistical Analysis Based Upon Five Hundred Case Records of Children Examined at the Michigan Child Guidance Institute*. Springfield, IL: State of Illinois.

Hinshaw, S. P. and Anderson, C. A. (1996). Conduct and oppositional defiant disorders. In E. J. Mash and R. Barkley (eds), *Child Psychopathology*. New York: Guilford Press, pp. 113–49.

Hinshaw, S. P. and Zupan, B. A. (1997). Assessment of antisocial behavior in children and adolescents. In D. M. Stoff, J. Breiling and J. D. Maser (eds), *Handbook of Antisocial Behavior*. New York: John Wiley & Sons, pp. 36–50.

Hodges, P. (1989). Itinerant support teacher (behaviour) program. In C. Szaday (ed.), *Addressing Behaviour Problems in Australian Schools*. Hawthorn, Victoria: ACER, pp. 36–9.

Holt, G. (1995). Students with conduct disorder. In R. Conway and J. Izard (eds), *Student Behaviour Outcomes: Choosing Appropriate Paths*. Melbourne, Victoria: ACER, pp. 67–85.

House of Lords Debate (2002, 23 July). Vol. 638, col. WA64, Mental Health Bill: Categories of Mental Disorder.

House of Representatives Standing Committee on Employment Education and Training (1996). *Truancy and Exclusion from School*. Canberra: Australian Government Publishing Service.

Huang, L., Macbeth, G., Dodge, J. and Jacobstein, D. (2004). Transforming the workforce in children's mental health. *Administration and Policy in Mental Health,* 32(2), 167–87.

Hultqvist, K. (1998). A history of the present on children's welfare in Sweden: From Fröbel to present-day decentralization projects. In T. S. Popkewitz and M. Brennen (eds), *Foucault's Challenge: Discourse, Knowledge and Power in Education*. New York: Teachers College Press.

Human Rights and Equal Opportunity Commission (1993). *Human Rights and Mental Illness: Report of the National Inquiry into the Human Rights of People with Mental Illness* (Vols 1 and 2). Canberra: Australian Government Publishing Service.

Husain, S. A. and Cantwell, D. (1991). *Fundamentals of Child and Adolescent Psychopathology*. Washington, DC: American Psychiatric Press.

Institute of Medicine (1999). *Report on Adolescents*. Washington, DC: National Science Foundation.

Irvine, J. (1988). Special education for educators – are we ready? *Australasian Journal of Special Education,* 12(2), 2–11.

Jackson, M. (1973). Special education: Contribution to the alleviation of human suffering in Victoria. *Australasian Journal of Mental Retardation,* 2, 189–96.

Jacobs, B., Youth Affairs Network of Queensland (2004). *Written Submission to the Inquiry – Attention Deficit Disorder and Attention Deficit Hyperactivity Disorder in Western Australia.*

Jahr, H. M. (1928). Mental hygiene and the physician. *Archives of Pediatrics,* 45(491–7).

Jenkins, R. L. (1960). The psychopathic or antisocial personality. *Journal of Nervous and Mental Disease,* 131, 318–34.

—— (1969). Classification of behavior problems of children. *American Journal of Psychiatry,* 125(8), 1032–9.

—— (1973). *Behavior Disorders of Childhood and Adolescence.* Springfield, IL: Charles C. Thomas.

Jenkins, R. L. and Hewitt, L. E. (1944). Types of personality structure encountered in child guidance clinics. *American Journal of Orthopsychiatry,* 14, 84–94.

Jones, W. and Patterson, B. (2000). Inside the mind of a killer. *Sunday Herald Sun,* 9 April 2000, p. 32.

'Joyrider broke his electronic tracer tag', *Eastbourne Today,* 11 June 2004. Retrieved 8 February 2005, from http://www.eastbournetoday.co.uk

Judge Rotenberg Center (2005). *Admissions/Programs.* Retrieved 16 March 2005, from http://www.judgerc.org/

Kanner, L. (1972). *Child Psychiatry* (4th edn). Springfield, IL: Charles C. Thomas.

Kaplan, H. I. & Sadock, B. J. (1998). *Synopsis of Psychiatry* (8th edn). Baltimore: Williams & Wilkins.

Kasanin, J. (1929). Personality changes in children following cerebral trauma. *Journal of Nervous and Mental Disease,* 69(4 (April)), 385–406.

Kazdin, A. E. (1996). Foreword. In E. Mash and R. A. Barkley (eds), *Child Psychopathology.* New York: Guilford Press.

Keenan, K. and Wakschlag, L., S. (2004). Are oppositional defiant and conduct disorder symptoms normative behaviors in preschoolers? A comparison of refereed and non-refereed children. *American Journal of Psychiatry,* 161(2), 356–8.

Keenan, K., Loeber, R. and Green, S. (1999). Conduct disorder in girls: A review of the literature. *Clinical Child and Family Psychology Review,* 2(1), 3–19.

Kendler, K.S. (1992). Twin studies. *Psychiatric Times,* 46(14).

Kevles, D. J. K. (1985). *In the Name of Eugenics: Genetics and the Uses of Human Heredity.* New York: Alfred A. Knopf.

Kirk, S. A. and Kutchins, H. (1992). *The Selling of the DSM: The Rhetoric of Science in Psychiatry.* New York: Aldine De Gruyte.

Koplewicz, H. S. (1996). *It's Nobody's Fault: New Hope and Help for Difficult Children and Their Parents.* New York: Time Books, Random House.

Kramer, M. (1968). The history of the efforts to agree on an international classification of mental disorders. In APA Committee on Nomenclature and Statistics (ed.), *Diagnostic and Statistical Manual of Mental Disorders* (2nd edn). Washington, DC: APA, pp. xi–xx.

Lahey, B. B., Loeber, R., Strouthamer-Loeber, M., Christ, M. A., Green, S., Russo, M. F., Frick P. J. and Dulcan, M. (1990). Comparison of DSM-III and DSM-III-R diagnoses for prepubertal children: Changes in prevalence and validity. *Journal of the American Academy of Child and Adolescent Psychiatry*, 29, 620–6.

Lahey, B. B., Applegate, B., Barkley, R. A., Garfinkal, B., McBurnett, K., Kerdyk, L., Greenhill, L., Hynd, G. W., Frick, P. J. and Newcorn, J. (1994). DSM-IV field trials for oppositional defiant disorder and conduct disorder in children and adolescents. *American Journal of Psychiatry*, 151(8), 1163–71.

Lahey, B. B. and Loeber, R. (1994). Framework for a developmental model of oppositional defiant disorder and conduct disorder. In D. K. Routh (ed.), *Disruptive Behavior Disorders in Childhood*. New York: Plenum Press, pp. 139–80.

Lapage, C. P. (1911). *Feeblemindedness in Children of School Age*. Manchester: Manchester University Press.

Lau, A., S., Garland, A., F., Yeh, M. and McCabe, K., M. (2004). Race/ethnicity and inter-informant agreement in assessing adolescent psychopathology. *Journal of Emotional and Behavioral Disorders*, 12(3), 145–57.

Laurence, J., and McCallum, D. (1998a). Disorder in the classroom: From the administration to the diagnosis of the student body. *Hysteric. Body Medicine Text*, 3, 27–50.

—— (1998b). The myth-or-reality of attention-deficit disorder: a genealogical approach. *Discourse: Studies in the Cultural Politics of Education*, 19(2), 183–200.

—— (2003). Conduct disorder: The achievement of diagnosis. *Discourse: Studies in the Cultural Politics of Education*, 24(3), 307–24.

Laws, C. and Davies, B. (2000). Poststructuralist theory in practice: Working with 'behaviourally disturbed' children. *International Journal of Qualitative Studies in Education*, 13(3), 205–21.

Lewis, T. (2003). The surveillance economy of post-Columbine schools. *The Review of Education, Pedagogy and Cultural Studies*, 25, 335–55.

Lindsay, W. (1990). Education services to disturbed youth through a tutorial centre. In S. Richardson and J. Izard (eds), *Practical Approaches to Resolving Behaviour Problems*. Hawthorn, Victoria: ACER, pp. 244–8.

Lindsey, B. B. (1908). Introduction. In T. T. Travis (ed.), *The Young Malefactor, A Study in Juvenile Delinquency, its Causes and Treatment*. New York: Thomas Y. Crowell & Co.

Linfoot, K., Martin, A. J. and Stephenson, J. (1999). Preventing conduct disorder: A study of parental behaviour management and support needs with children aged 3 to 5 years. *International Journal of Disability*, 46(2), 223–46.

Lipton, G. (1978). The current status of child psychiatry in Australia with special reference to training in general psychiatry. *Australian and New Zealand Journal of Psychiatry*, 12, 157–60.

Lock, J. and Steiner, H. (1999). Gay, lesbian, and bisexual youth risks for emotional, physical and social problems: Results from a community-based survey. *Journal of the American Academy of Child and Adolescent Psychiatry*, 38(3), 297–304.

Lorei, T. W. and Vestre, N. D. (1969). A set of factor analytically derived scales for scoring the m-b history record. *Multivariate Behavioral Research*, 4(2), 181–93.

Lynam, D. R. (1998). Early identification of the fledgling psychopath: Locating the psychopathic child in the current nomenclature. *Journal of Abnormal Psychology*, 107(4), 566–75.

McCallum, D. (1997). The uses of history: Mental health, criminality and the human sciences. In R. Bunton and A. Peterson (eds), *Foucault, Health and Medicine*. London: Routledge, pp. 53–73.

—— (1998). Dangerous individuals: government and the concept of personality. In M. Dean and B. Hindess (eds), *Governing Australia, Studies in Contemporary Rationalities of Government*. Cambridge: Cambridge University Press, pp. 108–24.

—— (2001). *Personality and Dangerousness: Genealogies of Antisocial Personality Disorder*. Cambridge: Cambridge University Press.

Machin, A. E. (1934). The problem of mentally defective children in New South Wales from the educational and vocational points of view. *Medical Journal of Australia,* (17 March), 370–6.

McLean, J. (2004). Disarming the classroom terrorist, *Times Educational Supplement*, 12 March 2004. Retrieved 4 November 2004, from http://www.tes.co.uk

Macpherson, J. (1926). The psychiatric clinic. *Medical Journal of Australia,* 2(August), 174–8.

Maier, N. R. F. (1949). *Frustration: The Study of Behavior Without a Goal*. New York: McGraw-Hill.

Marshall, J. D. (1997). Michel Foucault: Problematising the individual and constituting 'the' self. *Educational Philosophy and Theory,* 29(1), 32–49.

Maudsley, H. (1879). *The Pathology of Mind, Being the Third Edition of the Second Part of the Physiology and Pathology of Mind*. London: Macmillan.

Maughan, B., Brock, A. and Ladva, G. (2004). Mental health. In Office for National Statistics (ed.), *The Health of Children and Young People*. London: Office for National Statistics.

Meltzer, H., Gatward, R., Corbin, T., Goodman, R. and Ford, T. (2003). *Persistence, Onset, Risk Factors and Outcomes of Childhood Mental Disorders*. London: The Stationery Office.

Meltzer, H., Gatward, R., Goodman, R. and Ford, T. (2000). *Mental Health of Children and Adolescents in Great Britain*. London: The Stationery Office.

'Mental defect and delinquency' (1923). *Medical Journal of Australia*, 479–80.

Mercier, C. A. (1911). *Crime and Insanity*. London: The Home University library.

Metherell, T. (1989). *Excellence and Equity: New South Wales Curriculum, a White Paper on Curriculum Reform in New South Wales Schools*. Sydney: NSW Ministry of Education and Youth Affairs.

Midgley, C. (2004). Why was my self-destructive daughter sent to prison?, *The Times Online*, 26 November 2004. Retrieved 10/01/2005, from http://www.timesonline.co.uk

Miller, E. (1936). Classification of the disorders of childhood. In H. Rolleston (ed.), *British Encyclopedia of Medical Practice*. London: Butterworth & Co.

Miller, T. and Leger, M. C. (2003). A very childish moral panic: Ritalin. *Journal of Medical Humanities,* 24(1/2), 9–33.

Ministerial Council on Education, Employment, Training and Youth Affairs (1994). *National Report on Schooling in Australia* 1994. Carlton, Victoria: Curriculum Corporation for the Australian Education Council.

Mitchell, D. and Snyder, S. (2003). The Eugenic Atlantic: Race, disability, and the making on an international Eugenic Science, 1800–1945. *Disability and Society,* 18(7), 843–64.

Mitchell, N. (2004). Attention Deficit Disorder (ADHD) – Debate hots up in Western Australia, *All in the Mind, ABC Radio National,* Transcript Saturday 19 June. Retrieved 17 March 2005, from http://www.abc.net.au/rn/science/mind/stories/s1132023.htm

Moncrieff, V. (writer) (1996). *A Dangerous Mind* [Television], *Four Corners*. ABC, Sydney, Australia.

Monk, D. (2000). Theorising education law and childhood: Constructing the ideal pupil. *British Journal of the Sociology of Education,* 21(3).

Morse, W. C. (1961). A research evaluation of an action approach to school mental health-workshop, 1960 – the mental hygiene dilemma in public education. *American Journal of Orthopsychiatry,* 31, 324–31.

Murray, B. A. and Myer, M. A. (1998). Avoiding the special education trap for conduct disordered students. *NASSP Bulletin,* 82(594), 65–9.

Narrow, W., E., Regier, D., A, Goodman, S., H., Roper, M., T., Bourdon, K., H., Hoven, C. and Moore, R. (1998). A comparison of Federal definitions of severe mental illness among children and adolescents in four communities. *Psychiatric Services,* 49, 1601–8.

Nass, R. D. and Leventhal, F. (2005). 100 *Questions & Answers About Your Child's Attention Deficit Hyperactivity Disorder.* Sudbury, MA: Jones and Bartlett Publishers.

National Conference on Medical Nomenclature (1942). *Standard Nomenclature of Disease and Standard Nomenclature of Operations.* Chicago: American Medical Association.

National Crime Prevention (1999). *Pathways to Prevention: Developmental and Early Intervention Approaches to Crime in Australia – Appendices.* Canberra: National Crime Prevention, Attorney-General's Department.

National Health Service (2004). *Specific Mental Health Problems, Disorders and Illness.* Retrieved 15 March 2005, from http://www.wiredforhealth.gov.uk/cat. php?catid=890&docid=7261

Neal, D. (1982). The right to education: The case of special education. *The Australian Quarterly* (Winter), 147–60.

New South Wales Commission for Children and Young People (2002). *Prescription and Over-the-Counter Medication.* Sydney: NSW Commission for Children and Young People.

New South Wales Department of Education and Training (2003). *Community Grants Programs, Intervention Support Programs: Guidelines* 2004 (July edn). Sydney: NSW DET.

—— (2004). *Annual Report* 2003*: Vol.* 1*, Report of Operations.* Sydney: NSW DET.

—— (2005). *School Locator: Campbell House School.* Retrieved 17 March 2005, from http://www.schools.nsw.edu.au/schoolfind/locator/summaryschool.php?selectOption=5735

New South Wales Department of Education and Training Policy and Planning (1999). *NSW Department of Education and Training Annual Report,* 1998. NSW: NSW DETPP.

New South Wales Department of School Education (1990). *The Special Education Plan Year 3 – A Fair Deal for Students with Disabilities and Learning Difficulties.* NSW: NSW DSE.

—— (1996). *Directory of Government Schools in New South Wales* 1996. NSW: NSW DSE.

Noble, R. (1929). The mental hygiene movement and its possibilities in Australia. *Transactions of the Australasian Medical Congress,* 300–2.

Nudd, H. W. (1926). The purpose and scope of visiting teacher work. In M. B. Sayles (ed.), *The Problem Child in School, Narratives from Case Records of Visiting Teachers.* New York: Joint Committee on Methods of Preventing Delinquency.

Office for National Statistics (2001). *Prevalence of Mental Disorders Among Children: By Gross Weekly Household Income and Age of Child,* 1999*: Social Trends* 31. London: Office for National Statistics.

Offord, D. R. (1997). Bridging development, prevention, policy. In D. M. Stoff, J. Breiling and J. D. Maser (eds), *Handbook of Antisocial Behavior*. New York: John Wiley & Sons.

O'Leary, T. (2002). *Foucault and the Art of Ethics*. London: Continuum.

Ollendick, T. and Herson, M. (1998). *Handbook of Child Psychopathology* (3rd edn). New York: Plenum Press.

O'Toole, M. E. (2000). *The School Shooter – A Threat Assessment Perspective*. Retrieved 10 March 2005, from www.fbi.gov/publications/school/school2.pdf

Packenham, M., Shute, R. and Reid, R. (2004). A truncated functional behavioral assessment procedure for children with disruptive classroom behaviors. *Education and Treatment of Children,* 27(1), 9–25.

Patterson, G. R., Reid, J. B. and Dishion, T. J. (1992). *Antisocial Boys* (Vol. 4). Oregon: Castalia Publishing Company.

Phillips, K. R. (2002). Spaces of invention: Dissension, freedom, and thought in Foucault. *Philosophy and Rhetoric,* 35(4), 328–44.

Pigott, R., and Cowen, E. (2000). Teacher race, child race, racial congruence, and ratings of school adjustment. *Journal of School Psychology,* 38, 177–96.

Pinel, P. (1962). *A Treatise on Insanity*. New York: Hafner Publishing.

Pottick, K. J. (2002). *Children's Use of Mental Health Services Doubles. New Research – Policy Partnership Reports* (Vol. 1). New Brunswick, NJ: Institute for Health, Health Care Policy, and Aging Research, Rutgers University.

Potts, P. (1983). Medicine, morals and mental deficiency: The contribution of doctors to the development of special education in England. *Oxford Review of Education,* 9(3), 181–96.

Poulou, M. and Norwich, B. (2002). Cognitive, emotional and behavioural responses to students with emotional and behavioural difficulties: A model of decision-making. *British Educational Research Journal,* 28(1), 111–38.

'The problem of mentally defective children in NSW' (1934). *The Medical Journal of Australia,* 1, 390–1.

Raine, A. (1993). *The Psychopathology of Crime: Criminal Behavior as a Clinical Disorder*. San Diego: Academic Press.

Ramazanoglu, C. and Holland, J. (1993). Women's sexuality and men's appropriation of desire. In C. Ramazanoglu (ed.), *Up against Foucault: Explorations of Some Tensions Between Foucault and Feminism*. London: Routledge.

Ransom, J. S. (1997). *Foucault's Discipline: The Politics of Subjectivity*. Durham, NC: Duke University Press.

Rapoport, J. and Ismond, D. (1996). *DSM-IV Training Guide for Diagnosis of Childhood Disorders*. New York: Brunner/Mazel.

Rasmussen, M. L. and Harwood, V. (2003). Performativity, youth and injurious speech. *Teaching Education Journal,* 14(1), 25–36.

Rees, R. J. and Irvine, J. W. (1981). Responding to need: Special education in the 1980s. In R. J. Rees and J. W. Irvine (eds), *Responding to Need: Special Education in the 1980s*. NSW: University of New England Press.

Reid, R., Hakendorf, P. and Prosser, B. (2002). Use of psychostimulant medication for ADHD in South Australia. *Journal of the American Academy of Child and Adolescent Psychiatry,* 41(8), 906–13.

Reid, R., Riccio, C., Kessler, R., H., DuPaul, G., J., Power, T., J., Anastopoulos, A., D., Rogers-Adkinson, D. and Noll, M. (2000). Gender and ethnic differences in ADHD as assessed by behavior ratings. *Journal of Emotional and Behavioral Disorders,* 8(1), 38–45.

Rey, J. M., Morris-Yates, A., Singh, M., Andrews, G. and Stewart, G. W. (1995). Continuities between psychiatric disorders in adolescents and personality disorders in young adults. *American Journal of Psychiatry,* 152(6), 895–900.

Rhodes, E. C. (1939). Juvenile delinquency. *Journal of the Royal Statistical Society,* 102(3), 384–405.

Richardson, J. and Joughin, C. (2002). *Parent Training Programmes for the Management of Young Children with Conduct Disorders: Findings from the Research.* London: Gaskell, The Royal College of Psychiatrists.

Richters, J. E. and Cicchetti, D. (1993). Mark Twain meets DSM-III-R: Conduct disorder, development, and the concept of harmful dysfunction. *Development and Psychopathology,* 5, 5–29.

Riley, D. (1997). *The Defiant Child: A Parent's Guide to Oppositional Defiant Disorder.* Dallas: Taylor Publishing.

Robins, L. N. (1999). A 70-year history of conduct disorder: Variations in definition, prevalence and correlates. In P. Cohen, C. Slomkowski and L. N. Robins (eds), *Historical and Geographical Influences on Psychopathology.* Mahwah, NJ: Lawrence Erlbaum Associates, pp. 37–56.

Robinson, J. F., Vitale, L. J. and Nitsche, C. J. (1961). Behavioral categories of childhood. *American Journal of Psychiatry,* 117(9), 806–10.

Robotham, J. (2004). Adara wasn't pretending – it was cancer. *Sydney Morning Herald,* 31 March 2004, p. 1.

Rosaldo, R. (1987). Where objectivity lies: The rhetoric of anthropology. In J. Nelson, A. Megill and D. McCloskey (eds), *The Rhetoric of the Human Sciences: Language and Argument in Scholarship and Public Affairs.* Madison: University of Wisconsin Press, pp. 87–110.

Rose, N. (1985). *The Psychological Complex, Psychology, Politics and Society in England 1869–1939.* London: Routledge & Kegan Paul.

—— (1989). *Governing the Soul, the Shaping of the Private Self.* London: Routledge.

Ruffolo, M. C., Evans, M. E. and Lukens, E. P. (2003). Primary prevention programs for children in the social service system. *Journal of Primary Prevention,* 23(4), 425–50.

Ruggles-Brise, E. (1926). Introduction. In M. V. Waters (ed.), *Youth in Conflict.* London: Methuen.

Ryan, B. M. (2004). *Kool Kids Project Turns Naughty Kids Into Nice.* Retrieved 18 March, 2005, from http://hnb.dhs.vic.gov.au/web/pubaff/medrel.nsf/0/b15da32cad178a50ca25 6f4600004861?OpenDocument

Sadler, J. Z. (2004). *Values and Psychiatric Diagnosis.* Oxford: Oxford University Press.

Sadler, W. S. (1947). Preinstitutional recognition and management of the potential delinquent. In R. M. Lindner and R. V. Seliger (eds), *Handbook of Correctional Psychology.* New York: Philosophical Library, pp. 130–1.

Saltmarsh, S. and Youdell, D. (2004). 'Special Sport' for misfits and losers: Educational triage and the constitution of schooled subjectivities. *International Journal of Inclusive Education,* 8(4), 353–71.

Sandelowski, M. (1994). The proof is in the pottery: Toward a poetic for qualitative inquiry. In J. Morse (ed.), *Critical Issues in Qualitative Research Methods.* Thousand Oaks: Sage, pp. 46–63.

Saunders, J. (1987). Bad, mad or . . . sad? *Special Education Journal,* 2, 9–13.

Sawicki, J. (1991). *Disciplining Foucault: Feminism, Power and the Body*. New York: Routledge.

Sawyer, M. G., Arney, F. M., Baghurst, P. A., Clark, J. J., Graetz, B. W., Kosky, R. J., Nurcombe, B., Patton, G. C., Prior, M. R., Raphael, B., Rey, J., Whaites, L. C. and Zubrick, S. R. (2000). *Mental Health of Young People in Australia*. Canberra: Mental Health and Special Programs Branch, Commonwealth Department of Health and Aged Care.

Schowalter, J., E. (2003). A history of child and adolescent psychiatry in the United States. *Psychiatric Times*, 43–5.

Scott, S., Knapp, M., Henderson, J. and Maughan, B. (2001). Financial cost of social exclusion: Follow up study of antisocial children into adulthood, *British Medical Journal*. Retrieved December 22, 2004, 323, from bmj.com

Simonoff, E., Elander, J., Holmshaw, J., Pickles, A., Murray, R. and Rutter, M. (2004). Predictors of antisocial personality. *British Journal of Psychiatry*, 184, 118–27.

Simons, J. (1995). *Foucault and the Political*. London: Routledge.

Slee, R. (1995). *Changing Theories and Practices of Discipline*. London: Falmer Press.

—— (1998). High reliability organizations and liability students – the politics of recognition. In R. Slee, G. Weiner and S. Tomlinson (eds), *School Effectiveness For Whom? Challenges to the School Effectiveness and School Improvement Movements*. London: Falmer Press, pp. 101–14.

Slutske, W. S., Heath, A. C., Dinwiddie, S. H., Madden, P. A. F., Bucholz, K. K., Dunne, M. P., Statham, D. J. and Martin, N. G. (1997). Modelling genetic and environmental influences in the etiology of conduct disorder: A study of 2,682 adult twin pairs. *Journal of Abnormal Psychology,* 106(2), 266–79.

Snow, D. (1990). Historicising the integration debate. *Australian Journal of Special Education,* 13(2), 28–38.

Southam-Gerow, M. A. and Kendall, P. C. (1997). Parent-focused and cognitive behavioral treatments of antisocial youth. In D. M. Stoff, J. Breiling and J. D. Maser (eds), *Handbook of Antisocial Behavior*. New York: John Wiley & Sons.

Special Education Directorate, NSW DoSE (1993). *Special Education Plan 1993–1997*.

'Special education requirements in teacher training' (1983). *The Australian Journal of Special Education*, 7(2), 5–6.

'Spit test for future criminals', *BBC News Online*, 13 January 2000. Retrieved 16 January 2005, from http://www.news.bbc.co.uk

Spitzer, R. and Williams, J. B. W. (1982). The definition and diagnosis of mental disorder. In W. Grove (ed.), *Deviance and Mental Illness*. London: Sage, pp. 15–31.

Stearns, A. W. (1916). A survey of the defective delinquents under the care of the Massachusetts State Board of Insanity. *American Journal of Insanity,* 72(3), 427–37.

Stoler, A. L. (2000). *Race and the Education of Desire, Foucualt's History of Sexuality and the Colonial Order of Things*. Durham, NC: Duke University Press.

Stone, M. (1997). *Healing the Mind: A History of Psychiatry from Antiquity to the Present*. New York: W. W. Norton.

Strecker, E. A. (1928). Behavior problems of encephalitis: A clinical study of the relationship between behavior and the acute and chronic phenomena of encephalitis. *Archives of Neurology and Psychiatry,* 21(1), 137–44.

Sutton, H. (1911). The feeble-minded – their classification and importance. *Transactions of the Australasian Medical Congress*, 894–907.

Sutton, H., Greig, J. S., Fitzgerald, E. and Simpson, C. J. (1915). *Report on Medical Inspection and Kindred Subjects*. Melbourne: Albert J. Mullet, Government Printer.

Swalcliffe Park Special School (2005). *Referrals and Admissions*. Retrieved March 16 2005, from http://www.swalcliffepark.oxon.sch.uk/ReferralAdmissions.cfm

Swinson, J., Woof, C. and Melling, R. (2003). Including emotional and behavioural difficulties pupils in a mainstream comprehensive: A study of the behaviour of pupils and classes. *Educational Psychology in Practice, 19*(1), 65–75.

Szaday, C. (1989). Preface. In C. Szaday (ed.), *Addressing Behaviour Problems in Australian Schools*. Hawthorn, Victoria: ACER.

Tait, G. (2001). Pathologising difference, governing personality. *Asia-Pacific Journal of Teacher Education, 29*(1), 93–102.

—— (2005). The ADHD debate and the philosophy of truth. *International Journal of Inclusive Education, 9*(1), 17–38.

Talbot, E. S. (1902). Juvenile female delinquents. *Alienist and Neurologist, 23*(1), 16–26.

Tamboukou, M. (1999). Writing genealogies: An exploration of Foucault's strategies for doing research. *Discourse: Studies in the cultural politics of education, 20*(2), 201–17.

Thom, D. A. (1940). *Normal Youth and its Everyday Problems*. New York: D. Appleton-Century Company.

Thomas, G. and Glenny, G. (2000). Emotional and behavioural difficulties: Bogus needs in a false category. *Discourse: Studies in the Cultural Politics of Education, 21*(3), 283–97.

Todd, M. K. and Gesten, E. L. (1999). Predictors of child abuse potential in at-risk adolescents. *Journal of Family Violence, 14*(4), 417–36.

Tomlinson, S. (1982). *A Sociology of Special Education*. London: Routledge and Kegan Paul.

Tonge, B. J. (1998). *Common Child and Adolescent Psychiatric Problems and their Management in the Community*. Retrieved 22 February 1999, from http://www.mja.com.au

Travis, T. T. (1908). *The Young Malefactor, A Study in Juvenile Delinquency, its Causes and Treatment*. New York: Thomas Y. Crowell.

Turecki, S. and Tonner, L. (2000). *The Difficult Child: Expanded and Revised Edition*. New York: Bantam Books.

Twemlow, S. W., Fonagy, P., Sacco, F. C. and Vernberg, E. (2002). Assessing adolescents who threaten homicide in schools. *American Journal of Psychoanalysis, 62*(3), 213–35.

US Department of Health and Human Services (1999). *Mental Health: A Report of the Surgeon General*. Retrieved 4 March 2005, from http://www.surgeongeneral.gov/library/mentalhealth/chapter3/sec6.html

Van Waters, M. (1926). *Youth in Conflict*. London: Methuen.

Victorian Government (2002). *Victorian Government Submission to the Senate Employment, Workplace Relations and Education References Committee Inquiry into the Education of Students with Disabilities, Submission* 212, from http://www.aph.gov.au/Senate/committee/eet_ctte/ed_students_withdisabilities/submissions/sublist.htm

Vinson, T. (2002a). *Report of the Independent Inquiry in the Provision of Public Education in NSW, Second Report*. Sydney: Public Education Inquiry NSW.

—— (2002b). *Report of the Independent Inquiry in the Provision of Public Education in NSW, Third Report*. Sydney: Public Education Inquiry NSW.

Visser, J. (2003). *A Study of Children and Young People Who Present Challenging Behaviour*. Birmingham: School of Education, The University of Birmingham.

Visser, J. and Stokes, S. (2003). Is education ready for the inclusion of pupils with emotional and behavioural difficulties: a rights perspective? *Educational Review,* 55(1), 66–75.

Vogt, M. E. (1947). The Philadelphia procedure as used in the municipal court. In R. M. Lindner and R. V. Seliger (eds), *Handbook of Correctional Psychology*. New York: Philosophical Library, pp. 11–23.

Waddell, C., Wong, W., Hua, J. and Godderis, R. (2004). *Preventing and Treating Conduct Disorder, A Research Report Prepared for the British Columbia Ministry of Children and Family Development*. Vancouver: Children's Mental Health, Mental Health Evaluation & Community Consultation Unit, Dept. of Psychiatry, Faculty of Medicine, The University of British Columbia.

Wakschlag, F. S., Lahey, B. B., Loeber, R., Green, S. M., Gordon, R. and Leventhal, B. L. (1997). Maternal smoking during pregnancy and the risk of conduct disorder in boys. *Archives of General Psychiatry,* 54(7), 670–6.

Walker, H. M. (1984). The current status of classification, assessment, programming, and service delivery issues relating to children with externalizing behaviour disorders in the school setting. *Australian Journal of Special Education,* 8(2), 25–9.

Wallace, E. R. I. (1994). Psychiatry and its nosology: A historico-philosophical overview. In J. Z. Sadler, O. P. Wiggins and M. A. Schwartz (eds), *Philosophical Perspectives on Psychiatric Classification*. Baltimore: The Johns Hopkins University Press, pp. 16–86.

West, J. and McVeigh, T. (2001). Schools forcing children to take drug, parents say, *Observer,* 22 April 2001. Retrieved 8 October, 2004, from http://www.observer.guardian.co.uk/uk_news/story/0,,476595,00.html

White, S. (1996). Developmental psychopathology: From attribution toward information. In S. Matthysse, D. L. Levy, J. Kagan and F. M. Benes (eds), *Psychopathology: The Evolving Science of Mental Disorder*. Cambridge: Cambridge University Press, pp. 161–95.

Wile, I. S. (1926) The relation of intelligence to behavior. *Mental Hygiene*.

Williams, J. F. (1949). Child psychiatry. *The Medical Journal of Australia* (May), 675–678.

Working Party on a Plan for Special Education in NSW (1982). *Strategies and Initiatives for Special Education in New South Wales*. NSW: New South Wales Government.

World Health Organization (1974). *Mental Disorders: Glossary and Guide to their Classification for Use in Conjunction with the International Classification of Diseases, 8th Revision*. Geneva: World Health Organization.

—— (1992). *The ICD-10 Classification of Mental and Behavioural Disorders*. Geneva: World Health Organization.

—— (2003). *International Statistical Classification of Diseases and Related Health Problems, 10th Revision, Version for* 2003. Retrieved 13 March 2005, from http://www3.who.int/icd/vol1htm2003/fr-icd.htm

Index

Printed in the United States
65281LVS00002B/328-333

9 780415 342865